RON HALL

Workin' our way Home

The Incredible True Story of
a Homeless Ex-Con *and a* Grieving Millionaire
Thrown Together to Save Each Other

Praise for *Workin' Our Way Home*

It's a rare opportunity for an actor to be blessed with a role so soulful as in *Same Kind of Different as Me*. To embody Denver's spirit was at once an emotional challenge and an extreme privilege, learning the story of a man who came from so little and gave so much.

—Djimon Hounsou, Academy Award and Screen
Actors Guild Award–nominated actor

I have known and loved Ron Hall for over four decades and it was my joy to know and love Denver for a decade as well. Never have two men lived with each other, learned from each other, and loved each other in a more Christ-honoring way than Ron and Denver. There are lessons here for all of us. After all, we, too, are just working our way home!

—O. S. Hawkins, president/CEO of
GuideStone Financial Resources

This book is so powerful. It opens my heart and deeply touches my soul. Thank you, Ron Hall, for bringing this awe-inspiring story to my life and the world. I am forever changed—*I love this book!*

—Kym Yancey, cofounder and president of eWomenNetwork

Ron and Denver have done it again in this page-turning memoir about the two most unlikely friends. This will go down as one of the greatest buddy stories in history.

—Jon Gordon, keynote speaker and bestselling
author of *The Power of Positive Leadership*

For decades, legendary radio broadcaster Paul Harvey concluded one of his nationally syndicated programs with these enduring words: "And now you know the rest of the story." That's exactly what Ron Hall gives us in *Workin' Our Way Home*. Their authentic account is a powerful reminder that the journey from human crisis to human flourishing does not play out on a downhill highway, but rather on an uphill track through tough terrain with numerous turnouts and toll booths. And the book's abiding lesson for us all is this: it's a journey God never intended for anyone to take alone.

—JOHN ASHMEN, PRESIDENT OF THE ASSOCIATION
OF GOSPEL RESCUE MISSIONS

In *Workin' Our Way Home,* Ron Hall continues to remind us of the power and inspiration that can be found in unexpected friendships. In this new book, we have the gift of exploring Denver's unique wisdom and ongoing legacy that Ron keeps alive through his beautiful storytelling. What a joy to experience this journey!

—ANNE NEILSON, ARTIST, AUTHOR, AND PHILANTHROPIST

Workin' Our Way Home is a magical read and an important reminder that each day we get closer to the end of life. What will *you* do with this day and this moment? Ron and Denver, two amazing men, answered that question as they searched their souls, only to discover we are all simply working our way home. A must read!

—LOUIS UPKINS, ENTREPRENEUR AND AUTHOR
OF *TREAT ME LIKE A CUSTOMER*

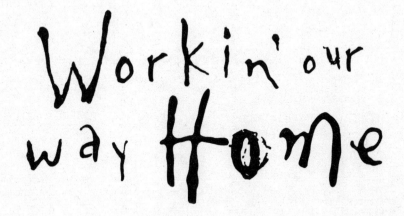

Workin' our way Home

The Incredible True Story of
a Homeless Ex-Con *and a* Grieving Millionaire
Thrown Together to Save Each Other

RON HALL

W PUBLISHING GROUP

AN IMPRINT OF THOMAS NELSON

Published in Nashville, Tennessee, by W Publishing, an imprint of Thomas Nelson.

Thomas Nelson titles may be purchased in bulk for educational, business, fundraising, or sales promotional use. For information, please email SpecialMarkets@ ThomasNelson.com.

Any internet addresses, phone numbers, or company or product information printed in this book are offered as a resource and are not intended in any way to be or to imply an endorsement by Thomas Nelson, nor does Thomas Nelson vouch for the existence, content, or services of these sites, phone numbers, companies, or products beyond the life of this book.

ISBN 978-0-7852-1985-9 (eBook)

Library of Congress Control Number: 2017918090

ISBN 978-0-7852-1983-5

Printed in the United States of America

18 19 20 21 22   LSC   10 9 8 7 6 5 4 3 2 1

Dedication

I'm dedicating this book to the memory of my father, Earl Hall. In my first book, *Same Kind of Different as Me*, I wrote some unkind things about him. Though they were true based on my understanding of his life, I own my part in the conflict we experienced given that I never found a way to love him until Denver forced me to "bless the hell outta him." It was then I discovered the father I'd wanted since my early childhood. I cherish the year we spent hanging out together the way best friends do and getting to know each other before he went to heaven at age ninety-one. I have just finished writing our memoir that can best be described as *Same Kind of Sorry as Me*—an apology and a celebration.

And to Denver, who moved into my home bringing nothing and gave me everything. I miss you.

As Denver was the first face I saw every morning and the last almost every night for nearly twelve years, I know his voice as well as mine. I have tried to faithfully recapture it here as best I could. For more than ten of those twelve years, we lived under the same roof and experienced the events and had the conversations I've written about in this book. Both are recounted as accurately as I remember them.

—RON HALL, SEPTEMBER 2017

Preface

I'm not really a betting man, though I am a gambler. That said, if you are reading this preface, you are probably one of the millions who read *Same Kind of Different as Me*, the first *New York Times* bestseller coauthored by a skitzy, homeless ex-con known as Suicide who could not read or write.

If that's not the case, then let me say welcome. I hope you will join Suicide and me on this untold journey that straddles a Texas canyon between insanity and hilarity for a long tumble in the whitewater until tragedy shows its ugly head. And hopefully, after you have turned the last page and said, "Dang, that was fun," you will circle back to our first book and make some sense out of all this craziness.

This story is for Debbie, who on her deathbed gave me a job to do, and for Beth, who years later encouraged me to write about it—then cracked the whip until I finished.

1

I am trav'ling tow'rd life's sunset gate,

I'm a pilgrim going home.

—"THE SUNSET GATE"

DENVER

I looked out over the crowd—mostly white folk. Wadn't nary a dry eye in the whole church. They was affectin me, and that ain't normal 'cause I seldom makes eye contact 'less I be thinkin 'bout takin care of bidness, if you get my drift. I paused, tryin to figure out what I was gonna say next. Maybe I done said enough—seemed like I'd been talkin 'bout thirty minutes. Then it come to me.

"I'm fixin to do somethin the Devil ain't never done for you—I'm gonna cut you loose. But before I do, I'm gonna leave you with a little somethin to think about. Whether we is rich or whether we is poor, or somethin in between, this earth ain't no final restin place. So in a way, we is all homeless—ever last one of us—just workin our way home."

A rich-lookin man 'bout fifty years old on the front row stood up and pointed his finger at me. That shut me down. I thought I might have made the fella mad tellin rich white folk they's homeless just like me. But the next thing I knowed, the lady next to him stood up, then Mr. Ron and his family stood up, and before I knowed it, the whole crowd, maybe a thousand or so, was on they feet clappin like they was at some kinda performance.

I never really wanted to know Miss Debbie. Miss Debbie forced me to know her. That was the stubbornest woman I ever met—black or white. That's sayin a lot for some skinny little white lady who wadn't scared of me, 'cause everbody else on the streets feared me—I made sure of that. I guess I'd have to say Miss Debbie was a stubborn angel, my angel that I wadn't never lookin for or never wanted. For the life of me, I never could quite figure the lady out, but she loveded me and never gave up on me.

Sad to say, she died before she seen me as the man she wanted me to be. She used to tell me, "Denver, you got a callin on your life, and you're gonna live to see it." That's why I be standin up here like a preacher in this big white-folk church to honor that lady in front of all these rich white folk. They was even a few fellas like me and some street ladies from the mission—God's people, Miss Debbie called 'em.

Miss Debbie wanted to bring about a change in my life—at least see me act a little nicer and help her help the homeless. Over and over, she kept tellin me I had to change places and playgrounds—leave my past. Bossy. She even offered me to move in with her family. For sure, I wadn't gonna be movin in with no rich white lady and her husband and kids and lose my status in the hood. I told her I was a bad man, but that lady was stone deaf to my objections. She say she didn't see no bad man—she seen a good heart. Seemed to me the lady was wearin Superman's glasses and was able to see plumb through all my anger and confusion to a heart only I knowed was locked up inside my scarred black skin. But now she's gone. I figure God needed her more in heaven than down here on the streets. God don't make no mistakes. Did you hear me?

Now, Mr. Ron—well, I figured the onliest reason he was bein

my friend is 'cause Miss Debbie told him to. That man didn't never want to disappoint his wife or tell her no. He'd done somethin he was payin for. But now that she's gone, I figure he's gonna cut me loose and go about his life. We's friendly, but to tell you the truth, I don't let nobody, I said nobody, get close to me. Never have, never will. Although Miss Debbie come real close.

After the service, I slipped out the back door to avoid havin to talk to nobody. I've always been skitzy 'bout talkin to folks—especially whites.

I'd borrowed a suit to wear, a real nice one so I wouldn't be an embarrassment to Miss Debbie's family. Now, what's a fella like me gonna do with a suit? I ain't got no place to go or no place to hang it, so I walked right back in the mission store and hung it back on the rack so it's there for someone else who need to look nice for just a day.

The clothes I wore before the funeral that mornin got throwed in the Dumpster, which ain't no big deal since I ain't never bought no clothes, not really. So I picked out a new pair of dark-brown britches and a brown belt to hold 'em up. A brown shirt, the same color, caught my eye, and I put it on. Then, quick as I slicked up for church, I slid back into my comfortable spot in the hobo jungle near the tracks.

Unless you ever walked in my shoes, you wouldn't understand how I could stay in the bushes in a cardboard box surrounded by hoodlums, crooks, killers, and thieves. Nobody never trusted nobody in the hobo jungle. That's why you never seen me without my base-ball bat. I enforced my own brand of justice. Why do you think everbody on the streets called me Suicide? It wadn't 'cause I was a nice fella! That's called self-protection-izin.

I found a big piece of cardboard in the Dumpster and laid down on the wet ground from the mornin rain in the shade of a big ol' oak tree. I hadn't really slept in the last three days since Miss Debbie passed. When I closed my eyes, I just be thinkin 'bout Miss Debbie.

Ain't nobody ever seen me cry—specially on the streets, where they thinks I'm the meanest man alive. So I put a rag over my head to hide my face from the other fellas that was layin up in the bushes. In fact, the last time I remember cryin 'fore that was when I was a little boy and watched Big Mama burn up in a fire. I tried to save her, but she just wouldn't wake up after takin them Red Devil pills. She was a large woman, top to bottom and back to front, too heavy for me to drag out.

Them red and yellow flames looked like the Devil hisself was fannin 'em and killin her. I heard her cryin out for Jesus as the roof come crashin down on her. That was the terriblest thing ever happened to me. You just don't never get over somethin so tragible like that.

But here I was in just about the same spot I laid forty years ago— two days after I hopped on a freight train as it was passin by the plantation. Life there was slow and easy. Listen to me: ain't nothin more beautiful than a black-land cotton field ready for the pickin. Slimy green alligator-filled swamps lined with cyprus trees don't sound too appealin to someone who ain't never sat on the bank with a fishin pole watchin snakes slither and listenin to the bull-frogs croak. It brings tears to my eyes thinkin 'bout the beauty and wonderment of Louisiana.

There was plenty of work for the coloreds till mochinery took all the jobs. Wadn't long after that our peoples was forced into city slums with no money, no education, and no hope. I hung 'round longer than most—till the Man cut everbody loose 'cept the Boss Nigger. When he cut off my credit at his store, I just walked across the blacktop road and climbed up inside that boxcar. I smiled till I fell asleep. That was freedom.

I'd never been more than thirty miles off that Louisiana plantation—the Man made sure a that. I knowed people on the out-side say we was free, but on the inside, I felt like his slave. I had no idea where that freight train was goin. A hobo layin up in there told me prob'ly California. Didn't matter. I had plenty of time to get there.

When that train finally come to a stop, I got off and walked right into this camp—it ain't changed much. I asked a fella where I was at, and he say Fort Worth, Texas. I knowed it wadn't California, but I figured it was a long way from the plantation—too far for the Man to come lookin for me.

The big city and me didn't get along very well. Too much confusion, hustlin, and runnin game. Things got bad in a hurry when a fella tried to rob me and shot me in the leg with a .357 Mag. I ended up on another freight train, runnin and hidin from the law, 'cause I gave him a taste of his own medicine. A few days later, one of the hobos I was ridin with say we was in Los Angeles. I stayed a purty good while out there, but I ain't wantin to talk 'bout that. There was a lotta allegations against me in that town, but the allegator didn't know the whole truth. So I eased on outta there on the next freight train goin slow enough for me to hop on.

I ended up back in Fort Worth and set up camp right here in the jungle. It was the onliest place I knowed. And to tell you the truth, I didn't have no other place to go—still don't. This is where I began my new life, runnin from the past with a secret I didn't want nobody to find out.

I been carryin this secret—a lotta secrets—a long time. Ain't never told nobody, and hoped I'd never have to. Miss Debbie got me to start talkin 'bout my past, and I almost spilled the beans once or twice 'cause she was the first person I ever trusted. But I still ain't told nobody. Now that she's gone, don't know if I ever will. But it's a load to carry. Did you hear what I said?

2

RON

I woke up to the news that George W. Bush had won the presidency. Just three weeks before, my wife, Debbie, and I had watched the last debate. Politics for her was a passion, and she was a big supporter of Bush. Now she was gone. But knowing her, I would not doubt that some of her new friends in high places might have helped with the election.

The kids and I were driving to the church about an hour before the start of Debbie's memorial service. I dialed Denver's cell phone over and over, but he wasn't answering. He'd already lost three phones since Debbie gave him his first one a few months ago. This was not a good time to lose another one.

Denver and I had talked early that morning as he drove back to Fort Worth from our ranch at Rocky Top. He said he was shaking with the chills and sadly would not be able to attend her service. Reluctantly, like it was a secret, he told me he had spent the whole night before keeping watch over Debbie's grave at the ranch, where we'd buried her the previous afternoon. I asked him why, since it had rained most of the night—a cold rain. But after living outside for so many years, he said the rain didn't bother him. "It was cleansing," he said, adding he had prayed for Debbie's service the whole night long and wasn't going to stop until it was finished.

I just couldn't accept that he wasn't coming, so I kept dialing his number, hoping he would answer, miraculously feeling better. He didn't. As we walked in the sanctuary and took our seats, through the blur and fog of my own tears, I visualized Debbie crying in heaven. One of her final special requests was for her friend Denver to say a few words at her service.

There was a commotion at the back of the church. The crowd all seemed to turn their heads at once to see who was arriving as the preacher began reading Debbie's eulogy. I'd never seen him so freshly scrubbed—wearing a suit and tie with shoes that shined like a mirror. He looked shockingly handsome, in contrast to his preferred vagrant style. After two years my heart and eyes were no strangers to this miracle transformation.

For the next few minutes a profound sadness lifted. Tears of joy flowed like the Brazos River as Denver walked down the aisle, followed by a few of Debbie's homeless friends—Mr. Ballentine, Hal, Clara, and two ladies I didn't know.

Though Denver and I had been friends for nearly two years, I'd never heard him speak more than a few words of wisdom. He was the silent type and had been most of his life, according to him. But this was a good day to break his silence. He spoke like a graduate of a master speaking class, inciting nearly a thousand mourners to stand and applaud—something I'd never seen nor heard of at a funeral. When he finished speaking, he slipped away as if he'd been an actor in a magician's illusion.

The next morning as my kids, Regan and Carson, and I were packing our car, I got a call from Don Shisler, who ran the Union Gospel Mission where we'd first met Denver. Immediately after Debbie's service, he'd received several calls from her friends. They wanted to donate money to build the mission of Debbie's dream, which Denver had spoken about at the service. Nearly five hundred thousand dollars was already committed.

I tried again to call Denver, but still no answer. I was uneasy about leaving for a week to decompress with my kids without at least letting him know. His words about friendship from one of our first meetings rang in my ears.

I had asked him to be my friend, and he'd told me he'd have to "thank about it." A couple of weeks after that meeting, I spotted him on the streets, taking trash out of a Dumpster and feeding the wild birds. I rolled down the window and asked him to go with me to Starbucks. Reluctantly, he slowly walked to the passenger side and opened the door without a word.

When he first heard the cashier ring up and say, "Four dollars please," he refused his cup, saying: "Coffee is free at the mission. Why pay for somethin that's free?"

A few moments later, sitting on the patio, he stared me in the eyes and said, "I been thinkin a lot about what you asked me."

"What did I ask you that required any thought?" I replied.

"You asked me if I'd be your friend."

"Yes, I did. So what do you think?"

"Before I decides if I's gonna be your friend, I need to ask you a question 'bout fishin."

"I don't fish much, Denver. In fact, I don't even own a rod and reel or a tackle box, so I'm not sure I can answer."

"Betcha you can." He seemed to stare deep into my soul.

"Well, ask."

"I heard when white folks go fishin, they do this thing called catch and release."

"Of course they do. It's a sport—don't you get it?"

"Nosir, I sure don't."

He went on to tell me that back on the plantation they would go out in the morning, dig a can full of worms, cut a cane pole, and sit on the riverbank all day long. When they finally got something on the line, they were real proud of it. They would take it back to the plantation and share the catch with all the folks.

Denver said, "So, it occurred to me, if you is a white man that is fishin for a friend, and you gonna catch and release, then I ain't got no desire to be your friend."

My body twitched at first, then relaxed as if an electrical shock of profound wisdom had coursed through my veins. Never had I heard something so wise from a scholar, much less an illiterate.

My mind flashed back to Debbie's dream about a poor man who was wise, and by whose wisdom our lives and city would be changed. Staring at my coffee, unable to look him in the eye, I took a minute or so to contemplate what he'd said—his blast of wisdom had fragmented my thinking. Could I actually be hearing from God myself? I considered that possibility before I raised my head and looked Denver in the eye. "If you will be my friend, I promise I will not catch and release."

"Then you gots a friend forever, Mr. Ron."

Those were the words that haunted me now as I prepared to leave town. For the last nineteen months during Debbie's battle with cancer, Denver had been at our home every day. Now she was gone, and the family was going away without him. I didn't want him to think I'd released him. But he wasn't answering his phone. He lived in the hobo jungle that no white man would dare to enter and live to tell about it.

So, sadly, we headed west on the interstate without ever telling him. Guilt rode shotgun for the next four hundred miles.

3

DENVER

Mr. Shisler seen me in line for supper and told me Mr. Ron told him to tell me he'd gone on a retreat with his kids. I figured somethin done happened. Wadn't like him to not be callin or comin by to pick me up. But Lord have mercy, that man and his kids needed a break after carin for Miss Debbie the way they did.

The funny thing is, Mr. Shisler laughed when he say the word *retreat*, 'cause he remembered the time Miss Debbie took *me* on a retreat.

I'll never forget that day when she showed up at the mission in her big ol' white-on-white fancy somethin or 'nother 'bout half the size of a bus, with four more white ladies in the back.

"Anybody seen Suicide?" she asked some of the homeboys sittin on the curb. They all pointed toward the hobo jungle, and she run across the street and right into the jungle like a hobo runnin from the law. I 'spect she be the first white lady ever to set foot in the jungle. I know she knowed how dangerous it was in them bushes, but she wadn't scared.

"Denver!" I could hear her callin out in her purty little voice.

"Denver!" she hollered again as I hung tight like a rabbit avoidin a coyote. I covered my head with a blanket tryin to keep her from findin me, 'cause I did not want to go to no retreat with a bunch of white ladies. But some fella, without sayin a word, pointed his finger and ratted me out. She jerked that blanket off my head and

10

grabbed my hand like I was a little boy and dragged me out of the bushes.

Some of the homeboys seen what was goin down, and they started snickerin and singin "Swing Low, Sweet Chariot." You know that's a funeral song.

I seen them other white ladies in her SUV, and I started thinkin about the time when three white boys put a rope 'round my neck and dragged me behind a horse for helpin a white lady change a flat tire on a dirt road near the plantation. I was purty sure they daddies was KKK. That was prob'ly fifty years ago.

Until Miss Debbie, I ain't never again spoke to no white ladies, not really—except Sister Bettie at the mission. But Sister Bettie ain't no real white lady; she a color-blind sure 'nough saint. I'm gonna tell you I was sweatin like a death-row inmate strapped down in Ol' Sparky as I wiggled my six-foot, two-hundred-seventy-five-pound self in the car with them ladies and headed out to a cabin in the woods for this retreat they'd been tellin me about.

It was hard for me to believe none of they husbands was goin with 'em. And even harder to believe them husbands would let they wives spend the weekend in a cabin with a dangerous, skitzy nigga like me.

But Miss Debbie, she knowed what she was doin, 'cause I come back a changed man. A free man—freed up from the Devil's prison. That's when I almost told her what I still ain't told nobody.

4

RON

Big Bend National Park was an elixir for three sore hearts. The kids and I floated the river—the Rio Grande—for a couple of days in pure solitude. That river's canyon, though smaller than the Grand Canyon, is the most magnificent stretch of river in Texas. The silence was healing after weeks of painful death cries and agony.

The three of us talked a lot about Debbie and her legacy. How as a family could we honor her life and use her death to make a difference? Regan debated her return to her job at a Young Life camp in Colorado. Carson would be heading back to New York City, where he was set to open his own gallery. Then there was me—a fifty-five-year-old wreck of an art dealer. What did life have in store for me now? Would I remarry? Would I ever be happy again? And where would I live? It seemed too painful to stay in our dream home, now full of ghosts.

And Denver? Catch and release—really? What could I do with that?

I considered him a friend—a good one. But with Debbie in heaven, I found myself reflecting on that day at Starbucks and wondering what I'd meant when I agreed to that. As I floated down the Rio Grande, all this seemed so heavy, so burdensome. Did I really want to be tethered to a homeless man for the rest of my life? More important, did God want me to be?

Starting life over at my age meant freedom to go and do as I pleased, I decided. *Yes, I'll provide for his welfare if he lets me. But he is stubborn, unreasonable, and skitzy, as he tells me constantly.*

And something else. Though we had spent a lot of time together, I really didn't know the man apart from a few personal things he'd told me—and prying that little bit of information out of him had been more difficult than pulling a railroad spike out of a cross tie. I suspected he was running from something a lot more troubling than picking the Man's cotton. Plus, I wasn't even sure his real name was Denver. It sounded too convenient for a man who rode the rails.

I didn't share this thinking with the kids or anyone else. It was embarrassing. Shameful. The past year had left me too exposed. Raw. My doubts and fears, for the present, would be my secret friends.

"Denver, is that you?" It was good to hear him laugh when I got back into cell-service range and answered his call. "Yessir, it's your amigo Negro," he chuckled. He was making fun of a time a few months back when I took him to my country club and he overheard one of the members refer to him as such. I dropped out of that club.

Curious about our retreat, he wondered if it was anything like the one Miss Debbie had taken him on. Then he asked if I'd come get him and take him to eat when we returned. There was something bothering him; it was obvious as his tone of voice flipped to another side of him. "We need to talk," he said.

"What are you doing in the morning?"

"I's homeless. Ain't got nuthin to do!"

5

Denver

I drove out to Mr. Ron's ranch to visit Miss Debbie. The white roses on her grave was all dead and brown, blendin into the dirt like clods piled up on her coffin. Can you believe that rich lady wanted to be buried in a pauper's pine box just like the homeless?

It was a peaceful site, high on a hill overlookin the Brazos River. I sat on a big, flat rock under a giant oak tree that leaned hard like the wind done tried to blow it down. But oak trees is strong, like Miss Debbie, and in all my days on earth, I ain't never seen one blowed down. I was tryin to make sense of why God blowed her down.

I asked God why he done took such a beautiful woman, who loveded the homeless and was makin a difference on the streets of Fort Worth. I told God if he'd let her rise up from this grave like Lazarus, I'd trade places with her. That's how much I loveded her.

I thought about how Miss Debbie ain't done none of the bad things I done over the years. I deserved a death sentence. She deserved more years of life. She deserved to see her kids all growed up and married. She deserved to teach her grandchildren how to love the unlovables like me. I ain't done no good for nobody. And there I was still alive—actin a fool sometimes, smokin all the time. It just didn't make no sense.

They was lots of rocks layin 'round that the gravedigger left, so I decided to pile 'em up on her grave so the wolves wouldn't dig her up and gnaw her bones. All the while I was thankin her for all the things she done for me, like fixin my teeth. I only had two or three when we first met, and both of 'em felt rough and rotten. Maybe you don't understand how I didn't know if it was two or three, but I never looked at myself in no mirrors. Looks ain't important. Courage and respect is all that matters, and you can't see them in no mirrors.

She bought me a car, too—not no junker, a nice Ford SUV—and Mr. Ron taught me to drive in his Mercedes. Even though I wrecked the first one she gave me, she bought me another one, even better, without so much as a scoldin word ever spoken. That's real forgiveness. Same goes for my cell phones that I lose purty often. She just say, "Oh, Denver," and buy me another.

6

Ron

Denver was sitting on the curb dressed in clean slacks and shirt—surprisingly right on time, but then he confessed he'd been sitting there since sunup. After tacos at his favorite Mexican restaurant, we headed out to the ranch. He specifically asked to go there but didn't say why.

We started winding up the dirt-road portion of Chestnut Mountain on the last leg of our journey when for some reason, unprovoked, he started laughing so hard he had trouble catching his breath. He grabbed his chest over his heart, and I started to pull over, but he told me to keep driving.

"What's so funny?" I asked.

"Mr. Ron, ain't nobody ever gonna believe our story. We gots to write us a book!"

"What's this 'we'? You don't read or write, so who is gonna write your part?"

"You know what I mean. I'm gonna tell you my part, and you write it down. You already know your part, so write that down. And when we finish we'll put the two together, and we'll have us a book!"

Debbie's horse, Rocky, ran along the fence like he was hoping it was her. She always brought him apples or carrots. We stopped at the barn, fed him and the others, and talked about the possibility of Denver's moving out to the ranch. He shot that down like a clay pigeon.

16

He walked up the stairs to the big hayloft and sat down on a
bale of alfalfa, then hollered down: "I like it up here. If you really
want me stayin out here at your ranch, then you can build me a little
sleepin spot up here in the loft."

Debbie would like that. That afternoon I called an architect and
asked him to make it a priority. He promised we could have it finished in no more than six months.

7

DENVER

Mr. Ron and me walked up to Miss Debbie's grave. He could see I'd been there, and he was happy about that. We sat on that big rock, starin at her grave without sayin nothin, when I got to thinkin to myself that this rich white man trusted me with his most valuable things, includin his wife and cars—that just ain't normal. Miss Debbie and him are the onliest people ever trusted me with anything. I sure 'nough didn't wanna let 'em down. But I couldn't help wonderin—if they knowed the real me, would they still be that trustin, takin me to church and clubs and all they friends' mansions? I figured if they knowed, they'd have armed guards protectin 'em from me. I wished I'd met somebody like 'em back 'fore things went down like they did.

I told Mr. Ron I wanted to gather lots of rocks and build a wall 'round Miss Debbie's grave, make it a proper graveyard. He said he'd help and we'd start the next mornin.

As the sun was goin down we sat on the big porch where it seemed to me you could look so far and see half of Texas—and California too. I asked Mr. Ron if he was okay, and he say he was, but I knowed he was lyin. The man didn't eat nuthin. He just sat 'round in his shorts drinkin wine and smoking them big cigars. Seemed to me he just wanna die and get buried up there on the hill next to Miss Debbie. I don't really like it that I gots to worry 'bout somebody, but the man ain't nuthin but a bag o' bones.

That night after supper I was headin outside to sleep on the ground when Mr. Ron said he wadn't gonna have none of that. He walked me up the stairs to Mr. Carson's room, showed me the bed and shower, and told me to sleep there.

I'd been at that house many times before, but never to spend the night. Miss Debbie would try and make me stay, but I'd always find a way to slip off. Never in my life did I think I'd be sleepin in some white millionaire's house, usin they toilet and shower. I ain't never knowed any colored folk that could boast about that.

After I showered, I found me a patchwork quilt in the closet like Big Mama used to make and decided I'd sleep *on* the bed—not *in* it. It just seemed too personal—sleepin in white folks' bed.

Now, I'd been layin there quite a while with the cover over my face like everbody do in the jungle—that's so nobody can see who you is, in case somebody be lookin for you. But I wadn't sleepin. Then the air started kinda whistlin and stirrin like somebody was movin 'round in the room—kinda scary. I gots animal instincts that comes from livin outside. I feels things normal folk can't feel. I was thinkin maybe Mr. Ron was checkin on me, makin sure I slept where he told me to.

You prob'ly ain't gonna believe this, but the stirrin air went stone-cold silent and still. I laid there still as a dead man till a peace come over me. Through the quilt I could see a bright light like somebody flipped a switch—but they didn't. That light was big and round, and in the middle of it the shape of a person was walkin toward my bed. There weren't no footsteps—no noise at all, silent as a morgue after closin time. I felt her soft hand as she pulled the quilt off my face, and there she was—Miss Debbie, dressed in white like an angel, all healed up and purty as ever.

"Denver, you are always welcome to stay in our home." It was her voice for sure—it ain't forgettable.

"Thank you, Miss Debbie."

Then she just evaporated like river fog at sunrise. It wadn't no dream 'cause I ain't never gone to sleep. It was straight up a visitation from an angel—Miss Debbie.

8

RON

Denver's perfect teeth looked like a piano keyboard as he grinned from ear to ear behind the wheel of our big green John Deere tractor. It was a beautiful clear morning with a slight coolness to the air as we began gathering rocks in the front-end loader. Denver reminded me about a conversation we had the first time I invited him to drive my tractor.

"Mr. Ron, did you know all the crime and problems we have in the hood can be traced right back to Mr. John Deere? He done made a mochine that could do ever job the black folk was doin. A few years later, even though they didn't have no cars, hunger drive 'em straight to the cities, where there wadn't no jobs for folks with no education. So they went to work for the gov'ment—it's called welfare, where they gets paid to do nothin!"

I marveled at his insight and perspective, especially since he was one of those who had never gone to school—had never even been given the opportunity.

I warned him to kick the rocks over with his boot before using his hands—Rocky Top was famous for its rattlesnake population. Luckily, none were hiding under the piles of rocks we stacked up that day. However, we found a few tarantulas, which he picked up and let crawl up his arm like ladybugs. He claimed to have had a pet tarantula as a kid.

We talked about a name for the cemetery we were building. He

21

didn't understand why it needed a name, and I explained that it had
to be registered with the state and mapped so anyone who wanted
to visit her grave could find it. I told him how Debbie loved that our
ranch was on the Brazos River, whose original name was *Rio de los
Brazos de Dios*. The River of the Arms of God.

"I think Miss Debbie might have named it herself 'cause she
be layin right here in the arms of God." So we agreed, and in the
dirt with a stick I sketched an arch that read "Brazos de Dios," with
gates to match.

That evening we fished from the river bank. I caught an alliga-
tor gar, the most disgusting fish that inhabited those waters. It has a
long snout like a gator, with hundreds of needle-sharp teeth that can
rip a man's arm off. Denver helped me get it off the line, and as I was
about to throw it back, he said, "We gots to gut and clean this fish,
Mr. Ron. You ain't never s'posed to catch and release!"

"Are you serious? Gut and clean a trash fish like a gar?" I laughed,
but he was serious—so we did it.

Those days I was really struggling with Debbie's final request,
spoken to me just hours before she died. "Ron," she whispered,
"please don't give up on Denver. God is going to bless your friendship more than you can ever imagine." Now, nearly two months
after she made that heartfelt plea, I was feeling it less as a request
and more as a command—in other words, a job.

Sometimes when I couldn't sleep I would get a little angry at
her for asking me to do such a ridiculous thing. Or was it really
ridiculous? What did "not give up" actually mean? If I stuck it out,
would people think I was a hero or an idiot? Did I really care? I
guess I did.

What was Debbie thinking? Did she even know? How did
heaven work anyway? I'd heard of rare occasions when people died
and went to heaven, only to find out God was not ready for them,
so he sent them back to earth. But from what I'd read about those

magical mystery trips, the returnees didn't ever talk about the loved ones they saw in heaven being angry about broken promises.

Did I even make that promise to Debbie anyway? I remembered her asking, but I couldn't for the life of me remember if I'd answered.

I hadn't shared my feelings about that with anyone. And I wasn't going to give up on Denver—didn't even want to. But how was I supposed to blend someone like him into my life—my future? It was out of the question for me to blend into his way of life.

After two days of working, Denver and I had gathered and piled enough rocks to build a fifty-foot square wall around Debbie's gravesite, with plenty of room for other graves.

We stood side by side, proud, as the setting sun filtering through the oak leaves seemed to cast a holy light on her grave.

"Denver, would you like to be buried out here with Miss Debbie?"

He looked at me, head cocked and tilted, one eye squinting closed like I was crazy, and replied, "Not yet!"

9

DENVER

Mister Ron and his kids was goin off to Mexico for Christmas. They invited me, but I ain't got no interest in goin someplace where I don't know what they is sayin. You know I gets a little skitzy when I think folks is talkin 'bout me. Plus, he said somethin 'bout a pass-port. Now, what's a fella like me gonna do with a passport? First of all, I ain't never wanted or needed to be flyin on no airplanes. I gots no place to go and plenty of time to gets there.

Sometimes, though, I feel like I need to burn off, 'specially when I ain't been doin right. And when that happens, I hops me a freight train. They ain't never asked me for no passports.

When we left the ranch after pickin up all them rocks and stackin 'em, Mr. Ron let me drive his big green four-by-four Ford pickup back to the mission. That's the same one he let me drive when I got my drivin license and took all his daughter's worldly goods up to Colorado. I slept in that truck the whole week 'cause I wadn't sure if other states wanted black homeless fellas stayin in they motel. One day I drove the whole day and ended up back in the same place I started that morning. It's hard to make it from Texas to Colorado when you can't read no road signs. Finally I figured out if I stopped at ever fillin station along the way and asked which way it was to Colorado, I'd finally get there—and I did.

I really like that truck. It be a real man's truck, though I come

24

real close to drivin it off the side of a mountain 'cause I didn't really understand what a mountain really was.

Anyway, on the way back into Fort Worth from the ranch that day, Mr. Ron asked me if I'd like to drive it for a bit. It's hard for me to believe the man would trust me with a fifty-thousand-dollar truck like that, 'specially after I done wrecked the Ford SUV they gave me.

I only had it a coupla months when I wrecked it. And that wouldn't be so bad if I ain't forgot to pay the insurance payment. Ain't nobody to blame but me for that. Miss Debbie done give me the money to take to the insurance man, but I kinda forgot and kinda spent it on a few other things that I didn't want to tell her about. Now I know why you is s'posed to pay the insurance bill *before* you stop off at a liquor store—'cause I ended up with no truck.

That little accident caused Mr. Ron to run hot when I asked him to give me a ride and he asked me why I couldn't drive myself. Guess I shoulda thought about that before I asked him, but I knowed I was gonna have to tell him some time or 'nother. Miss Debbie overheard him kinda raisin his voice at me and asked what the problem was.

"He wrecked his truck and the insurance wasn't paid, so it's a total loss. And now he has nothing to drive."

"Oh, Denver," she said, "you are going to have to learn to be a better driver and learn about responsibility. And you, Mr. Ronnie Ray—you are going to have to learn about forgiveness, mercy, and grace!"

10

RON

Christmas that year was one of the worst days of my life. I was too depressed to get out of bed, though we were on one of the most beautiful beaches in the world. It had not even been two months since Debbie's death, and the sting was still as painful as a fresh hornet bite. Sitting in a pool lounger, drinking margaritas, and listening to "Feliz Navidad" with strangers from New Jersey made me realize it had been a mistake to run from the extended family and friends who had been our source of comfort and understanding for the last two years.

An old cowboy once told me good judgment comes from experience—and a lot of that experience comes from bad judgment. I was living out the results of my bad judgment that Christmas.

Finally, by late afternoon, Regan and Carson convinced me to join them on the beach and get massages under a grass *palapa*. That evening we shared our favorite Christmas stories in an outdoor restaurant with a spectacular view of the hot orange sun dipping into the blue Pacific Ocean. God's art at its best.

The subject of Denver finally came up—again. What should I do about him? What part would Regan and Carson play? I told them about building him his own place in the barn at Rocky Top. We all agreed that was a good start. But did Denver really want to be with us? We hadn't really thought about that. Would he prefer just sliding back into his comfort zone as Suicide, king of the jungle?

26

At least twice Debbie had asked him to move in with us. On both occasions he'd sternly refused, citing freedom as the reason he did not want to live any way but the way he had lived for more than twenty-five years—homeless, by a Dumpster, or in a cardboard box in the hobo jungle. He claimed it was an honor to have the respect of every single homeless person on the streets—something he had not only earned, but demanded. The bloodstains on his Louisville Slugger bat were evidence of his demands. How else could he have earned the nickname Suicide—the only name he'd been known by for most of the years he'd spent homeless? Would he be likely to give that up now, especially now that Debbie was gone?

We discussed his mental state. Would our lives be endangered by bringing a homeless man into our home—a man who, by his own admission, was a skitzy alcoholic prone to bursts of violent anger? Surely there were too many unknowns, too much risk to leave someone like him alone in our million-plus-dollar home filled with a multimillion-dollar art collection. Would our insurance company drop us if I revealed this kind of information?

But even more important than all these considerations was this: What would Debbie want us to do?

The only decisions we made that evening were that Carson would return to New York City and continue to run our art business and Regan would pick up where she had left off in Colorado. As for me, I decided I would spend the next few months in Italy. I had always wanted to study painting and sculpting. Now seemed the perfect time to get away and contemplate starting life over—and figuring out what to do with Denver.

11

DENVER

DENVER

Before Mr. Ron left for It'ly, I reminded him we need to write us a book. Well, I'm thinkin he agreed with me, 'cause he bought me a tape recorder and gave me some lessons in usin it. He told me to find a quiet place, and ever time I thought 'bout somethin, to record it. He wanted to know everthing I could remember 'bout my life, includin the plantation and streets.

Now, if I told him everthing 'bout what I done on the streets, I'd scare the livin daylights outta the man. I ain't gonna lie—the streets'll turn a man mean, and ain't no rich white folks gonna want be hangin with a fella like me if they knowed all the stuff that went down in the hood. If a man tells it all, he ain't got nothin else to say. So I decides I'm gonna leave out a few things so I don't run outta stuff to tell him if he starts diggin.

To tell you the truth, if Mr. Ron was gonna be tryin to dig up stuff on me, he ain't gots to dig too deep! But I gots things, and plenty of 'em, that I don't plan on ever tellin nobody—book or no book. I be takin 'em to the grave.

It wadn't too long after Mr. Ron left I ended up back in jail. I been in and out of jail so many times I done lost count. I'd been tryin to be good since Miss Debbie met me, but I did spend a coupla days in jail while she was sick. I sure didn't want her to know that, though.

The po-lice say I was drivin the wrong way on a one-way street in somebody else's truck. They run my license through they computer

28

and seen they was several tickets I ain't paid. Truthfully, I ain't never paid no kinda ticket for two reasons. One, I ain't never had no money, and two, you ain't gotta pay nothin if you is willin to go to jail for a few days. So sittin in a jail cell is just like makin money to me.

Actually, I was mighty thankful for the opportunity to have three hots and a cot back then on account of the big ice storm we was havin. Most of the time in terrible weather I would check into the mission, but it fills up fast when the temperatures head below freezin. There's been times when it was so cold I'd show up at the jail and beg 'em to arrest me. So I figured if I sat out my fine in jail, it would mean more room for another fella to take cover in the mission. To me, I was doin somebody a good deed like that good Samaritan in the Bible.

Once, when the mission was full durin a snowstorm, I slept in a graveyard—in a fresh-dug grave. Now, I know that sounds crazy, but it ain't nothin but the truth. Some colored ladies was waitin on a bus right after sunrise the next mornin when they seen me come up out of that grave all covered in snow. Them two ladies took one look at me, and they both screamed at the same time, "He risen from the dead!" They took off runnin like they feet was on fire, even faster than them fellas in the O-lympics. I gots a good laugh outta that myself.

While I was coolin my heels in the cell for a few days, some fella in the next cell flashed me a sign—a secret one, known only to a few. He knowed who I was, and that was fixin to be a problem. I act like I didn't see it 'cause, for sure, I didn't need nobody spewin no trash about me. I done put that stuff in the past.

When my time had been served, I walked back to the jungle to check on Mr. Ron's truck, and I thought my eyes was lyin. They was six or seven more tickets stuck under the windshield wiper. Since I don't know how to read, I asked Mr. Shisler at the mission what I'd done wrong. Seems like I'd parked Mr. Ron's truck in a no-parkin zone. In my mind, there wadn't no meter, so I figured it was a free spot. But the po-lice didn't see it that way. They came by ever day and put a fresh ticket on the windshield until I come back to claim it.

The good news is I could sit them tickets out in jail the next time a big cold spell blowed in. That's the good thing about Mr. Ron bein off in some foreign country. He ain't callin to check on me ever day. Plus, I done lost another cell phone, so I don't has to tell him till he gets back home.

For the next several weeks, I'd drive out on the interstate toward Rocky Top and sit on a picnic table at the roadside park and talk into the tape recorder. After the highway patrolman seen me there several days in a row, he pull up, turn on his flashin lights, and order me lean up against Mr. Ron's truck with my hands above my head and spread my legs. He was actin like I done robbed the First State Bank. I guess a homeless-lookin fella drivin a fifty-thousand-dollar truck stick out like a chunk of coal in a snow pile.

He wanted to know what I was doin there. I says, "I'm writin me a book," and he kinda smarted off, "I'm sure you are!" Then he started stickin his hands in my pockets, so I asked him what he was doin. "I'm just lookin for the keys to my solid-gold Rolls Royce." We both started laughin. I knowed he was just doin his job. After that, when he seen me, he'd stop and ask me about my book. He always say he wanna read it.

12

RON

Grief is personal. Everyone experiencing the unavoidable consequence of a loved one's death must choose a path to get through it. It never occurred to me to write a book about grief because I ran from it—never wanting to get good at it, never wanting to medicate my way around it or through it.

A fun ship with a cruise director forcing me to interact with strangers was never an option. Being holed up in a mountain cabin would have driven me insane. I needed to see life and the living to get over death and the dying.

Boarding the plane to Rome, my heart seemed to have gone into hiding—numb. Yet my mind was well aware I was leaving my hometown and several grieving friends who were fully invested in Debbie's life. In our lives. They wanted to be a part of my grieving, which I only wanted to see in my rearview mirror. I knew in my heart that facing my grief with them could have provided a shortcut. However, facing anyone, strangers included, left me feeling too exposed.

For the last several weeks, I had slept in Debbie's closet in the contemporary dream home we'd build in Fort Worth just two years earlier to showcase our art collection and be closer to Rocky Top. That was the place where she dreamed about Denver, and where she met the angels who took her to heaven just two months before. On a pile of Debbie's clothes that still held the scent of her love,

I doubted God and battled the enemy. Night after night, I stayed in that closet so dark I felt like I was all alone in the world, falling down a shaft with no bottom and no end in sight. There was no one I wanted to see and no one I wanted to share this with. No one I trusted—not even God.

I read the celebrity gossip rags in grocery store lines to avoid eye contact and breakout pity parties. Sometimes I felt like a crazy old man as I smoked cigars naked in my backyard by the pool so I wouldn't have to answer the doorbell—not even for Denver, who often sat on my front porch for hours, even into the night. Every hour or so I'd stand on the commode and peek out a tall bathroom window and see him—usually on the steps, until his habit got the best of him; then he'd be sitting on the curb smoking. Finally I'd open the door because I knew he wouldn't leave until he saw my face and blessed me with an encouraging word.

Sadly, most of the time he waited, I secretly contemplated wiggling out of any real, lasting relationship with the man of Debbie's dream. To be honest, that was a big part of my leaving town.

It's funny, but not really—since her death I had dreamed of Debbie every single night. Some nights I dreamed I went to heaven to see her, and she would not speak to me because I had cut Denver loose. Other times I saw the three of us together in a brilliantly colored garden, laughing about how God threw us all together to save each other.

After a twelve-hour flight, a change of planes, and a two-hour train ride, refuge came in the fifteenth-century Villa Angeli, a former monastery and part-time residence of the pope near the tiny Etruscan village of Fiesole, tucked into the hills above Florence. My artist friend Julio, the current resident, offered me a room and a car and made available their Colombian nanny, Ché, as a tour guide and language coach.

Winter in Italy is about like winter in New England, cold and overcast most of the time, and a little sleepy. Debbie and I had made many wonderful trips to Italy, but always in warm months. I guess it was those memories that made me want to go. However, Florence looked so different in the winter—especially without her. Its ancient beauty was now cloaked in smoky grays and cold shades of black, the colors of mourning and grief.

Night and day, day and night, Debbie and Denver never left my mind. Or, let me be clear, her final request never left my mind as I chewed on it without ceasing, like a piece of gum that could not be spit out.

Florence, the city that inspired the world's greatest masters, Michelangelo and da Vinci, was Debbie's favorite city. As I strolled aimlessly through the narrow streets, I looked for her in the Piazza della Signoria and the Uffizi Gallery, the museum she loved the most. I stood in front of the pastry shop near the Ponte Vecchio and recalled her sitting on her suitcase waiting for hot *bombalonis* to drop from the fryer into a basket of powdered sugar. (We wagered the bill on who could eat the most before we boarded a train to Rome.) I said a prayer for her in the Basilica di Santa Croce and rubbed the nose of the bronze boar at the market for good luck.

One day, as I dipped a biscotto in my espresso, a realization slapped me upside my head. Pasta, pizza, and Chianti had to be better for me than the Prozac and Zoloft my doctors had prescribed. Best of all, here there would be no casseroles sitting on my front porch with perfumed notes of sympathy—and, thank God, no more pity parties and stares from those who knew me without really knowing me.

Truthfully I wanted no pity, for though I had endured great sadness and the physical pain of grief—losing thirty pounds, with skin left hanging on exposed bones—I was a blessed man. I grieved for the thousands of others who bury spouses on Sunday and have to show up at work on Monday, facing huge debts to hospitals and mortuaries, with nothing to show for their loss. Knowing my situation was different was the faint light that encouraged me as I sought the exit from the dark tunnel of grief.

Night and day, day and night, as I'd promised Denver, I wrote our story. I imagined him doing the same—but of course he couldn't write. So I imagined him sitting on the quiet riverbank at the ranch or on the big rock by Debbie's grave, speaking into his recorder.

Between fits of writing, under Julio's instruction, I did my best to learn something of the fine art of painting. Between the frustrations of contemplating first and last brush strokes on a canvas, I took long, soul-searching, and often inspirational drives through Tuscany and the Amalfi Coast. In Positano I drank limoncello. In Greve I learned how to make pesto and pasta. In Pietrasanta, a town Michelangelo put on the map in the fifteenth century when he selected Carrara as his marble of choice for sculpting the David, I got inspired to try sculpture—the first activity that seemed to take my mind a little off myself and the scarred earthen mound at Rocky Top.

Julio and a friend shared a studio just off the plaza in Pietrasanta near the atelier of legendary Italian film star Gina Lollobrigida, and I was privileged to be introduced to her. Late in life she had given up acting to become a sculptor. Unlike any artist I've ever met, she worked the clay while wearing elegant dresses instead of smocks; she was adorned with enough jewels to open a boutique. She claimed to enjoy my Texas accent and swagger, and of course I enjoyed hanging with the 1960s heartthrob of every red-blooded Italian male—though by this time she was pushing eighty.

Gina and I hung out for a couple of days, and I wowed her with tall tales of wild broncs I'd ridden and rattlesnakes I'd charmed like cobras with my poetry. She laughed at my story of how her lookalike had seduced me into buying not one, but two very expensive cashmere topcoats twenty years earlier. She raised her pinky finger slightly above her head and extended it for me to touch with mine— her germophobic Italian version of an American high five.

Hanging out with Julio and my new Italian friends helped distract me and mask the pain, but in my heart I was still alone. Time spent alone in the most beautiful place in the world is still time spent alone. As I lamented that thought one night to Julio at an outdoor trattoria, the waiter passed me a note with an invitation to a romantic dinner that evening. It was signed in red lipstick, "Love, Gina." Luckily, before I presented myself at her door, I recognized the handwriting—Julio!

Making my own sculptures and assisting Julio with his was the most enjoyable task I had undertaken in years. But writing, though cathartic, was frustrating. I filled countless trash cans with sloppy starts until I had more than a hundred pages of a first draft. I wondered about Denver's progress and tried to call him several times, but he never answered—probably he'd lost yet another phone. Sometimes my mind would drift off, wondering if we would be able to find a publisher. Probably not, because my part at least read like the world's longest thank-you note.

Day after day, in the cafés near the Piazza della Signoria, I told my story to Ché, who lent a sympathetic ear. She was intrigued with my stories about Denver and asked to read my manuscript, but I was not ready to share it. Ché was fascinating—spiritual, young, and beautiful—giving me cause to guard my heart. During the weeks we spent together, I gave her art-history lessons in museums, and she taught me to read Italian road signs while riding on the back of her Vespa.

After three and a half months, I awoke in Florence knowing it was springtime in Texas. The eagles would soon be flying north. I'd seen twelve of them in the big cottonwood tree below our house last Christmas morning. *How many are still there?* I wondered. The mockingbirds by now were building their nests, and Debbie's long-horn calves needed naming before they were branded.

After months of pizza and pasta, I longed for the smell of a big old chicken-fried steak wafting from the kitchen of a West Texas greasy-spoon café.

It was time to go home.

13

DENVER

"I know it ain't none of my bidness, but what do that say?" I asked Mr. Ron as we stood in front of the big arch and gates to the cemetery we built for Miss Debbie. A cross was on the top, pointin straight up to heaven.

"*Brazos de Dios.* That's Spanish for 'the arms of God.' Remember? It's the full name of the river."

"Sure do. I'm glad you put the cross on there, too, 'cause that stand for Jesus."

We stood there together, not sayin much but just restin in the beauty of bein there. This rough ol' hilltop was now a place of peace and beauty. They was yellow and purple wildflowers coverin all the rocks, dirt, and that big ol' brown scar in the earth.

"What do you think, Denver?"

"Nice. Real nice."

To tell you the truth, I was thinkin I was real proud of what I helped do. That's sayin a lot for a man that ain't never found nothin to be proud of. But I just keep my trap shut and give God the glory, 'cause it was Him that created all them rocks we stacked and planted all them purty wildflowers.

It was a beautiful Sunday morning, about six months since we laid Miss Debbie to rest. Mr. Ron said we was consecratin the cemetery and asked me to say a few words. I'd picked out a nice suit at the mission store—it fit me real good.

Cars, a bunch of 'em, was streamin down the ranch road kickin up dust. I could see 'em comin for a mile. I know a lotta Miss Debbie's friends and family was worried that Mr. Ron just left her out there unprotected. So the Brazos de Dios arch was a welcome sight, 'specially since it was topped with the cross that pointed up to heaven and the most beautiful blue sky Texas ever seen. There wadn't no sadness that day.

"As I stands here this mornin, I wants to say a few last words. Miss Debbie was a close enough friend of mine that I prayed and prayed and prayed for her day and night. Ain't nobody ever in my life that I prayed for like I prayed for her.

"I even prayed to God to let me take her place—let me go on in and let her stay here. I felt she was more worthy to be here on this earth and I'd be better off goin on up to heaven, 'cause I wadn't havin no good luck or good time at all down here. I was pleadin to let her stay on the earth 'cause she was the one that was bearin fruit.

"Now, Miss Debbie done cross the river to the other side. Sometime we just gots to be thankful for the things that hurt us, 'cause sometimes God does things that hurt us but they helps somebody else. If I holds on to Christ, when I end my journey here on this side, I's gonna sprout up on the other side of the river. That's where I'll see Miss Debbie again. And everbody that knowed her here, if you stays bound and rooted with Jesus, then we'll all get to heaven, and what a day of rejoicin that'll be.

"I'm thankful to be able to speak to y'all here today, and I thank God for Miss Debbie and Mr. Ron, Miss Regan and Mr. Carson, 'cause they's all been such a great inspiration in my life. One of the most precious things Miss Debbie taught me was that ever man should have the courage to stand up and face the enemy. She stood up with courage and faced me when I was dangerous—changed my life. It was the Christ in Miss Debbie that became the hope of glory for ol' Denver. Because of her, I'm gonna pick up her torch for the homeless and be a servant of God for the rest of my life. I praise God for her life. Now, I'm fixin to do somethin for y'all that the Devil ain't never done for you—I'm gonna cut you loose. God bless you and good-bye."

14

RON

Denver's new hayloft apartment above the barn turned out much better than expected. Filled with Western antiques and memorabilia, it appeared as if Debbie had picked out every single lamp, bedspread, and frying pan. Everyone who saw it wanted to stay there. Most of all, he was proud of his new home away from home!

The cemetery dedication was beautiful, and with Denver having his own place here, maybe I'd want to stay more and run less. Hopefully the stinging pain that kept me away would fade, and I would be left with all the good memories that would one day make me want to stay. But that day had not arrived.

Denver wanted me to listen to the eighteen hours of recordings he'd made in my absence. In the cool shade of a spring afternoon, we sat on the patio overlooking the Brazos with a glass of iced tea, and with great anticipation I turned on the recorder.

"Er . . . er . . . er . . . *zzzzzzzoommmmmmmm.*" The sounds of Denver hesitating to speak were followed by the roaring sound of one eighteen-wheeler after another passing the roadside park. It took more than ten minutes of this before I heard, "When I was just a little boy, I growed up on a plantation in Louisiana." Then another ten minutes of the same *ers* and *zooms*, followed by, "We had us a garden."

For one solid hour I listened to the same sequence of nothing until I was so frustrated I wanted to throw the tape recorder off the balcony into the Brazos River three hundred feet below.

I paid my aunt Vida, my long-time personal assistant, to listen
to the other seventeen hours. Three days later she was ready to kill
me and Denver. She had listened to every word spoken and came
away with less than half a handwritten page naming vegetables in
the garden and two mules, Jenny and Joe.

I'd been in Texas just two weeks when once again I bade fare-
well to Denver. This time he seemed sad. I felt that sadness, though
it was not spoken. He told me I didn't look good and thought I
should stay and get healthy—put a little fat on my bones. But after
buying him a new cell phone I promised to stay in touch. The next
morning, Carson and I left on another journey to Europe. This
time we planned a grand art tour to visit all the homes and studios
of our favorite artists of the past century: Picasso, Matisse, Léger,
Giacometti, Monet, Cézanne—the list went on and on. I was on the
run, who knew from what or for how long.

15

DENVER

I was standin there with a coupla hundred of Miss Debbie's friends, sweatin through they clothes in the hot sun as they turned over the dirt to begin buildin the mission she dreamed about. Mr. Shisler told me her friends give nearly five million dollars to build it. I didn't think there was that much money in all of Fort Worth—'cept maybe in the banks.

I was worried Mr. Ron had forgotten about the groundbreakin. Far as I knowed, he was still runnin from something 'cause I ain't seen him since we consummated the cemetery a couple months ago. Mr. Shisler seen me in the dinin hall a few times and ask me when Mr. Ron was comin back to Texas. I told him I didn't know 'cause he ain't been a callin.

But sure 'nough, Mr. Ron show up right on time.

I ain't never met no mayors or senators. So when Mr. Ron introduced me to 'em, I wadn't sure why they was there at the groundbreakin for a homeless mission. I ain't never thought important white folks care about the homeless, but I found out they do. Some of 'em anyways.

They was all talkin 'bout some foreigners that had flown they airplanes into some tall buildings in New York City a couple of days before. Even in Fort Worth, the po-lice was racin all over town with their sirens blasting, lookin for suspects. They even searched the hobo jungle, but they didn't find nobody 'cept fellas like me.

Anyways, even though the groundbreakin was for the mission, we prayed lots of prayers for our country and the families of the people that died in New York City. Somebody asked why did God let this happen. I told 'em God be all good, and since this be bad, it come from the Devil, so don't be blamin God.

Mr. Ron still wadn't quite right, kinda throwed off—couldn't figure out nothin, and ain't put no fat on his bones since I seen him last. We talked a bit 'bout Miss Debbie. I reminded him how God gave her some keys she used to set me free. Maybe I could put them keys to good use on him. The man was blind, can't see he be locked up in his own prison. We shared a meal that he pushed 'round the plate, not really eatin. Then he told me he was goin away again—he just got home—and wadn't sure when he be comin back. He looked shame-faced and wouldn't look me in the eye.

I always knowed the reason Mr. Ron was my friend is 'cause Miss Debbie told him to. But I figured now he was gonna cut me loose and move over to the other side of one of them big oceans.

He said I was welcome to stay at Rocky Top. And the man was real surprised to find out I ain't even spent one night in that barn since he left the last time. What he don't understand, maybe 'cause I ain't told him, is I don't like bein out there without him. He's my friend.

Before he left, Mr. Ron took back his truck but gave me a Jeep. He done bought his mama a new red Jeep, so he give me her old one and pay the insurance for a whole year. I have to say that Jeep was a whole lot easier to drive than that four-by-four truck. I ain't doubtin the man's kindness. But to tell y'all the truth, none of us on the streets could really figure him out—includin me.

But ain't none of us ever knowed no rich folk neither.

16

RON

I witnessed the sunrise burn off the low-hanging fog that tried to hide my view of the vineyard bearing new fruit on the Italian hillside below my room. The scene was Turneresque and glorious. Though I had been in Italy just five days short of a month, this was my third visit since Debbie's death. For the first time in almost a year, softly I said, "Thank you, God, for waking me up."

Debbie and I had said that without fail every morning for the last two years of her life. Then one day she hadn't woken up, and in protest I had gone silent. So this little surge of gratitude was a strange yet familiar feeling that took a minute or so to move from my body and my heart to my brain.

Miraculously, the grieving seemed to be over. At least for today I could imagine a new beginning, a blank canvas on which I could add the strokes of color and texture that would define the last half of my life. I wanted purples, pinks, and red for sure—no more blacks and grays. Well, except for Denver, who now had gray hair. I laughed at the thought, wondering if all these dreams of a new life were wishful thinking for a fifty-five-year-old.

After lunch I was in the studio writing when my cell phone rang—a very infrequent occurrence those days. Jerry, an old friend from Dallas, was calling to offer me a job.

Thinking it was a joke, I laughed and let him know I would not be a good employee even before he gave the job description. But

I listened as he told me the job was to sell a huge art collection belonging to the estate of one of the most famous women in Texas.

"I've closed my gallery, and I'm living in Italy writing a book," I told Jerry. "I haven't sold a single painting or sculpture since Debbie was diagnosed—probably lost my touch."

Undeterred, he described an incredible opportunity—truly an art dealer's dream come true.

Lupe Murchison was a socialite known and talked about around the world. In the '40s and '50s, her late father-in-law, Clint, was among the wealthiest and most powerful people in the world; his sons, Clint Jr. and John, had taken up where he left off. Lupe was John's wife, and together they threw parties of such note they still cannot be topped, with stars like Frank Sinatra in attendance. But those days were long over. John and Clint Jr. were dead. So was Sinatra, for that matter. Now Lupe had passed away, the last of her generation. And just before her death, Lupe had directed Jerry, her executor, to find a bachelor who loved and knew art to move into her home, sell the collection, and donate the proceeds to charity.

I promised to consider Jerry's offer and get back to him in a month or so. But did I really want to do this? Had I so quickly forgotten the miracle of the morning's sunrise—the new beginning, the blank canvas? I was making sculptures and paintings that would never sell and writing a book that would probably never get published. And Denver?

Two weeks later, Ché and I were having an espresso near the Ufizzi, and I described my job offer with great animation. She smiled as always at my stories, then asked me how my book was coming.

"I'm stuck but near the end," I offered.

"I saw it lying on a table in the studio," she confessed. "So I read it. But there is more to the story."

"Are you my editor?" I asked, curious as to what she was implying.

"Are you really the author?" she asked.

"What does that mean?"

"It's a tragedy. You have run away from the real story of hope and redemption, and that story cannot be written here in Italy."

17

DENVER

I could hear 'im from a distance hollerin, "Denver! Denver!" I knowed immediately who it was, and I knowed his life was possibly in danger. Ain't no white men 'cept homeless ones come in the jungle—not even the po-lice.

Next thing I knowed, he was standin there right in front of me as I stirred some sardines in the skillet over my campfire and drank the juice from a can of Vienna sausages.

"Where you been so long?" I asked. I kept on stirrin and starin at the pan without lookin up.

The man pause for a second to figure out what he's gonna say, then pop off, "A Klan meeting!"

Man, I'm tellin you, the both of us started laughin so hard the fellas in the bushes 'round us started hollerin for us to be quiet. Mr. Ron is the onliest white man that could say that and get away with it, 'cause he done learn it from me. When I'd go missin for a few days, I'd tell him the same thing just to make him laugh. And that would stop him from askin any more questions.

"So you just gonna show up here? For what?"

"I want you to come live with me."

"Man, I thought you done cut me loose!"

"I know. But I promised not to catch and release. So I've come back for you . . . you know . . . what do you think about living with me?"

I thought to myself, *The man think he just gonna walk in my house here in the jungle and haul me off to live under his rules.* I'm a man—a real man who don't need nobody or nothin. And I don't need no slick, white, art-sellin man that I coulda whooped with both hands tied behind my back thinkin he be takin care of me. This life in the jungle is freedom, and what he be offerin wadn't no different from the plantation, 'cept he live in a million-dollar house. But it wadn't mine, and it ain't feel like home to me. And I wadn't sure if he really want me in his home or he just tryin to put a Band-Aid on his guilt.

I stared him straight in the eye and said, "I 'preciates your offer, but you gots things to attend to. You know what I'm talkin 'bout." I been tellin Mr. Ron for a while he need to get things right with his daddy. "After that, maybe we can spend us a little time sharin a meal and get to know each other again."

As he walked away, I hollered at him: "What you wants from me? Miss Debbie's gone. You ain't gots to be my friend no more."

18

RON

Earl answered the door, surprised to see me. In better days I would have just walked in without knocking.

I had only seen my father once since Debbie's funeral. In fact, we had hardly spoken since the Christmas before Debbie died, when he foolishly told her that cancer was no big deal. To me, to her, and to our children, it was bigger than a big deal—it was life, our future, and our happiness all bundled up in a time bomb. Alcohol showcases fools.

Since I was a little boy, I'd had a problem with my father's drinking. In December of '45, when he walked in the door of my grandparents' farmhouse as a victorious war hero still in uniform, my mama whispered to her sister that he wasn't the same man she'd married three years earlier. The young soldier looked as handsome as ever, with his wavy auburn hair and wearing that green army uniform covered in battle-campaign ribbons and patches. But he bore the kind of deep wounds and scars that don't earn a soldier the Purple Heart—wounds that never seemed to heal.

I had never neglected my mother, a teetotaler who'd endured a lifetime of anguish being married to a chain-smoking alcoholic. However, I'd made a point to avoid conversations and encounters with my father, with the exception of birthdays, holidays, and an occasional guilt-massaging Sunday-afternoon visit with my children in tow.

My father was jealous of my friendship with Denver, asking me once why I treated a homeless Negro better than I did my own father. Strangely, Denver asked me the same question early in our friendship. Even on the Christmas Day when Earl insulted Debbie, when he spotted Denver driving up, he'd asked, "Does he have to be invited to every family gathering?"

Denver had told me on many occasions I would have no peace in my life until I could find a way to forgive Earl. "The man gave you life," he would say. "Bless him." Another time my wise friend had asked a very thought-provoking question: "If the man who gave you life gets kicked off your ranch and told to never come back for sayin somethin foolish, how you gonna treat a man that ain't never give you nothin? What's gonna happen if I slip up and do the same thing?"

I told him that wasn't the same thing at all, but he just shook his head.

To Denver, it was a precious thing for a boy to have a daddy. However, a lifetime of resentment had clogged my forgiveness faucet. "Your ol' daddy's got a lotta hell in him, Mr. Ron," he said. "You just gotta bless the hell outta him."

———

"Well, lookie who's here," Earl said with a surprisingly warm and welcoming smile when he answered the door. "I never expected to see you again."

"Who is it, Earl?" my mother called.

"Ronnie."

"Ronnie? Oh my goodness, bless your heart, son."

For eight-five years, this woman had blessed the heart of every human and small dog she ever encountered. My stubbornness about Earl had caused me to miss that blessing for at least a year. My heart immediately let me know that.

I sat down at the kitchen table with Earl as Mom dished out some chicken and dumplings—my favorite meal. For more than fifty years I'd sat in my spot at the same table, eating the same thing. It's family.

Then the miracle happened. Before I could say anything, Earl began to apologize to me—his first apology ever, totally out of character for him. He was about to turn eighty-five, and I sensed I was just about to get to know him for the first time.

———

The next day I drove to Dallas and met with the Murchison estate executors. The north Dallas estate once seemed to grow giant modern sculptures on the nearly one hundred wooded acres winding along White Rock Creek. But eighty-five of those acres had been sold and would be the site of a new housing development called Glen Abbey.

On the remaining fifteen acres sat Clint Murchison's original ranch house, a stately three-story white limestone structure surrounded by giant, ancient live oaks, reflecting pools, and fountains. Back in the '30s it had been the most spectacular home in Texas, with the largest spring-fed swimming pool ever built for a private residence. That spring still spewed hundreds of gallons of crystal-clear Texas water per hour. Modern and contemporary art had hung floor to ceiling in every room of that mansion—too many to count. On any given weekend in its glory days, royalty, heads of state, governors, presidents, and movie stars would have been weekend guests, flown in by a private fleet of DC-3s to the Murchisons' adjacent private airport.

Fifty yards away from the mansion, through the oak forest, sat Lupe's award-winning contemporary glass and stone residence, a one-story masterpiece of Texas architecture recently completed at a cost of more than seven million dollars. At almost seven thousand square feet, it was more museum than home. Lupe had lived just one year there when she died in her all-glass bedroom overlooking rolling manicured grounds dotted with massive modern sculptures.

Across the courtyard from Lupe's house was a three-thousand-square-foot guesthouse and art gallery. Enormous paintings by Morris Louis, Helen Frankenthaler, Roy Lichtenstein, Sam Francis, Kenneth Noland, and many others covered every square inch of its walls—some stretching twenty feet from floor to ceiling.

In the three homes altogether hung more than five hundred magnificent works of art. And all were to be sold, with the money distributed to Lupe's favorite charities. It was truly an art dealer's dream.

I wondered how I could have been so cavalier as to dismiss this opportunity when Jerry first called. I certainly wasn't dismissing it now. I wanted to do this.

Standing in the sculpture-filled courtyard we made a deal the old-fashioned Texas way: we shook hands—but not before I laid out my requirements. First of all, Regan and Carson would both move in and work on this together with me.

No problem. Deal.

But the next requirement was one I was sure would kill the deal. I hesitated and gut-checked my integrity. Was I prepared to walk away if they rejected my terms?

"My only other requirement—remember the homeless man who spoke at Debbie's funeral? I want him to move in and live here with me."

Without hesitation Jerry extended his hand, and we shook again on our deal.

Things were moving quickly. The executors wanted me to take over in a matter of days, and I had a lot of business to take care of first. Since I would be living on the Murchison estate for a while, maybe years, I decided to put my Fort Worth home up for sale—not the ranch—and move my belongings out of the place in Santa Fe I'd been leasing. I needed to move away from our Fort Worth dream home. Debbie's death had caused it to become my nightmare.

I realized I had spoken up for Denver without consulting with him. He would need some convincing to leave Fort Worth, where he reigned as king of the jungle. Dallas was a foreign country to him.

19

DENVER

I figured I done made Mr. Ron mad. He ain't called or come to see me since I told him I wadn't interested in his offer to come live with him.

While I was gettin somethin to eat at the mission, I asked Mr. Shisler if maybe somethin was wrong with the phone Mr. Ron give me. It ain't rung, even though Mr. Ron and Miss Debbie was the onliest ones that ever knowed the number—not even me!

Mr. Shisler say the battery is dead.

Now, that ain't made no sense to me, since it wadn't but a few months old. But he say you gotta charge it ever day to keep it up and runnin. Maybe I done lost all them others 'fore they runned outta gas. Now I ain't very smart, but listen, as many smart peoples as there is in the world, how come the fellas who make batteries for trucks and cars is smarter than the ones that make 'em for telephones?

That night I was nearly asleep when some commotion was stirrin in the hood. I heard some of the fellas hollerin, "White boy, white boy," and the jungle bull, the toughest fella other than me, yelled, "What that white boy doin in here?"

That's about the time I hear someone hollerin, "Denver!" But it wadn't Mr. Ron this time. I knowed Mr. Carson's voice, and it scared me that somethin was about to go down that wadn't gonna have no good endin for him. It kinda peeved me that the boy was actin a fool—about to get hisself killed. I done warned him and his whole family never to come in there day or night. And now I gots to get up and take care of some bidness.

The fact that he was hollerin my name was the thing that saved his life, 'cause ain't nobody gonna mess with somebody they thinks is my friend. Then a fella who knowed where I stay peeked in my camp and told me there was one bad white boy lookin for me, and he wadn't even scared. "What you done do to that white boy to make him come chargin in here thinkin he gonna drag you outta here?" Now that made me laugh.

About that time, Mr. Carson was standin in front of me. "Boy," I said, "what you doin here in the jungle? You 'bouts to gets yo'self killed!"

He started flappin his lips 'bout he and his daddy just moved to Dallas and Mr. Ron told him to come get me and not to come home without me. His daddy was smart and knowed he couldn't drag me outta there, so he sent his boy.

Well, I packed up my stuff and rode to Dallas with Mr. Carson in his truck. *Dallas?* I thought. I didn't know nuthin 'bout no Dallas 'cept Mr. Ron drove me over there to his art gal'ry when we first got to bein friendly. To tell you the truth, the onliest reason I got in Mr. Carson's truck was to save his life. I didn't want to go to his daddy's old house or new house—not really. But I couldn't let Miss Debbie's only son walk back through the jungle by hisself.

20

RON

It was after midnight when Carson showed up at the Murchison estate with Denver. I heard them parking in the garage of Lupe's glass house, where I had moved in the day before.

"Let me help you get your things out of the truck."

"I ain't left nothin in the truck. This is all I gots." He held up one small, black, plastic trash bag.

"What do you mean that's all you got?"

"Mr. Ron, listen to me real good. Thank God for nothin! When you can do that, he'll give you everthing. So everthing I owns is in this here garbage bag, and it ain't much of nothin."

What he said caused me to take a lightning-fast inventory of my possessions and shake my head in disbelief—even shame. Here stood a man with next to nothing who was able to thank God for just that and nothing less.

I made a pot of coffee. We sat in the kitchen and talked for a little while. I told him about the Murchison deal and expressed that I wanted him to be a part of it. But he made it clear to me that he hadn't come to stay. He'd only come so that Carson would not have to leave the hobo jungle by himself.

I made it clear he was here as a friend of the family. I was not the Man, and I would never order him to do anything. I might ask him to do certain things that might be good for him or even me, explain the pros and cons as I saw them, then let him chew on it until it was his idea. It was clear he valued his freedom, and I assured him I would protect and defend that. But I was going to be all alone on this huge estate, I said, and I would really appreciate having him there with me.

He thought about that for a minute, then he said: "Mr. Ron, you needs to listen to me real good. Do you hear me?"

"Yes, I'm listening."

"You don't really wants me to be livin with you, and it's got more to do with me. It ain't nothin 'bout you. You see, Miss Debbie was the first person I ever gots close to or let get close to me since my uncle James died when I was a boy. Seemed like ever time I gots close to somebody like Big Mama, my daddy, and Uncle James, they died. So I wadn't never gonna let that happen again. Then 'long come Miss Debbie. I didn't wanna know that woman, or any white woman. Then after we got to be friends, I sure didn't wanna care 'bout her, even love her, 'cause I knowed that if I did, God would take her."

"Denver, I don't think God works that way. It was just their time to go and had nothing to do with you loving them. So what are you trying to tell me?"

"You is a good man, Mr. Ron, and I likes you. So don't you worry 'cause I don't loves you. Miss Debbie, she was the first person I loveded in fifty years, and look what God did to her. Now that she's with the Lord, I ain't wantin to get close to nobody, 'cause my heart can't take that kinda pain no more. That's not a warnin. It's just the way it is. So I'll stay here with you for a couple of days, but I be leavin soon."

The flashlight lit the path as we walked through tree-tall hedges across the yard to the big mansion, where I planned for him to live for the next few years until our job was finished. He was nervous—skitzy, in his words—and I was making small talk to smooth the edge off that last conversation. I led him through the sculpture-filled grand entry and down a hall half the length of a football field toward his bedroom, which just happened to be the master, adorned in silk and gold. A red-lacquered bathroom, larger than a starter home, with gold faucets, sinks, and commodes completed the suite. I thought he would get a kick out of knowing he was moving into the home and even the giant bedroom formerly occupied by one of the wealthiest men in the world.

To my surprise, he stood frozen like one of the statues we had passed in the entry. His eyes, bright as a full moon on a clear country night, reflected fear. Chill bumps covered his body.

"Are you okay?"

"I be fine," he answered, his eyes fixated on the life-sized portrait of Lupe Murchison, who appeared to be watching his every move.

"Just one thing, Denver. No smoking in any of the houses."

21

DENVER

After Mr. Ron walked back over to his house that didn't look like no house to me, I went out on the back porch to smoke and take me a leak. Now, I knows that sound crazy to a sane person, but I just ain't feelin right 'bout peein in the man's solid-gold shitter with that smilin lady hangin on the wall watchin.

I had to get me some 'couragement, and that take nearly half a pack 'fore I slip back in the mansion. I pull back the covers, and the sheets was bright red and shiny like they been buffed out after a new paint job. They was slippery too. I tried to lay my head on the pilla, and I slid off like a hog on an ice pond. Even though I knowed I wadn't s'posed to smoke in the house, I lit me another cigarette, wonderin what in the world is a fella like me doin in a place like that. If the homeboys and fellas in the jungle knowed about this, they'd be laughin and talkin trash like I done turned sissy. It took me a good while, but I finally dozed off.

Maybe I been asleep an hour or so when a fella standin beside my bed started shakin the headboard, tellin me to get outta his bed 'cause he don't like no niggers stayin in his house. This ain't no joke. That man was as serious as a widow-maker heart attack. So I come on up outta there and laid down in the bushes outside. If it ain't been so late, I'd have walked back to the jungle, but this wadn't no neighborhood for a black homeless man to be walkin down the street at three in the mornin.

59

And you prob'ly askin how in the world I wadn't 'fraid to live in the hobo jungle with thugs, killers, and thieves, but I's scared in a neighborhood with skillion-dollar mansions and armed guards at the gate. Well, let me 'splain it to you.

In the jungle, I's the lion.

Here, I's the prey.

22

RON

The sun woke me up early. I was feeling like a mannequin in a department-store window in Lupe's all-glass bedroom. I was the first person to sleep there since Lupe died more than a year ago—in the very bed where I slept. I'd been told by the property manager that the curtains were all computer operated, but the computer obviously needed booting up, and I never saw a mouse.

That didn't bother me so much—the woods around the house were pretty thick. But twice in the night I'd been wakened by big band music playing throughout the house. I'd gotten up to turn it off, only to realize I hadn't hooked up my stereo yet. Besides, I've never listened to big band music. That was my father's music, not mine.

Maybe the neighbors are having a party, I'd thought. So the second time I got up I had stepped outside on the patio that adjoined my bedroom and the pool. Under a sky full of stars and a bright moon waxing to full, I'd heard coyotes, cicadas, and crickets, but no big band music.

Exhausted from my interrupted night and not being an early riser anyway, I stumbled into the kitchen to make coffee. The sight of Denver sitting at the table with his black plastic garbage bag in hand surprised me.

"How was your first night in a mansion?" I smiled as I asked.

"Mr. Ron, what was the fella's name that used to stay in that big house?"

"You mean the owner?"

"Yessir."

"His name was Clint Murchison Sr."

"Well, I done met Mr. Murchison last night."

"Impossible, Denver. He died in 1969."

"I don't care when he died. He still stayin over there."

"Are you crazy?"

"Nosir, but *he* might be! That man come in my room and start shakin my bed, tellin me to get outta his house 'cause he don't like no niggas stayin in there! So I come on up outta there and slept in the bushes with the coyotes."

I started laughing, but Denver was not laughing with me. He was dead serious as he described the intruder as a stout-looking man about his size with black round glasses and short, straight hair, greased up and parted. I googled Murchison's picture on my iPhone, and Denver confirmed it was a match.

"When Mr. Carson wake up, I'm gonna get him to take me back to the jungle. I ain't spendin no more nights here in no Dallas mansion."

I was shocked, but then I wasn't. I had learned that Denver lived in a spirit world that I'd never inhabited. He heard and saw things no one other than spiritual beings could hear or see. I recalled the times he would show up at our door after talking to God all night long by his Dumpster. He spoke of things no one could possibly know except me and Debbie, and he was rarely wrong.

In this case, however, I was convinced that staying with me was what he needed—and what I needed too. It had taken me a year to reconcile Debbie's last wish and my willingness to fulfill it. Now, finally, I was at peace with it and anxious to see what God had in mind to bless our friendship the way Debbie spoke of it. For the length of their friendship, she had encouraged him to begin changing his people, places, and playgrounds and become the man God wanted and Debbie prayed he would become. Now was the time, I believed, and this was the place.

"Denver, please don't go back. I need you here. You are the only man I trust who can help me guard all this valuable art."

Shooting from the hip, with no prior thought of what I was saying, I offered him what he called "three hots and a cot" plus a thousand dollars a month to be our security guard. He thought about that for a while. Then finally, dropping his chin and fixing a one-eyed stare on me, he asked, "What kinda gun is you gonna give me?"

Laughing at first, then realizing he was serious, I told him none. I would buy him some khaki pants and some blue button-down shirts. He could carry his bat if necessary, but no guns.

He pushed back. "Brothers don't wear no khakis and button-down shirts." He wanted a uniform and badge and a "po-lice-lookin hat." I, however, prevailed in my choice of uniforms, not fully trusting his reasoning behind the police-lookin hat.

Later in the day, Walmart had the perfect size slacks and shirts for the perfect price, though he could not understand why I wanted to pay for clothes when the mission had piles of them for nothing. Standing in front of the full-length bathroom mirror in his new clothes, after he had showered and shaved his face and head, he looked like a new man—an executive on casual Fridays. He was proud, and it showed through the beautiful smile that showcased the pearl-white teeth Debbie had arranged for him, compliments of our dentist friend, Glen.

23

DENVER

The man got to me when he say I was the onliest person he trusted to guard that million-dollar art. He didn't know it, but if I'd knowed 'zactly where I was, I woulda already walked halfway to the jungle by the time he woke up. But I didn't, and that's a God thing. The man needed me, and I wadn't gonna let him down. So I started bein the guard at that great big ol' estate.

One day as I was walkin the property, I seen some wild bobcats, a mama and two babies, walkin alongside the creek. We used to see those back on the plantation, but I ain't never heard of no bobcats walkin 'round no skillionaire's mansions in the city.

I found a can of tuna fish in the kitchen and tried to make friends with 'em. I been doin that for years, back in the jungle. I'd find trash in the cans and Dumpsters and save it for the wild cats, dogs, and birds that hung 'round lookin for scraps left behind by the homeless. They was my friends, my onliest friends for many years. I 'spected I's about to make me some new ones right there. Animals ain't scared of folk with animal instincts.

Another day, while Mr. Ron was visitin some of his friends, I checked out some of the rooms I ain't been in yet and found a closet with wine stacked floor to ceilin, and ever bottle gots its own hole and a cold motor runnin in the wall. I pulled out a few and found nary a bottle of Mad Dog, and there wadn't none with no screw top. But I's thinkin I could put some of that wine to good use.

Mr. Ron didn't know that sometimes when he was gone I'd drive back over to the mission and do a little drinkin there with some of the homeys. Now, you prob'ly don't know this, but the police won't bother a fella that's drinkin on the street if he be drinkin his Mad Dog outta a water bottle.

One time, when I gots in the car to come back to Dallas, the po-lice walked up to me and asked me what was I drinkin. "Water," I told 'im. He take that bottle right outta my hand and stick his nose on the top and say it smelled like wine to him. I tried my best to look like I didn't really believe what he was sayin.

"Officer, is you jokin, or is you tellin me that Jesus done performed another miracle and turned that water into wine?"

That po-liceman laughed so hard, then he just poured out the bottle on the ground and let me go on 'bout my bidness!

It didn't really make no sense to me to walk 'round that mansion all night long guardin that art. It would take four men and a semitrailer to haul it outta here if they liked it—and I didn't see how anybody could like somethin that looked like a bucket of paint got spilled and they tried to clean it up with a weed eater. So I figured that if I gots tired, I'd just lay down and take a little nap in the bushes. So I did.

The cracklin sound of tires on gravel woke me up. There wadn't no moon, and the night was black as coal. The hair on my arms was standin up straight as a cornstalk. The car was rollin in with the lights turned off.

Oh Lord Jesus, help me, I was thinkin. *I ain't believin my eyes, 'cause here comes a robber.*

The car door shut without much noise. *I done beat many a fool down on the streets, so this is gonna be easy.* That's what I was thinkin as I raised my bat.

Through the bushes I made out a man in dark clothes—black, I thinks. The streetlight casted a shadow, and it was movin right up on me when I jumps outta the bushes and takes a swing that was meant to take 'im out with just one.

"Denver, it's me!" the man scream as he hit the gravel. "Mr. Ron, Mr. Ron!"

I was standin there, bat cocked for another strike if needed. Then I saw that the man layin in the gravel really was Mr. Ron.

"Man, don't you never sneak up on me like that in the bushes. You'll get yo'self killed!"

"Denver, this is my house!"

I had to think about that for a minute. Then I smiled. "Welcome home!"

24

RON

The night seemed to never end as I tossed bedcovers in fits of bewilderment mixed with hilarity. After the initial shock passed, I broke out in laughter enjoyed only by myself. Sleep was slow in coming. There was no counting sheep. I stared at the ceiling for hours, seriously questioning my sanity for taking a crazy homeless man in as a roommate. What should I have done differently last night? Instead of trying to be quiet and respectful of my not-so-close neighbors, maybe I should have announced my arrival with the Texas Christian University (my alma mater) marching band.

I rubbed the sleep from my eyes, recalling the death stare from Denver's glassy yellow eyes as he stood over me with his bat cocked for a final swing—one that could have ended my life. Then my first smile of the morning came as I recalled seeing him break into a sweet Southern smile and welcome me home.

My first call of the morning was to Mr. Shisler at the mission, who had known and observed Denver for many years. He told me something I had already figured out: that Denver had serious mental-health issues and was prone to violence. Some of the mission people thought he might be bipolar or schizophrenic.

Then he told me about a time when Denver had wanted to use a pay phone that was already being used by another homeless man. When the man refused to hang up, Denver had taken the receiver out of his hand and cracked his skull open, shattering the hard plastic receiver. Mr. Shisler cautioned me not to make any aggressive moves. Before we hung up, he encouraged me not to feel bad if it didn't work out—it was okay if I wanted to drop him off at the mission. He would give him a bed there.

The kids, who were staying temporarily in the guest house, and I talked it over before breakfast. We had discussed the potential violence and risk on several occasions. Now it was real and present, actually living on the premises. But after a serious discussion, we decided as a family to move forward and show Denver grace by not even mentioning his infraction. That's what Debbie had done for me a few years earlier when I violated our marriage vows. It had been her grace, mercy, and forgiveness that lured me back into a loving, faithful relationship. Now the three of us agreed that Debbie would want us to do the same for Denver.

For the next several days, our security-guard roommate showed exemplary behavior. We were not robbed, burglarized, or accosted again. Denver settled back into the big house but seemed to struggle with the idea of sleeping on red satin sheets, so I bought him some cotton ones, knowing his affinity for the product that for years defined his life. We'd say our good-byes at night, and Denver would walk the perimeter of the property before settling in the big house.

Curiously, every morning when I'd walk into the kitchen of Lupe's glass house to make coffee, he'd be asleep on the kitchen floor. "Bed's too soft," he complained. He said it was hurting his back after years of sleeping on the ground.

It was about the end of the second week when I was rudely awakened by a pounding on the glass of my bedroom. Denver was panicked, sweating profusely and out of breath, with eyes as big and bright as two new silver dollars.

"Mr. Ron, there is some kinda gathering goin on in the big house, and they is planning to bring down the gov'ment of the

U-nited States of America." He pounded his fist into his palm, with a heavy emphasis on *bring down the gov'ment of the U-nited States.*

"What in the world are you talking about, Denver? A dream?"

"Nosir, it wadn't no dream 'cause I ain't been to sleep yet. I can hear 'em all talkin, and I gone lookin, but I can't find nobody. They is all gathered in the big lodge room, all angry and cussin 'bout the president."

"Okay, let's go. I want to hear all this myself."

"You can go over there if you want to, but I ain't never goin back in the big house. I'd rather sleep in the bushes in Fort Worth than spend one more night over there."

"Come on. You gotta go with me," I said, adrenaline pumping as I quickly slipped on jeans, a T-shirt, and flip-flops, then motioned to him to follow.

We walked slowly, cautiously, in the bright moonlight as I led the way through the trees and along a big hedge where we could take cover if needed. Denver, bat in his trembling hand, reluctantly followed about ten feet behind. We reached the side of the nearly one-hundred-foot-long front porch and paused to listen. All was quiet except for wind-tossed branches and leaves crunching under the weight of our shoes.

"Okay, let's go," I repeated quietly as I took the first hesitant steps, tiptoeing toward the imposing front door maybe fifty feet away.

"Nosir, this is as far as I is goin," he whispered sternly, and I could tell he meant it.

So I proceeded cautiously across the porch until I was standing at the ten-foot-tall, half-glass front door, looking into the pitch-black foyer. Still, I saw or heard nothing, so I said to Denver in a normal voice: "It's nothing, Denver. Come on in with me."

I grabbed hold of the large, brass front-door handle, and ZZZZZZZZZZZZZaaaaaaappppppppp! An electric current raced through

my body as if I had grabbed the live end of a 220-volt execution-
er's wire.

I let out a bloodcurdling scream like a teenager at a Frankenstein
movie and hollered at the top of my lungs, "Let's get outta here!"
We both took off running like there was a venomous snake nipping
at our heels.

We locked every door in my house, lowered all the electric curtains, and collapsed on the sofa in the living room, out of breath and
unable to speak. After a minute or so, unnerved and still trembling, I
asked Denver, whose eyes were frozen wide open, "What was that?"

"Spirits," he said with a scowl.

"Okay, I understand the voices you heard could have been spirits, but what about the near electrocution I survived?"

With both eyes trained like lasers on mine, he said very matter-
of-factly, "Mr. Ron, the Devil's got a flyin mochine!"

25

DENVER

Ain't no man can scare me—you better believe that. Don't matter if they come at me with a .357 Mag or a switchblade knife. I done faced 'em all and lived to tell 'bout it. In fact, I ain't scared of nothin I can see. It's the unseen that'll take you down.

Now you ain't gonna believe this, but one time I stared down a black-funnel killer tornado that was takin down the tallest bank in Fort Worth. Folks was hollerin: "Come on inside. Is you crazy?" Sirens was howlin like a pack of wolves in the night. But I stood there, the onliest person on the street in broad daylight, and told that tornado to bring it on, 'cause I wadn't scared. I don't know why they don't name no tornados like they do hurricanes, 'cause this one sure felt personal to me.

They was glass and metal and ever kinda trash, includin the Dumpsters, swirlin 'round me, and ain't none of it touch me. Did you hear me? I said none of it touch me.

I knowed the people watchin thought I's a crazy man. But listen to this—I had a plan. When the tornado finished blowin all the glass outta that bank, I'd be snatchin hundred-dollar bills outta the sky like butterflies. Or even better, all that cash would be knee-deep on the ground in all directions. I could fill a trash bag full before the po-lice got there.

Now I ain't no dummy, so I had a backup plan, and that was for the tornado to pick me up and drop me off in heaven. I was 'bout sixty years old at the time, and I figured nothin good was gonna happen to me.

So I stood my ground. I didn't flinch or move a muscle. You prob'ly ain't gonna believe this, but that tornado didn't wanna mess with Suicide, so he took a left turn and spoiled my plan.

Like I done told you, I wadn't scared 'cause I could see it. But them evil spirits in the big house was like what was in my sister Hershalee's house that terrible night long ago, and they ain't nothin to be messin with.

Mr. Ron made me promise we'd start writin our book that mornin. I didn't have far to go to work since we was gonna write it at the kitchen table, so I slept on the floor under that table just in case the Devil in the big house come lookin for me. 'Sides, in the night I gots a vision for a name for the book, and I was wantin to tell Mr. Ron 'fore I forgot it.

'Bout that time Mr. Ron come walkin in, and when he see me, he and I just looked at each other and started laughin.

"Was that real?" he asked me. "It sure was," I told him. But then I told him somethin he wadn't 'spectin to hear.

"Mr. Ron, we don't never need to be talkin 'bout last night never again, 'cause everbody that s'posed to be dead ain't dead yet!"

"What do you mean?"

"Just 'zactly what I said. We ain't gonna write no book about it, either, you hear me? And speakin 'bout books, what do you think 'bout this name? You ever heard of Stevie Wonder, the blind brother?"

"Sure. He's one of my favorites."

"Then how 'bout *Ebony and Ivory, Livin Together in Perfect Harmony*, by Mr. Ronnie Ray Hall and Denver T. Moore?"

We got a real good laugh outta that, but to tell you the truth, I was serious.

Lord, I tell you that man be hardheaded, 'cause it wadn't but an hour or so later that a fella knock on the door. Mr. Ron say he's the engineer for the Murchison family and he come there once ever few days to check on the place. I told him I thought engineers was the ones that drove trains. He thought I was tryin to be funny, but I wadn't.

"Tell Steve what happened last night," Mr. Ron say. And if I'da had my bat, I woulda whacked him upside his head. But I looked him dead in the eye and told him, "He who knows don't tell, and he who tell don't necessarily know." And that's all I really had to say 'bout that subject.

But Mr. Ron went ahead and told the engineer the whole story, maybe puttin our lives at risk. That peeved me, and I was just about to get up and walk outside when the engineer said he knowed what we was talkin 'bout. That got my attention.

He told us 'bout spendin a few nights in the big house twenty years ago and hearin the same voices. In fact, he say one of 'em was the voice of Mr. J. Edgar Hoover. And he say Mr. Hoover had his own bedroom next to the big lodge room and visited there once a month. Mr. Ron laughed and asked the man if Mr. Hoover was still in the closet or had he come out? Him and Mr. Ron laughed. They don't know it, but I done checked all the closets, and to tell you the truth, I found out everthing I wants to know 'bout all that bidness. We gonna put this subject to bed, and you ain't never gonna hear me talkin 'bout it again.

26

RON

For the next few months, we made good progress on our book. Denver and I would talk every morning over breakfast and most days all the way into lunch. I was curious what he knew about history. He'd lived under eleven presidents, so I asked him, "How many presidents can you name?"

"Abraham Lincoln is the onliest one I ever heard of that I remembers." Then after scratching his head, with squinted eyes, he added, "And the one that got shot in Dallas."

At times we'd just sit on the porch or the deck at Rocky Top and make small talk about our pasts, old friends, and dogs—things we wished we'd done and things we wished we hadn't. Our friendship had become real and often raw. Denver wasn't very good at small talk and usually circled back to spiritual things. Outside the mission, the only friend he ever mentioned was a preacher.

Pastor Stafford, years ago, had found Denver sleeping in the bushes behind a funeral home where he was about to conduct a service and had invited him inside for coffee. Sometimes when Denver had been gone most of the day, he'd say he'd been to see Pastor. I'd met the man a few times on the rare occasions when Denver invited me to ride the streets with him—he usually didn't allow anybody to ride in his car.

Denver was changing and loved to preach on the streets to the homeless near the mission and occasionally to gangbangers at a carwash in the heart of the Stop Six neighborhood, the meanest streets in town. I showed up there once with Denver, and the bangers all scattered like flushed quail at the sight of a bird dog. According to Denver, I ran off all his customers for spiritual food because I looked too much like the CIA.

Twice I heard Pastor Stafford preach to a packed-out crowd at his church, Riteway Missionary Baptist, which stood near the car wash. Church lasted all day there. Denver said it was the only safe place in the hood.

Though Denver resisted watching TV at first, the History Channel became his classroom. He was excited to learn that someone in Israel found a stone box with some bones and writing on the side that said, "James, son of Joseph, brother of Jesus." He was glad no one had found the bones of Jesus, because he said that would mean the Bible wasn't true.

———

Most of our work on the book consisted of interviews about his life on the plantation and the streets, which had comprised his whole life. But he spoke in way too many generalities and gave too little detail. I knew we needed more, so I proposed doing something we had talked about but had not yet done. We would visit the Louisiana plantation where Denver grew up. To my knowledge, he hadn't been back there since the day he hopped the train headed for Fort Worth.

It was nearly a three-hour drive from our home to Red River Parish, a pleasant one in my brand-new, four-wheel-drive Suburban. On the way, we talked about the war in Afghanistan. He never really talked about politics, but he said he was glad President Bush wasn't a coward and was standing up to the bullies. And he wished he was a little bit younger. He would like to join the army to go over there and kick some butt.

When we passed a sign informing us that we were now in Red River Parish, Denver rolled down the window and inhaled the warm, moist air deeply. As we traveled the back roads we could see cotton in the fields, ready to be picked. We stopped for a photo op.

"I done chopped and picked ever square inch of that big field for a lotta years—yessiree, a lotta years," he said with pride. Then the smile vanished when he recalled not ever getting paid for the job. "The Man give us credit at his store, but I scarcely ever saw any foldin money."

We turned off the blacktop onto a one-lane dirt path with deep bar ditches on both sides. It was a little muddy from an earlier rain, and there was no way to turn around. Denver suggested backing up, but I had come too far on this long-overdue mission not to plow on through.

Passing a relic of a former slave cabin, Denver pointed and said, "I used to stay in that shack." Again, another quick photo op. Driving became more difficult because the tires were coated in mud that was kept at the maximum by the fender well knocking off the excess.

Denver pointed again. "That's my sister Hershalee's house." We turned off the engine and got out, leaving the car in the middle of the road.

Johnson grass taller than our six-foot frames surrounded the house, leaving it barely visible until we had pushed through at least fifty feet of it like parting a curtain. Reaching the front porch, we stopped to take in the sight. Denver was in a reverent mood, thinking about his sister, who had died there just two years earlier after spending a lifetime in the same house. After their uncle James died, Denver had moved in with Hershalee and stayed for several years until the Man—the plantation owner—gave him the shack we had just passed down the road.

We climbed up on the porch, watching our step because many boards were either rotten or missing. A rotting smell filled the air.

Denver said it came from the swamp back behind the house where the poor folk emptied their slop jars every morning.

As we entered the open door, I was shocked to see the little house was fully furnished. To one side stood a hand-cranked record player with gospel and blues records stacked and ready to play. Denver smiled when he saw that; he said it brought back memories of fun times on Saturday nights after the work was done and the moonshine chilled. His uncles paid him a nickel per night for keeping the Victrola fully cranked. A well-worn sofa, a hand-me-down from the Man according to Denver, was covered in raccoon droppings and old newspapers. Surprisingly, the bed was made and the pillows neatly stacked atop a log-cabin quilt his sister had stitched. It had been two years since anyone had lived there, and Denver remarked that not much had changed, although the glass in every window had been broken. Rodents scurried around at the sound of our voices. Creepy.

With a broomstick we slashed away at large, active spiderwebs blocking our way to the back of the house, where Denver wanted to show me the potbelly stove and the bathtub on the back porch. He'd bought the tub at Home Depot for his sister's last birthday after I "blessed" him with a little money for driving Regan's worldly goods, as he called them, to Colorado. Just weeks before Hershalee died, for the first time in her life, she'd taken a bath in a real bathtub, the stickers still on it. It wasn't hooked up to any plumbing, though. The water had been drawn from the well and heated on the potbelly stove in the room we were about to enter.

"Did you hear that?" I asked as I reached out to block Denver from taking another step in that direction. The hair on our bodies spiked like steel bracelets on a goth. We stood side by side in silence as the thump of footsteps in the next room—heavy ones—moved in our direction, then stopped, followed by a low growling that quickly escalated to a lion-like roar.

We locked eyes and at the same moment hollered, "Let's get outta here!"

The man I had only seen move in slow motion now raced out the front door. Then, like Superman without a cape, he flew across the porch to the grass as I drafted behind him. Stopping to catch my breath, I picked up a large stick and raised it above my head in attack mode, fully expecting to see an alien-appearing swamp monster with flashing eyes spit fire as it hurtled toward us.

When it didn't immediately appear, we turned and raced back through the tall grass to the car and locked ourselves inside, throwing up a prayer like feeding a slot machine, hoping for a jackpot.

I turned the key, and—nothing.

I turned it again and heard the slow rolling of the engine with no ignition. It sounded like a dead battery, except I knew the battery was good. Denver's sweating head was turning quickly back and forth, keeping one eye out for the monster and the other on the perfectly good keys that seemed to have fallen under the spell and wouldn't start the car.

"Impossible," I screamed while banging my fist on the steering wheel. "The car is a week old!"

Again and again it would not start. Then finally, after a minute, it coughed and cranked but would not run. I jerked hard on the gearshift and pressed hard on the gas, but it only puttered, spitting and coughing like an old tractor on bad gas, with just enough power to turn the muddy wheels very, very slowly. We moved away at approximately one mile an hour.

The road came to an end in a grassy pasture where we could hopefully turn around without getting stuck. The car died.

For the next minute we repeated the same steps, hoping for better results, but after several frantic turns of the keys we got nothing but the same. *Putt . . . putt . . . putt*—we managed to turn and roll back very slowly the way we had come.

We passed right back in front of Hershalee's house, our hair again spiking even from our ears and noses. But then miraculously, a hundred or so feet past her house, the car seemed to revert to factory conditions and ran like it didn't know what we were talking about. If we'd reported it, that car would have made us look like liars.

Denver wiped his face with a towel he carried in his pocket and erupted into a long bout of howling laughter. "You gonna put this in our book?"

"I sure am."

Then, slipping back into the laughter, he added, "Ain't nothin keep you honest like a witness!"

———

We spent the rest of the day visiting every site that had shaped who Denver became—good and bad. For a good while we sat on the porch of the Mary Magdalene Baptist Church, which sported a fresh coat of white paint. Denver said the "coloreds" from many plantations would gather there every Sunday—some walking, others on mule-drawn wagons—and listen to sermons that lasted all day. At the pastor's discretion, at some point they would break for a covered-dish dinner and a game of stickball for the young'uns. Supper came later—always leftovers.

Denver laughed as he told me how one of the parishioners asked the preacher, "Brother Bill, why you keep preachin the same sermon over and over?"

"Well," the preacher said, "I knows all you peoples and what you is up to. So when I see some changin outta you, you'll hear some changin outta me!"

BB, Denver's daddy, used to sit in the front seat of his Pontiac, with Denver in the back seat, and listen to the sermon through the open windows. BB was banished from sitting in the pews inside because he was courting a married lady who sat on the third row. (He claimed she was not the only one.) When Brother Bill passed the plate, he'd stick it out the window. BB would attempt to atone for his sins by dropping in a handful of change, making enough noise to sound like a tambourine, hoping to get the ladies' attention and a wink.

Sunday visits with BB made Denver happy because he was more like an older friend, not a real daddy. He worked on the railroad and was gone a lot. So when he'd pick up Denver, he always brought candy. "He never whupped me," Denver told me with a smile.

We got back in the car, and a few minutes later we passed the Grand Bayou Social Club where, on a dark night in 1945, Denver's daddy was stabbed to death on the parking lot in a fight with what witnesses claimed was a jealous husband. Denver saw the whole fight and heard the dying screams from the front seat of his daddy's Pontiac—though it was too dark to identify the killer. He was only eight years old.

Just a mile down the road we parked in front of the Man's store, now boarded, and walked across Highway 1 for a photo op on the railroad tracks. "This be the spot where I hopped the train to escape the Man and the bill I owed at his store. No matter how hard I worked, it wadn't never gonna get paid off."

Then he laughed a little and told me, "The Man kept the books, and nary a colored man on the plantation knowed how to count. There was a sayin back then: 'An aught's an aught, a figure a figure, all for the Man, and none for the nigger!'"

27

DENVER

I never believed that one day I'd be standin on that track again gettin my picture made. Mr. Ron said one day it would be historically important—the picture where I hopped that train with the Man's store behind me. In my mind, it sure 'nough would be a good one to use on the cover of our book. To tell you the truth, I was glad to see his store was all boarded up, though I done ate a lotta cheese and crackers from there—baloney too—that I ain't never paid for. I couldn't help wonderin if he seen me pokin 'round, lookin through them boards over the windows, would he run 'cross the road tryin to empty my pockets and make me pay?

That whole trip, Mr. Ron kept scoopin up the dirt like he's diggin potatoes, lookin for a little somethin he can sink his teeth into for our book. But hear me real good—there is just some things I ain't gonna tell. He wanted to meet the Man against my better judgmentalism. He kept on pesterin me till I told him the Man's name, and I'll be if his cell phone didn't tell him the Man's phone number faster than a barn cat can slap a mouse. I listened as he talked to him on the phone.

He musta been pushin a hundred, but I still could hear 'im from fifty years ago, hollerin. It'd be 'bout the time the evenin train was passin and a night moon was risin. "One more row—it's still light," he'd holler through his bullhorn. "You niggers gotta pick one more row if you is 'spectin to get paid for a day's work tonight."

I heard him tell Mr. Ron over the phone that he had a lotta good niggers but he never heard of no Denvers. "How about a boy the folks called 'Li'l Buddy'?" Mr. Ron knowed that's what my PawPaw call me when I's just little bitty and he carried me in the front pocket of his overalls. All the other folk call me that too.

You know what I heard the Man say? He say I was a good li'l nigger. Now, that made me laugh. Mr. Ron smiled and just shook his head.

Mr. Ron wanted to see where I got dragged by them three white boys. They was prob'ly connected with the KKK, but I told him not to be sayin nothin 'bout that to the folk 'round there. This here's the Klan headquarters, and they still as hateful as ever. Him and me got in a little fuss about puttin the draggin in our book, 'cause it make the white folks look bad. I's worried that if the Grand Dragon of the Klan get mad, he might send some fellas in white sheets with burnin crosses after my kin that still lived on the Man's land. Peoples that ain't from here might not believe it, but they is still buildin fires and chantin evil out in the woods here in Louisiana. Did you hear me?

They's a big oak tree in the next town where the Klan hung a black man years ago, and they left him hangin till his skin fall off his bones for all the coloreds to see. Folks down there say on a warm, windy night the smell still float out over the cotton fields and swamps. I know that's real, 'cause I done smelled it. I's reminded of that when I seen Mr. Saddam Hussein hangin on the TV.

Walkin through the graveyard where Big Mama and Uncle James is buried made me hurt in the heart. Ain't nobody cared enough to take care of it. We had to kick mud and grass off they headstones, and they was layin flat on the ground. I plan on comin back here by myself to fix up the place.

Near Aunt Pearlie May's house, I saw a man I was hopin I'd never see again walkin down the road, comin straight at me. He had the goods on me, and I ducked down in the seat as we passed.

That caused Mr. Ron to start askin a bunch more questions. But 'fore I told him too much, I needed him to 'splain somethin to me.

"Mr. Ron, can you tell me about that statue they call Lamentations?"

"Do you mean the Tower of Babel, that made folks talk crazy?"

"Nosir, I mean the statue that keep a man from goin to the pokey for somethin he done did in his past."

Mr. Ron thought that was funny and started laughin, but it wadn't funny to me. I was dead serious.

"You must mean the statute of limitations."

"That's it. Tell me 'bout it 'fore I let any cats outta the bag."

28

RON

The sun was setting as we drove out of Red River Parish. For both of us, it had been a trip of a lifetime. I understood Denver more and felt a great amount of compassion for him. The cotton fields and swamps, shotgun houses and attitudes, and of course the poverty are just the way he described—maybe worse.

For most of the ride home he sat in silence, head bowed. The day had been a blessing and a curse. I watched him slip into depression as he told the story of how his grandmother, overmedicated on her Red Devil pain pills, burned up in a fire and how he had desperately tried to save her. His cousin Chook had died in the same fire, started by embers from the fireplace landing on a wood-shingle roof of the former slave cabin the Man rented to them for twenty-five dollars a month. Denver and his brother had been carted off to a neighbor's plantation in a mule-drawn wagon to live with his uncle James—a sharecropper, a man of faith, and the only person in his family who could read the Bible, King James Version.

After we got home, we lit a couple of Cuban cigars and sat on the back porch for an hour or so, talking about our trip some but also decompressing for a bit in silence. Denver hemmed and hawed, trying to get something out, then fell quiet again. As he crushed out his cigar on the bottom of his shoe, without lifting his head or making eye contact, he told me in a soft voice that he had a pretty good idea who'd killed BB sixty years before. "That's the onliest thing I'm gonna say 'bout that." Then we said our good nights and retired to our rooms.

The piercing screech of the fire alarm started just after midnight. From a dead sleep, panicked, I raced from room to room throughout the house. Nothing. I thought maybe it was a false alarm until I reached Denver's bedroom in the connected guest house that he now preferred over the big house. Standing over the bed, he was slinging and slapping the smoldering mattress with a wet towel. Smoke filled the room. I was opening all the windows and doors when the firemen arrived.

"Looks like we've got a case of falling asleep in bed while smoking," the fireman said, looking at me.

"Not me. Him." I pointed to the guilty one, who quickly quipped, "It sure do," with a wink shot my way.

Like a school kid who spilled his milk, Denver got his wrists slapped by the fireman and another reminder from me that smoking in the house was never allowed.

The next morning he was much more forthcoming with information. Instinctively I knew he was hiding something, maybe a lot of things. Our trip had triggered memories that he'd stuffed away. The man who caused him to duck down in the seat—what did he know? Was he BB's killer? Whole years of Denver's life were missing and unexplained. I just couldn't crack the case, but at least he was now talking. I was looking for anything, hoping for everything.

Visiting Hershalee's house had triggered the memory of his first paid job—turning the crank on the record player. He'd been paid a nickel per night to make sure it didn't stop playing the blues during late-night gatherings at Hershalee's house. His favorite job, he claimed, was rolling cigarettes while his uncle James plowed the cotton field behind a team of mules named Jenny and Joe. Denver's job was to have a fresh cigarette ready and lit every trip around the field. If he lit them too quickly, he'd smoke them himself. That was the start of his lifetime pack-or-two-a-day habit, which I'd been unsuccessfully encouraging him to break.

Drinking was the other habit that had caused a lifetime of problems for my friend. He claimed it began when the Man paid him to climb up a giant oak tree and keep watch for revenuers looking to shut down the Man's moonshine still. He never spied a single revenuer but still got paid—no jingle in the pocket, but free cheese and crackers at the Man's store. And when the Man wasn't looking, Denver would sneak a little taste.

Even knowing that Denver had a taste for alcohol, I wasn't worried when I started finding him asleep on the kitchen floor every morning. I attributed it to his job description of around-the-clock protection of Lupe's multimillion-dollar art collection. Denver would "alter the truth," in his words, trying to convince me he walked the perimeter until the break of dawn, then crashed and burned on my kitchen floor. All this, he claimed, was just to keep from having to sleep in what he called a ghostly mansion.

His convincing words were proven false when, after months of not drinking myself, I decided it was time to enjoy a glass of a fine cabernet. Walking into my wine closet, I was struck by the absence of some of my finest and favorite bottles. "Some" is an understatement. "Most" is more accurate.

Using detective skills I'd picked up watching cops-and-robbers shows on TV, I paid a visit to the garbage cans lined up behind the garage. Luckily, it was the day before the weekly pickup, so there was a full week's worth of evidence.

My heart sank when I saw the most recent victim, an empty ninety-five-point Opus One bottle, lying on top—strangely, with a broken neck. The bottle for a ninety-six-point Château Lafite cabernet, one of Mr. Rothschild's finest, lay buried beneath empty bags of fried pork rinds, which apparently pair well with fine cabs. Its neck was broken off too. I chose not to dig any deeper.

In the storage shed attached to my garage I found the laboratory where Denver had experimented with removing the corks—or should I say not removing them. A trash can that had obviously not been emptied in weeks, maybe months, was nearly filled with just the necks of a number of bottles, corks still in place.

A venti-sized Starbucks cup half filled with a dark-red liquid stood next to a bottle whose neck was severed. A workbench covered in emerald-colored glass fragments, with a claw hammer lying on top, was the last piece of evidence needed to solve the case of the "sleeping" security guard and the disappearing wine collection.

Of course, my hat comes off to the ingenuity of a man who had drunk a lot of wine in his life but had also never encountered a bottle with a cork. Using his street smarts, he'd accomplished his mission and elevated his taste.

29

DENVER

Mr. Ron didn't show up to cook breakfast, so I figured I'd let the man sleep in and I'd make breakfast for us. He ain't never taught me how to use the stove in his house, but let me tell you, it's bigger'n a jail cell. And since I wadn't wantin to blow the place up, 'specially after the night before, I figured I'd put together a little somethin that didn't require no cookin. I figured he'd 'preciate that.

I was enjoyin a real nice breakfast and readin his newspaper when he come in. Well, not really readin, 'cause I ain't learned very well yet, though Mr. Ron and his aunt Vida been teachin me to read little chilrens' books. At first I resisted 'cause learnin comes from books, but wisdom comes from God—that's the way I operate. But now I kinda like to do a li'l readin.

So what I's really sayin is I was mostly lookin at the funny pages when he come in dressed in a suit and tie and sit down to talk. I was 'spectin he be tellin me to pack up and leave, but he was smilin and just shakin his head.

He never said nothin 'bout no smokin. What he wanted to know was what I was eatin. He was laughin as he looked over what I'd fixed up. He say he wanted to write down my recipe for our book, so I carefully 'splained how I cooks hobo style. We calls it that 'cause in the camp everbody brings in somethin, and we throws it all in one big pot, kinda like a washtub on a wood fire.

This mornin I took a bag of oatmeal that don't need cookin and opened a can of sardines and dumped it on the top. Then I gots a hot dog bun, and I smears some mayonnaise and grape jelly on it to make a little sandwich. But the bun's kinda dried up, so I dips it in my glass of Gatorade to make it nice and soft. You may think it's funny that even though Miss Debbie got me a whole mouthful of teeth, they gets in my way while I'm eatin', so I takes 'em out and sits 'em on the table.

Mr. Ron thought that was funny and say they look like they wanted a bite. Then he got serious and say he concerned 'bout my drinkin. Then the subject come up 'bout the missin wine. I told him it wadn't missin—I knowed 'zactly where it gone. He was a little hot I drank all his wine. But truthfully, I didn't know it was his 'cause I ain't never seen him take a drink. So when I stumbled on it in that big closet, I figured the lady that died here done left it behind, and it was goin to waste. It just took me a while to figure out how to get the lids off, 'cause I ain't never seen no bottle of wine 'cept screw-tops.

Mr. Ron was real nice 'bout it. He even laughed 'bout me hammerin the necks off and pourin that wine in the coffee cup in case he seen me drinkin it. I ain't no dummy, and though I don't wear no watch, I knowed what time it was. You gots my drift?

Anyway, he say he gots a solution to the problem. The man say he gonna teach me to be an artist like all the ones he be selling. A few hours later I was facin a blank white canvas and tubes of paint with more colors than a box of crayons. I did my best to try and convince him I wadn't no artist, but he just wouldn't listen. He stubborn that way.

I stared at that white canvas lyin on the kitchen table, and it seemed to stare right back at me. Mr. Ron put on some fancy-sounding music with no words and told me to squeeze out a color, dip my brush, and move with the rhythm.

"Blues is the onliest music I likes," I told him. "Maybe a little gospel too."

"It doesn't matter," he say. "Go on . . . move." But I just plumb froze up. So he takes the brush in his hand with no paint on it and show me how to move with the music. "Now, pick a color and start movin," he said again.

I chose red.

3 0

RON

The next morning Denver was sober as a deacon on Sunday, sitting at the breakfast table and eagerly awaiting my arrival.

"Come out to the garage. I gots to show you somethin."

I followed him to the same garage room where he learned to open wine. And there lying on the broken glass was a painting, a childlike abstract, though clearly the image of an angel.

"Dang, that's really good. How much do you want for it?"

"One million dollars."

"*One million dollars?*" I repeated in disbelief, then asked him where he'd come up with that price.

"Well, I seen over there in your livin room you gots a paintin that looks kinda like this one, but not this good. I heard you tellin a customer it was painted by Jackson the Polack and costs a million dollars. So I figured since mine is bigger and better, I'll make the man a deal and sell it for the same price."

"Good deductive reasoning, my friend. I was thinking about buying it, but I can't afford it."

"Mr. Ron, I ain't askin you to buy it. I just wants you to sell it."

31

Mr. Shisler called and told me Mr. Ballentine wadn't doin very well and wanted to see me real bad. The old man was my friend, 'cept he didn't really wanna be my friend—kinda like I didn't wanna be Miss Debbie's and Mr. Ron's friend. Growin up under plantation rules like I did, I been slow 'bout mixin the races. Miss Debbie helped me see whites with fresh eyes. But Mr. Ballentine sure wadn't no Miss Debbie.

I's standin by the gate to the mission one night when I seen a young man drive up in a late-model Ford. He open the other door, pull a drunk man and a old suitcase outta the front seat, and toss 'em both on the sidewalk. He left that ol' man layin there, screamin and cussin, as he pop the clutch and drive on outta sight.

That was four or five years ago. The man on the ground was Mr. Ballentine. I found out later it was his son that kicked him outta his house for drinkin too much.

The poor man was scared and cryin his eyes plumb out, so I offered to help him get a room at the mission. You prob'ly ain't gonna believe this, but that skinny little ol' man sat straight up, spit on me, and said he didn't need no help from a nigger. If the man had been anywhere near my size, I might have opened a can of whoop-ass on 'im. But I just laughed 'cause I thought it was funny he didn't know my name was Suicide. So I drag his skinny little drunk butt into the mission and carry him up to a room.

The man had a bad habit. Ever time he seen a black fella, he'd holler, "Get away from me, nigger!" Most would just laugh and make fun, but a few sent him off to the hospital in the ambulance for stitches. He even told folks he was a Nazi. It got so bad, he was banned from the dinin hall, so I'd get two plates and take one up to his room so he wouldn't starve to death.

Anyway, Mr. Shisler finally had to send Mr. Ballentine off to a gov'ment nursin home 'cause the man was pushin ninety, couldn't walk, and was just too ornery.

I decides I wants to go see that ol' man. So I talk to his nurse on the phone, and she say I better hurry, 'cause he ain't got long to live, and I's the onliest person he wanted to see.

His room smelled real bad, like he done messed in his bed. He was naked 'cept for a bright-orange huntin vest. I thought he might already be dead, except I could see the vest movin and I could hear a little breathin. I touched his cold toes—they used to be white but now was nearly black as mine—and that caused him to open his eyes.

"Denver," he said in a whisper, "I'm so glad you came."

He told me how much he 'preciated me takin good care of him at the mission and he was sorry for the times he spit on me and called me a nigger. I knew he was crazy and told him I forgive him.

He asked 'bout Mr. Ron and remembered the time Mr. Ron's friend, Mr. Scott Walker, bought him a carton of cigarettes. He said Mr. Scott was the first Christian he ever met. Them cigarettes changed his opinion about Christians.

We had us some good laughs. Then we talked about the time I took him to Mr. Ron's and Miss Debbie's church. That was the onliest time he ever been in a church in his whole life. He enjoyed it. It made him wanna act better.

"Denver," he said. "There is somethin else I wanna tell you before I die."

"Yessir?"

"Denver, you are a good man." Then he paused a few seconds before he say, "But you're still a nigger!"

I knew he was bein funny, and we both died laughin—'cept he really did. I know you ain't gonna believe this, but the man laughed so hard he began coughin and coughin till the alarm went off. The nurse come in, unplug him, and pull a sheet over his head.

I stayed for a few more minutes and said a prayer for Mr. Ballentine. I couldn't help wonderin if he prayed that prayer the preacher asked everbody to pray the day we went to church. I'm believin he did, 'cause he was a smart man—used to work at General Dynamics buildin airplanes.

32

Ron

Denver slipped into a sort of funk after Mr. Ballentine's funeral service. Chef Jim from the mission and Mr. Shisler had been about the only other ones there. The old man had been buried in a Tarrant County pauper's grave in a pine box like Debbie's. I asked Denver why he hadn't told me, and he said he didn't think rich folks had time for homeless funerals. I assured him I did.

By now Denver had made at least twenty-five paintings. Some, like the one of him picking cotton, were more interesting than others. Unfortunately, the art experiment had not caused Denver to stop drinking. More wine went missing. And most mornings I'd find him drunk on the kitchen floor, needing to sober up before we started our daily task of plowing up his field, searching for words that would fit in our book.

There were a lot of things about his story, especially timelines, that just didn't add up. "Mr. Ron," he told me, "I ain't never had no watch or kept no diary. I ain't never had no place to be, and I always had plenty of time to get there. That's it. They ain't nothin missin."

It was obviously painful for him to relive being dragged by those horses, witnessing the stabbing death of his father, and seeing his uncle James drop dead from a heart attack at the plow, just as Denver was handing him a freshly lit cigarette. "Them mules just keep on plowin . . . draggin him. I guess they didn't know he was dead. Them kinda things just hang on you like moss on the swamp trees," he said.

Surprisingly, he had nothing bad to say about the plantation owner. He even praised the Man for giving lots of "coloreds" a job and a place to stay. "If everybody was rich, who gonna do the work?" he said in the Man's defense.

Maybe a week or so after Mr. Ballentine's death, I walked into the kitchen one morning expecting to see him dead asleep on the floor. Instead, I found him sober and bright-eyed—clearly different, though smelling of Pall Malls as usual.

"What's gotten into you?" I questioned. I'd not seen him this alert in the six months we'd lived together.

"Miss Debbie come to visit me last night and sacked me out real bad."

"In a dream?"

"Nosir, a visitation."

Seems that after I retired for the night he'd driven to the filling station and bought a six-pack of Natural Light. He'd just opened his first beer on the way home when Miss Debbie appeared in the seat beside him.

"She ain't come in through no windows," he told me, "and she ain't open no doors. She just appear, and she say: 'Denver, you promised me before I went to heaven you were gonna pick up my torch and carry it for the homeless. But I've been watchin you. You haven't helped anybody but yourself. In fact, all I see you doing is sitting on your butt getting drunk every night. It's time you kept your promise to me . . . and God.' Then she disappear into the night like smoke after the fire is gone.

"If you don't believe me, just go out behind the garage and look in the trash can. There be a whole six-pack that ain't been touched 'cept one swig from the open can. The lady was right. I ain't gonna be drinkin no more. After breakfast, just watch and see. I gonna slide over to the hood and do a little street preachin by the mission."

———

I answered the phone with, "Hello." After that I was unable to get in another word for at least a minute because the lady on the other end of the line was berating me for turning Denver back into a slave—my slave.

I quickly put her on the speakerphone so Vida could share in this laughable moment. That was one angry and self-righteous woman. I'd met her just once at a church event. Seems Denver had talked to her about his painting, and she and her husband had inferred that I was forcing him to do it. She thought he'd become my art slave. And she was sure that God was not only going to judge me, but would actually strike me down for selling all Denver's paintings and keeping all his money for myself. "I'll bet you even make him mow your big yard," she accused. According to her, I was no different than the Man who never paid him for working the fields and picking his cotton.

When she finally stopped to catch her breath, I politely asked her if she was sober or if this was a drunk call. I proceeded to inform her that as of that day, Denver had been a guest in my home for more than two years. He had never paid rent, bought groceries, or made a car payment. In fact, I had given him three vehicles and also paid the insurance. Far from being my slave, he was given a thousand dollars a month to do absolutely nothing, since he had resigned the night-watchman job to become an artist. He had never mowed my yard, chauffeured me anywhere, or cooked my meals, and he never would as long as he lived there.

In addition, I bought all his art supplies, including the frames. Aunt Vida sold, packaged, and shipped his art by FedEx free of charge. He kept 100 percent of the proceeds and paid exactly nothing for nothing and received anything and everything he wanted.

"Now, what is your problem?" I asked before inviting that woman and her husband to spend a few days with us to monitor and, if necessary, report to the authorities my dark side as a slave master. She hung up before I could tell her about his nearly setting the house on fire!

At that point, Denver hadn't left our home in days. I'm sure the lady was telling people I had him chained and locked in his studio. But that wasn't even close to the truth. On a typical day, after our morning reading lessons and writing sessions, sometimes he'd go into the studio to paint. But other days he'd just relax on a chaise lounge in the shade by the pool, working his way through his daily pack of Pall Malls—his preferred form of work. But he wasn't just doing nothing, he'd told me on occasion, because he was always thinking or listening for God.

By now Denver had made friends with a mother bobcat and her babies and fed them twice a day. If he forgot, they would walk out of the bushes and press their noses against the big glass walls in the living room. On one of those days I was showing art to a former ambassador who was my client. She was standing with her back to the glass when she heard something scratching. Turning around, she let out a scream and hastily scooted away from the wall, sure that the mother bobcat was about to attack.

Later that same day, when I asked Denver to make a run to the store to pick up something I needed for our dinner, he asked to borrow my car.

"Where is yours?" I asked.

"It's lost," he said in a dead-serious tone.

"How does a car become lost?"

"Well, it stopped workin, so I just left it on the side of the road."

"Which road?"

"I don't rightly remember."

I quizzed him on how it was possible to not remember where you left a ten-thousand-dollar vehicle. And he did his best to convince me that since it had quit running, abandoning it was the best strategy. That way it would be someone else's problem, not his.

He wasn't sure *why* the car had quit. He seemed to remember it had been running hot, and that in turn had run him hot.

I asked Aunt Vida to check with the police in all the surrounding towns to see if the car had been towed. No luck. So I quizzed Denver on his best guess about the location.

He remembered street preaching to some gangbangers near the mission, making a wrong turn when he left, and getting lost. After the car stopped, he had walked to a filling station and taken a taxi home. The fare had been about one hundred dollars. So I estimated the distance that a hundred dollars would have taken him and drew a circle around our location representing the outer limits of where he could have left the car.

For two days we drove the highways and freeways within that circle, trying to trace Denver's route home from the mission. "Go this way. . . . No, that way. This way don't look right. I can't remember. . . . Turn 'round. Go back. . . . Start over again!"

Finally, after two full days of driving, we found his Jeep on the side of the interstate about thirty miles south of our home. It had been ticketed and vandalized, with broken glass covering the seats and the radio missing. I dusted the glass off the seat, turned the key, and saw it was out of gas. We got five gallons at a nearby station, and it started right up.

"Praise the Lord and pass the plate," Denver exclaimed, shaking his head before breaking into a belly laugh. "I guess it done cooled down sittin out here in the hot sun!"

33

DENVER

Miss Regan walked in the kitchen while I was waitin on Mr. Ron to start work on our book. I had somethin on my mind.

"You gotta movie camera I can borrow?" I asked her.

She say she didn't got no camera, but she was purty sure her daddy would buy me one if I asked him. She asked me what I was gonna do with it, and I told her I was gonna make me a movie. "Gonna call it *From a Mission to a Mansion*."

We both had a good laugh 'bout that. Miss Regan's a lot like her daddy. Her and I been good friends since I moved all her worldly possessions to Colorado while Miss Debbie was still livin. That was the first day I got my drivin license and the first time I ever seen a mountain. I studied it for a good while and tried to figure how I was gonna drive 'round it, but the lady at the fillin station told me I had to drive straight up and over it. Oh Lordy, I ain't never gonna forget drivin over that mountain.

Now Miss Regan was gonna be movin to Austin in a week or so, and I knowed I was gonna miss her. Me and her daddy was gonna drive her stuff down there. She graduated from college in that town. Since Miss Debbie passed, she been havin a hard time gettin back to work. Losin a momma is hard on a young girl. She told me she wanna take pictures with a camera and sell 'em, and Austin she say is real purty.

That night Mr. Ron call me and asked where I was. I told him I was in my bedroom. Then he say he seen somebody smokin in the bushes where the bobcats stay.

I knowed who he was talkin 'bout. And I done told the fella when I let him in the back gate not to be smokin at night 'cause Mr. Ron could see real good from his glass bedroom.

He was a homeless man I met at the fillin station. I didn't even know his name. All I knowed was he was livin in his car and the police kept makin him move it. So I figured I'd be a Good Samaritan and invite him to stay with me and Mr. Ron—'cept I ain't had the courage to tell Mr. Ron 'bout it. The man and his car been hidin back in the bushes 'bout two weeks without no problems. But now there was fixin to be a problem.

Mr. Ron is a very trustin man, and he ain't never told me, "Denver, don't ever let no homeless folk sleep on our property." So since he ain't told me that, I been lettin a few here and there stay over in the big house since I moved to the guest house to avoid the ghosts. I just brings 'em in the back of my Jeep and throws a blanket over 'em when I be comin by the guard house through the security gates. Me and the guards was purty tight. Sometimes I'd stop and have a smoke with one of 'em. They was always askin 'bout how I gots a job with a millionaire. So they never bothered me much and never asked if I was bringing somebody in.

I helped the man gather his stuff after Mr. Ron seen him. The fella done set up camp back there like in the hobo jungle. He told me he thought he figured out when Mr. Ron was comin and goin so he could cook hisself some food without gettin caught. But he did get hisself caught, so he had to leave.

Mr. Ron watch from his bedroom as the man drove outta the bushes, through the yard by the big red statue, and out the back gate. Then, back in the kitchen we had us a come-to-Jesus meetin about rules and somethin Mr. Ron's been preachin to me since the day I arrived 'bout two years ago—'countability and responsibilimy.

"Mr. Ron, you missed somethin very important," I told him. "We's writin us a book to help the homeless, and that's 'zactly what I was doin for the man you just run off. I heard on the Christian TV where two hundred million peoples live on less'n a dollar a day. That man was one of 'em. Did you hear me?"

"I know Denver, but. . . ."

"Don't be comin at me with no buts! Now, I ain't gettin smart with you, but I needs to have a talk with *you* 'bout some 'countability and responsibilimy. If we's gonna change the world, we's gotta start right here in our own backyard."

34

RON

After nearly three years of work, I finally wrote "The End" in cursive on page 356 of our manuscript. For weeks I'd been sending out letters to publishers and agents with zero success—not a single returned call. In fact, the partial manuscripts I'd sent to publishers had come back unopened and marked "Return to Sender." So I decided to swallow my pride and self-publish under the title *Denver Bound: A Journey with Miss Debbie*.

It surprised me that God—not that I'm blaming him—closed every front, back, or trap door to agents and publishing houses. I had not written the book for profit. I simply wanted to honor Debbie and raise a little money for the mission of her dreams. But with buyers as scarce as water in the desert, I gave away the self-published books to family and friends until they were all gone.

But even without sales, it seemed that word was getting out. Almost daily, Denver and I were asked to tell our story to small groups, book clubs, and Bible studies. It was the Bible studies that birthed a brilliant nugget of his wisdom—specifically after one persistent Bible study leader would not take no for an answer.

As she walked away from the sidewalk café where we were dining, Denver asked, "Do all white ladies gots Bible studies?" I agreed that it sure seemed like it, as we had spoken at too many to count.

"Well, it be curious to me that nary a one of them white ladies ever invited us to a Bible doin. So, what I wants to know, is they

103

just sittin 'round studyin, or is any of 'em out there doin?" He was
serious. "Think about it, Mr. Ron. A fella like me that don't read and
write don't know nothin 'bout studyin, so I ain't goin to no more
Bible studies. But if they wants to invite me to a Bible *doin*, tell 'em
to call, and I's gonna show up!"

———

The fall of 2005 was a busy time, but also quite profitable for the
man of Debbie's dream. After we poured our hearts out on stages all
across Texas, most of the hosts passed the hat to bless the man they
found fascinating and entertaining. Those blessings were overrun-
ning his gallon-pickle-jar piggy bank, so I opened up a bank account
for him.

A few days later he walked into my office frustrated and angry
and threw his debit card down on my desk so hard that it bounced
off to the floor. "I tried to put some gas in my Jeep, and the pump
wouldn't let me have no gas. So I took it into the man at the cash
register, and he say my card ain't no good 'cause it ain't been
aggravated!"

For Christmas that year, Denver asked Santa for an electric
piano keyboard. He'd banged around on one at the mission a few
years back. Now, in a matter of weeks, he taught himself to play. In
fact, he got good enough that he was asked to perform at several
events where we were speaking. His renditions of old spirituals,
plantation songs, and blues brought audiences to their feet, unwill-
ing to sit again until he performed an encore. There was a direct
correlation between his singing and the size of the blessings that
were piling up in his personal account after I called the bank and
"aggravated" his card!

I was enjoying some blessings of my own in those days. Three
days after Christmas that year, Regan and her husband, Matt

Donnell, blessed me with my first grandchild—a beautiful little girl named Griffin, with blue eyes and dark hair that stood straight up like a Mohawk. She'd been named after Matt's favorite pasture on his family ranch just west of Rocky Top.

Denver went with me to welcome Griffin to the world. He teared up as he held his first white baby and declared her to be his grandbaby too. For his gift to her, he painted her a small angel painting. He told me she was his little angel since she was Miss Debbie's first grandbaby.

The next month was Denver's birthday. He was certain he'd been born in January but only fairly certain of the date, so we always celebrated his birthday for the whole month, starting on New Year's Day. Santa had left a gift that year with instructions not to open until after he ate his black-eyed peas on New Year's. So he opened the box as we watched the Rose Bowl Parade and stared at the contents with the eyes of a cow looking at a new gate. "What's I s'posed to do with this?" he asked, holding up a tuxedo and an invitation to join me in Washington, DC, for President George W. Bush's inauguration.

35

DENVER

I never dreamed I'd be goin to the White House. The coloreds
use to say that they called it the White House 'cause no coloreds was
allowed there. But now I knowed that's a joke, 'cause when I was
standin in the front yard of the White House, I seen lots of brothers.
In fact, me and Mr. Ron was sittin on the very front row, and there
was a black fella and his wife real close by. The president sat on a
stage 'bout the distance from the front door to the back of a shotgun
house—real close.

Mr. Ron was talkin to some movie star and a astronaut sittin
next to us, and I seen that nobody was talkin to the president 'cept
his wife, so I decides I'm gonna go up and talk to 'im. I took 'bout
five steps in his direction, but then a big black fella like me—'cept he
had a wire stickin out his ear—stopped me and said he was a Secret
Service agent. I tried to shake his hand. I ain't never met one of them
fellas. But he look at me real serious-like and say I need to sit back
down 'cause I was in violation of the security space.

Now, this ain't nothin but the truth—a blind Eye-talian fella got
up and sang a song in a foreign language that nobody knowed what
he was singin. Now why in the world would a blind Eye-talian be
singin at the White House of America? He coulda been sayin somethin bad 'bout our president, and ain't nary a person there woulda
knowed it. But I clapped like everbody else.

The next mornin we watched the president put his hand on the

Bible and swear to protect us all. And later Mr. Ron showed me that big statue of President Lincoln. I took my hat off in his honor, said a prayer, and thanked him for settin us free. Big Mama done told me 'bout him and say the white folk kill him for doin just that. As I touched the cold stone statue, Mr. Ron took my picture. I wished Big Mama coulda seen me.

Later that night we went to the tuxedo party, where I got to wear mine for the first time. Now I figured out why Mr. Ron bought it. I told him everbody there was gonna think I was a waiter. He laughed and told me I was wrong. Then he say everbody was thinkin I was the president of Africa. That made me laugh. And for the third time in two days, I got to see the president again. This time he was dancin with his wife all by hisself on the big dance floor.

36

Denver had never been on an airplane, so he was not concerned when we made a very wobbly landing in a near-whiteout snowstorm. I, on the other hand, was britches-wet scared. I kept that to myself because Denver almost hadn't boarded the plane, claiming he really wanted to ride the bus. That had not been an option.

Actually, I had been surprised to get invited to the inauguration. I'd made a small donation, put a bumper sticker on my car, and stuck a sign in our yard. But Debbie had been the political one in the family. She'd been addicted to C-SPAN, known the name of every senator, and called their offices to voice her opinion on nearly every bill.

One of the greatest days of her life, and our lives together, had been attending President Reagan's first inauguration with VIP privileges. We'd sat behind the great actor Jimmy Stewart. So I found it a bit melancholic to be back in Washington without her. Hopefully she was watching and pleased to see the man of her dream living a dream. I knew she'd be happy to know that Denver was well on his way to becoming the best friend I'd ever known.

Back in Dallas, the call we'd been waiting for had come just a few months after our self-published book, *Denver Bound*, got passed around. One copy had ended up in the hands of a highly respected author, Ken Gire. He'd felt our book was worthy of a major publisher, and after a couple of calls to his brother-in-law, agent Lee Hough, we'd been visited by executives from Thomas Nelson Publishing.

They'd been among the many who previously returned our manuscript unopened. But now they were offering us a contract and money, more than we had ever dreamed of. The caveat was that I needed to cut out more than one hundred pages and rewrite several chapters. A writer named Lynn Vincent would be brought on board to shape the book up to Thomas Nelson standards. And, of course, we'd have to grant them our story rights.

"What's that mean?" Denver asked.

"They want to buy the rights to tell the story about our lives."

Denver balked. "My life ain't for sale," he said emphatically. "My peoples was sold on the slave block." He'd slipped back into his fight-or-flight mode. "Ain't nobody gonna turn me back into they slave."

I tried to explain that in order to have our story told by a publishing house, both of us had to sell them our life-story rights. That's just the way it works.

"Mr. Ron," he said with his trademark one-eyed squint, "did you know that I knows about trickonometry."

Unsure if he was joking, I replied: "I didn't know that, since it's a subject we have never discussed. I thought you couldn't even add and subtract."

"I can't, but hear me good—I knows plenty about when somebody tryin to trick me, and I ain't fallin for Mr. Nelson's tricks."

"Denver, you gave me the right to tell your story, our story. And that's exactly what Mr. Nelson wants, except he's going to pay you a lot more than a grand a month plus room, board, and a car."

"Maybe so, but when I come here I didn't gots to sign nothin I can't read."

Denver dug in. But I dug in deeper, tugging on his heart by reminding him that we were doing this for Miss Debbie and that my part of the money would go to help build the mission of her dream. And he'd get his part in folding money—lots of it.

"Okay," he said after some cajoling. "They can give me a hundred thousand dollars, and I'll let 'em tell our story."

This seemed out of character for my humble friend. Money had never been that important to him, but now he was talking like a rock star. I suspected someone outside our circle had spied some low-hanging fruit and was trying to pick it—and Denver was letting himself be picked.

I reminded Denver that he'd lived with me for three years and was getting paid for it, plus I'd bought him three cars and paid all his living expenses. "Listen, my friend, if you find a better deal, whether it's a publishing offer or a living arrangement, I encourage you to take it. You may be a wise man, but you're acting like a fool!"

This was the first time since we'd known each other—and we'd been through wrecks, fires, disappearing acts, and a near assault—that I was really angry with him and him with me. I heard the gravel crackle as he drove away. But a few hours later he walked into the kitchen, smiling and claiming he'd talked to some friends in Fort Worth who knew about legal stuff. They'd told him he'd be a fool not to sign.

"So, Mr. Ronnie Ray Hall, you ain't lookin at no fool!" He laughed as he extended his hand to shake.

As usual, he'd just needed to smoke a few Pall Malls and blow off some steam to get back to the man who just wanted to honor his friend and stubborn angel, Miss Debbie.

37

DENVER

Miss Lynn Vincent come to visit us right after we signed us a contract to publish our story. She wanted to see ever place I lived. Now, she didn't never say this, but I thinks Mr. Thomas Nelson ain't believed all the things we said I'd lived through. Not that they was ever gonna know it all. Everbody gots secrets.

The writer lady wadn't even scared when we walked the mean part of the streets and the hobo jungle. But we didn't stay long 'cause she was itchin to see the Man's plantation. So Mr. Ron and I drive her to Louisiana. On the way she was pryin, and that cause me to shut down some. I knowed it was her job, but I still didn't like all the questions.

After a bit Miss Lynn asked me what the coloreds ate on plantations. She nearly busted a gut laughin when I told her the Man give us a hog once a year and we ate his feet, ears, skin, and everthing from the rooter to the tooter!

We stopped for lunch at a café just down Highway 1 from the plantation. I told 'em it was whites only, and they thought I was jokin. Just read an encyclopedia 'bout the Coushatta uprisin, a Klan rally that the FBI drive down from Washington to shut down. The FBI ain't never run into nobody as bad as them hooded monsters. The Klan stood 'em down at the city-limits sign. A hundred FBI mens turned and run like whooped puppies with they tails between they legs, and they ain't never showed they faces here again.

111

I knowed better than to go in that café, just like I knowed it the time Mr. Ron take me to his country club. I was sittin on the pot and heard a fella in the men's room askin him not to be bringin his amigo Negro 'round the club. 'Bout that time I finished my bidness and walked out. Mr. Ron told the man he could tell me hisself.

That's called havin my back. That's what me and Mr. Ron does for each other. But I still didn't wanna go in that café.

Sure 'nough, it didn't take five minutes before the three-hundred-pound deputy sheriff come walkin in wearin his cowboy hat and six-shooter. I seen the waitress go call him when she seen me walkin in.

He looked me straight in the eye and asked what we boys was doin in there. The Louisiana law always calls the coloreds "boys." That's disrespect. Mr. Ron told him: "My friend Denver and I are visiting your town and writing a book about it. And we brought this lady who is an investigative reporter."

She smiled. "Nice town you got here."

The deputy didn't know what to say, but he didn't take his eye off me when he said, "Y'all behave yo'self and stay outta trouble."

The lady was mighty anxious to see Hershalee's house. To tell you the truth, Mr. Ron and me was purty leery 'bout goin back there after what happen to his car. I did my best to tell her that evil surrounded the whole place, from the road to the slimy green swamp off the back porch.

You ain't gonna believe it, but that made her want to go even more.

The lady rub her hands together real fast, like she was warmin 'em up on a cold day, and she say, "Yummy."

We pulled up in front of Hershalee's house. It looked 'bout the same. The weeds was just as tall and the air still smell bad, like somethin be dead. Like a man hangin from a tree. But Miss Lynn marched herself right on up on the porch and stuck her head in the

door. The lady had courage. She done been in the armed services—
the navy, I believe.

Everthing inside was still a mess. I showed Miss Lynn the bed
I'd laid in for days recoverin from the draggin. My auntie, the witch
doctor, done cooked up a potion with some mud, mushrooms, and
swamp moss and packed my whole head in it. My eyes was swol-
len plumb shut, and when they finally opened a week or so later, I
was near blind. That's the reason I gots to get my eyes deleted ever
month or so.

We was on the back porch showin Miss Lynn the bathtub when
we hears a noise outside—not the swamp monster like last time. A
big dog was barkin, and we hear a motor runnin.

"What are y'all doin on this property?" a man hollered. Mr. Ron
walked outside. A big ol' Rottweiler chained in the truck growl and
bare teeth like a gator. A redneck in a gimme cap with his belly
hangin over his buckle said he was the Man's relation and he was
runnin the whole outfit now that the Man done got too old. I heard
the conbersation from inside the house, but the redneck still ain't
seen me till Mr. Ron asked me to come outside.

"This is my friend Denver. He used to live in this house."

"He sure didn't," he said like he knowed it—but he didn't. "An
old nigger woman named Hershalee lived in there most of her life.
She was sorry as they come—never paid a dime's worth of rent.
The Man let her live here way past the days when she could earn
her keep."

"Hershalee was Denver's sister," Mr. Ron say. His face was turnin
red as a ripe tomato. "He lived with her when he was a young man."

"Well, he musta left here before I come along in 1970, 'cause I
ain't never laid eyes on him."

The redneck looked at me with a kinda snarl, runnin his eyes
from my head to my toes and back up and down again. I never seen
him before, either, and if Mr. Ron and Miss Lynn ain't been standin

there, I'da whooped 'im like a mad dog for talkin bad 'bout my sister. She picked his cotton, washed his wife's and daddy's and mama's
clothes, and scrubbed they floors and toilets from the time she was
ten years old till she died. Don't be talkin no trash 'bout Hershalee
not earnin her keep.

Then Mr. Ron told him we was writin us a book 'bout me and
Hershalee. That seem to run him hot, like he knowed what time it
was. He double up his fists like we was fixin to rumble. "Get off this
property now, and don't come back," he ordered.

Then the redneck really show his evil side. He say he gonna
torch the place right now to make sure we wouldn't have nothin to
come back to or write 'bout.

We got back in Mr. Ron's Suburban, the same one that was
under some kinda spell and wouldn't run the last time we was here.
Mr. Ron laugh and say, "Cross your fingers." But the car started
right up this time. Drivin off, we looked back and seen the redneck
take a torch outta his vehicle and light it up just like the Devil.

———

'Bout that time Hurricane Katrina was blowin hard down south in
Louisiana. I knowed peoples down there. I sat for hours watchin
the TV and lookin to see if they showed anybody I knowed. Like
Mr. Ron promised, we got a chunk of money for the book, so I sent
some down there to a lady whose house got swallowed up like
Jonah in the belly of the whale.

Mr. Ron had a girlfriend that come by the house with this li'l
white, furry dog that been rescued from the hurricane. She said it
was a homeless dog. And that snapped somethin in my mind that
caused me to get throwed off and act crazy. I got in her purty face
and screamed: "Don't you never call the homeless dogs. We ain't
no dogs!"

She started cryin and tryin to apologize, but my mind shut plumb down like the Devil flipped off the switch, and my ears was ringin *homeless dogs, homeless dogs*. That run me hotter than a V-8 Ford with a busted water hose. I needed to get outta there 'fore I hurt somebody. So I headed out to the car.

She and Mr. Ron followed me, sayin they was sorry and tellin me I misunderstood, but I never turned 'round. I got in my car, and they was foolishly thinkin they was gonna block me from drivin off.

Sometimes crazy folk do crazy things, and Lord help me, but I tried to run 'em down with my car. That was the old me from back 'fore Miss Debbie, the me I hoped had done died. But I'll be switched if the Devil hadn't just jump back in my skin—he's got a flyin mochine, you know.

Mr. Ron push the lady back. So when I push the gas pedal to the floor, he was my onliest target, and I fix my eyes on him like a hunter lookin down the barrel of a rifle. I'm sure thankful I missed. God musta took control of the wheel. I coulda killed 'im—both of 'em.

An hour or so later, after I smoked me a few Pall Malls, I cooled down. I shoulda smoked a few *'fore* I jumped in that car, 'cause now I was feelin real bad. I went back to 'pologize, but they was gone.

You ain't gonna believe this, but smokin saves lives.

38

RON

An act of kindness to take in a rescue dog from Katrina nearly cost my friend her life. Still shaking from the near-death experience, we drove to Fort Worth to seek counsel from a friend who was also Denver's doctor.

Temporary insanity was his diagnosis. "Denver isn't a fool, though he just did a foolish thing." He thought everything would be all right by the time I got home.

His advice was not reassuring. I was afraid to go home. I even contemplated having the police remove Denver from the premises and send him back to the jungle. I stayed in a hotel for two nights, then reluctantly returned to the scene of the crime.

Denver was sitting shirtless in his boxers at the kitchen table, eating a can of sardines with crackers. "Where you been?"

"Hiding from you."

I wasn't trying to be funny, but that made him laugh. I added, "If anything like that ever happens again, your things will be tossed to the curb like Mr. Ballentine's son did to him."

"I's sorry I tried to run over you and your friend. That wadn't nothin but the Devil."

He had gone back to the jungle and sought advice from some of his old acquaintances. Then what he said next broke me out in laughter.

"Mr. Ron, one of the fellas in the jungle called me a crazy ol' fool and asked me why I'd wanna kill the goose that laid the golden egg. He told me he seen a movie 'bout a broke black man that traded places with a millionaire. Then the man started laughin and told me he'd be happy to trade places with me—he sure would!"

After a good laugh we shared a rare hug and made up. For the next several days and weeks, Denver was contrite, helpful, and appreciative. I was slower to warm back up to him than he was to me. Like Debbie, he was quick to forgive, but I locked my bedroom door at night for the next few weeks.

On several occasions he offered to cook for me. I reminded him about the last time I returned home from Italy bearing two bottles of the gold-medal-winning olive oil wrapped and sealed in gold foil. I had set them on the kitchen counter before going to bed, only to awake in the morning to find them in the trash, empty. Come to find out, he'd used both two-hundred-dollar bottles of first-press, gold-medal, extra-virgin olive oil to "fry him up a batch of chicken gizzards." He told me later they didn't taste like Big Mama's. He wished he'd used hog lard instead.

A few days later, Denver got word that his daughter from Los Angeles was looking for him. Strangely, he had never told me about any children, though I suspected he was hiding a lot of things. We talked about going to California to meet her, and through her conversations we discovered there were two sons as well—all by different women.

Apparently he fathered all three in the mid-1960s while living homeless for a year or so in Los Angeles. And the reason he'd landed in Los Angeles was that he'd gotten into a shoot-out in Fort Worth not long after he landed there from the plantation.

He'd turned a man's own gun on him. "Self-defense," he told me and showed me the huge scar on his thigh—more hole than scar—where the assailant had shot him first. Bleeding profusely, he'd stuffed a T-shirt in the hole, tied a shirt around his leg to stop the bleeding, and tossed the gun in the river. Then he hopped a freight train before he found out if the man lived or died. Denver suspected he might not have made it.

While on the lam in California, he'd been arrested for battery and sentenced to six months hard labor on an army base. "I got my stripes," he told me with a laugh, "but they wadn't on no army uniform. They was black-and-white prison clothes!"

Word got back to him after that about babies being born—two in the same hospital on the same day by different mamas who were looking for him. But that turn of events caused him to "burn off," his term for hightailing it out of town on the next freight train going in any direction.

We had some real serious heart-to-heart talks about his responsibility to those children. He hung his head low, admitting "it was a low-down thing to leave them babies with no daddy." And the good news, I told him, was that he still had time to make things right. He assured me he would.

Lynn and I finished the book in a matter of weeks. A few weeks after that, a set of galleys arrived via FedEx. For the next two days I read to Denver from cover to cover, asking if there were any additions or corrections. "I think it's all there," he replied, slapping the tabletop as if taking an oath of office. Then an afterthought: "Take out the part of me and Bobby playin KKK in the Man's basement. I don't want none of my kin to suffer for that."

Denver and I returned to Louisiana to get signed releases to use the names of his family members who would appear in our book. And we couldn't help but sneak back on the plantation to see what had happened to Hershalee's house. It was gone. So was Denver's little shack. But Aunt Pearlie May's, Uncle James's, and hundreds of others were still scattered on the dirt roads within a stone's throw of modern interstates and brand-new Walmarts. It's hard to believe so many Southern black families still live in such poverty, forced on them by racist landowners who seem to want to keep it that way.

———

Denver sat at the kitchen table reading a kids' book called *Where the Wild Things Are*. He was laughing at the story and waiting for me to put a pot roast, turnip greens, and cornbread on the table when my phone rang. The voice was Southern black. I turned off the stove and walked to another room out of earshot of Denver. "Can I help you?"

"Is this Mr. Ron Hall who is writin a book?" The man stuttered badly. I was unsure if he was just nervous or if it was a condition.

"Yes."

"Do Thomas Moore from Louisiana live with you?" The stutter was so strong, it took him seconds to say what should have come out instantly.

"Do you mean Denver Moore?"

"I heard he changed his name. We all knowed him as Thomas."

Vida, a genealogist, had found Denver's birth certificate at Louisiana Vital Records office. It stated that he had been born on January 30, 1937, in Red River Parish and that his name at birth had been Denver Thomas Moore. But I'd never heard him referred to as anything but Denver or Li'l Buddy.

I wasn't sure what the caller was fishing for—he didn't ask to speak to Denver. So I simply listened.

"Mr. Hall, I need to let you know that your life is in danger. Thomas is a crazy killer. We served time together in Angola. You better get outta your house while you still gots a chance."

That hit me like an assassin's bullet in the back. I was blind-sided, unsure where this conversation was going. I walked outside to a clap of thunder, maybe symbolic, and prayed for ears to hear and words to defend my friend.

"Let me tell you," I said, "I know Denver Moore better than anyone, and here is what I'm sure of: Denver confessed everything and is a born-again Christian who surrendered his life to Christ. He now lives in peace under the grace and mercy of his Lord and Savior. He's lived with me for nearly four years and has told me everything. You can read it in our book. Now, why are you calling?"

His stuttering got worse, and it took him a full minute to line out the next sentence.

"When he get outta prison in '76, my mama let him stay at her house 'cause she lived in Denham Springs close to the prison and he could walk there. She took care of him, and he never paid her no rent or nothin. She know a lot more stuff 'bout Thomas that I'll betcha ain't gonna be in your book."

"Where is this conversation going?"

"Mr. Hall, she ain't doin very well, and she need a few thousand to help her out and keep her quiet."

"Okay. By law, I must inform you that I have recorded this conversation. In a court of law, what you just said is considered extortion and blackmail. If I proceed, you will be going back to Angola instead of staying with your mama and taking care of her. It sounds like she could use your help. Give me her name and number, and I'll ask Denver if he has anything to say to her."

I wrote down her name and telephone number on a piece of scrap paper and ended the conversation with a warning not to call back.

Denver saw me walk in. "Where you been? I'm hongry!"

I sat down at the table facing Denver. "I was on the phone with a man from Louisiana who called to warn me that my life is in danger. He said he served time in Angola with a known killer named Thomas Moore. And he was told that this Thomas Moore was living in my house."

Denver started wobbling, eyes expanding in a blank stare like he was going to faint. He dropped his face onto his crossed arms, knocking his hat off to the floor.

I continued, "The man said Thomas stayed with his mama after he got out of prison, and now she is down on her luck and needs a little help."

Denver slowly raised his head. "Did the man stutter?"

"Real bad," I said as I laid the paper with her phone number on the table and pushed it under his face.

He stared at it for a few seconds, then raised his head. "That low-down snake," is all he could say.

It took a minute or so for both of us to process what was happening. In my heart I'd known something like this was lurking in this mysterious man's past. There were just too many holes in his story. I had hammered on him to dig deep and search his memory to make sure we were telling the truth in our book. And more than once I had asked him point-blank: "Have you been in prison? Not jail—prison?" Just days earlier he had certified the galley proofs as true in a sworn deposition.

Sitting there, he couldn't meet my eyes. I was so angry, I could not look at him either. But I knew what had to be done. Before I spoke another word to Denver, I called our publisher and told them to *stop the presses.*

39

Oh Lordy, that was the day I hoped would never come. It felt like Judgment Day right here on earth. Them stutterin words done opened up a whole can of night-crawlin worms that was thirty years old. I was plannin on takin ever one of 'em with me in my coffin. I'd have to say this was a worse day than when the judge slammed his hammer on his tall wood desk and hollered, "Mr. Moore, I hereby sentence you to twenty years in the Louisiana State Penitentiary"—Angola.

I ain't never told nobody 'bout my time in Angola—not my friends, not my family, I mean *nobody*. The onliest ones that knowed was the other prisoners and the stutterer's mama. Remember the man that flash a secret sign when I was coolin my heels in jail, payin off them traffic tickets? He recognize me from prison, and I avoided him 'cause I didn't want him runnin his mouth 'round Fort Worth.

Remember the fella that caused me to duck when he was walkin down the road in front of Pearlie May's house? He was in Angola for murder—not my daddy's but another fella. But the stutterer told me after I got paroled that man is the one who killed my daddy. He was not anybody I ever wanted to see again 'cause I given revenge over to the Lord and I's afraid if I ever saw 'im I might try and take it back.

Think about it. Mr. Ron and Miss Debbie was showin me off 'round the whole town like I was a show dog in a beauty contest.

122

They was draggin me—not really draggin, but you know what I mean—to they country clubs, churches, resterunts, and the mansions of nearly ever skillionaire in Fort Worth.

Now, listen to me real good. If all them fancy folk knowed how bad I been for most of my life, do you believe for one minute they'da been sayin: "Oh, Denver, it's so nice to meet you. Welcome to our home, and the bathroom is down the hall by the jewelry box in the master bedroom"? I don't think so. They'da had a armed Brinks guard tailin me to the bathroom to make sure I wadn't haulin off all they diamonds and Rolex watches.

So I had my reasons for not tellin nobody. But now I gots to be a man and tell Mr. Ron everthing he want and need to know. It was a big load I been carrying, and it was time to unload.

I ain't cried since Miss Debbie passed. But facin Mr. Ron, I started wipin tears, knowin how I lied. Well, not really lied, 'cause everthing I told him was the straight up truth. I just withheld some truth, but I withheld a lot of it. Like I always say, "He who know don't tell, and he who tell don't necessarily know."

"Okay, what you wanna know?" I pushed back my plate and wiped away the tears with my napkin. This wadn't no time to be eatin. It was time for confessin—for being a man. A real man.

"Everything, Denver, I want to know everything. We were about to publish a book of lies and ruin Miss Debbie's good name. God had that man call me tonight to save her the pain of tears in heaven."

"Oh Lordy. I never thought 'bout that." But I s'posed Mr. Ron was right. So I asked him what he wanted to know.

He just look at me for a minute. Then he say, "The man on the phone told me you're a killer."

"Well, I ain't positive, but I been told that."

"What do you mean, not positive?"

"I ain't denyin nothin, but after somethin bad went down, I

always burned off while they was still breathin. I knows that ain't nothin to be proud of. But the streets'll turn a scared man mean."

He consider that, then look me in the eye. "You served time in Angola. Tell me about it."

So I told him.

———

When I left Los Angeles, I was in a gang called Satan's Saints. The name mean we could be good or bad, dependin on who was lookin. But we was all facin trouble, mostly drugs—heroin. Then I found out I done fathered three babies. I was young, about twenty-seven or eight, and I didn't have no money for child support. So I decided to burn off.

It took a while and a lotta of boxcars, but I made it back to Shreveport. I was afraid to go back to Fort Worth 'cause I wadn't sure if the law was lookin for me. Wadn't even sure I'd done anything wrong 'cept defend myself. But I didn't think I could go back there yet.

I was hongry, livin in the hobo jungle near the tracks in Shreveport, and I found a rusted old pistol—didn't even have no trigger. A bus stopped right where I was sittin on the curb. It wadn't planned, but I pulled the gun outta my pocket, stuck it in the bus driver's face, and told 'im to gimme the money from the money box. It was this glass jar where folks dropped they quarters, and I seen two or three lyin on the bottom.

Truthfully, all I was wantin was fifty cents for a hamburger, but the driver didn't have no key to the money box. Then a colored lady in the back of the bus got scared and started hollerin, "Help me, Jesus." So I just walk away, bein as she was callin on the name of the Lord. You know He say vengeance be His. But when I stepped off the bus, a po-liceman just happened to see me with the gun. And the next thing I knowed, I was starin down the barrel of a loaded gun, and he was callin for backups.

I landed in jail in Shreveport. Then the judge sentenced me to twenty years in Angola for holdin up a bus with a gun that didn't work. I went there in '66, and I come out ten years later. The judge cut ten years off my sentence for good behavior. I guess he didn't know what all went down in the Oak dorm, the one all the inmates call Bucket of Blood. You can try and figure that one out, but the name say it all.

While I was still in a Shreveport holdin cell, there was a parole violator on his way back there. He schooled me on what to 'spect. We became podners. He told me to look for him on the first day, when I'd be walkin down the fresh-fish welcomin line, and he'd slip me a weapon—a little knife some folks calls a shiv. He already done spent time there, and he told me ain't nobody, no matter how bad you thinks you is, gonna survive Angola without a weapon. Folks get killed there ever day and nobody care. Some is fed to the gators.

My podner wadn't lyin.

The first night some fellas decided to make me they woman. They surrounded my bed and told me to take off my drawers. When I stood up, they was lookin for a woman, but they got a man of steel. I pulled out my weapon and commenced to slicin 'em up like they was sticks of boloney.

The ones that could, ran. The ones that couldn't laid moanin on the floor in a river of blood. The warden showed up and asked me nicely if I'd take a ride with him. He convinced me it wadn't gonna be safe for me there.

"I ain't givin up my weapon," I told him, and he say I could bring it with me. I was covered head to toe in blood. I had to lick it off my lips—tasted like death.

He drove me to the place named the Red Hat. That's where they kept Ol' Sparky, the 'lectric chair. He strap me down in it and told me if I ever did that again he would turn on the juice and fry me like a chicken.

The next mornin four white guards come with ropes and chains and hauled me off to the Hole. It wadn't really no hole. It was about twenty or thirty cells in another buildin where they put the bad-dest of the bad. Them cells didn't got no windows, 'lectricity, or plumbin. It was black as a moonless night there twenty-four seven. They was a straw mattress full of maggots on the dirt floor and a hole in the middle for a toilet with no paper. I heard some prisoners survived by eatin the maggots, but I never done that.

Two times a day the guard would open a tiny door in the big steel door and hand me a cup of water, a piece of chicken, and a slice of bread. Once a week or so they passed me a wet cloth to wipe myself off with, and the guard waited for me to hand it back.

You know when you don't never see no light or hear no sounds 'cept convicts screamin, you goes blind and crazy. Ain't nobody to talk to, nothin to see.

I spent more than a year in the Hole. When they let me out, I wadn't nothin but a bag of bones—weighed 'bout ninety pounds. Then they sent me to the prison mental hospital, where they kept all the crazy niggas. They kept me dosed up on Thorzine till I could see and talk again.

Most folk judge me as a crazy man, and they ain't wrong. But certain things in life can cause a man to jump track and get completely throwed off. This was just one of 'em.

40

RON

After the initial shock of the phone call passed, I felt peace. In all the years Denver and I had lived together, I'd never feared he was a killer, only a sinner like me whose sins happened to be different than mine. But I'd been almost certain that Denver was holding something back. And many times over the last three years, I had worried that if our book were successful, some investigative reporter might find the missing ten years that my buddy had never been able to explain adequately. I knew it was God who dialed that phone and allowed a fallen stutterer to save our book.

After about three hours I finally put supper on the table, but we never stopped talking until the bobcats scratched on the window at sunrise. Stories, enough for a long TV series, flowed one after the other like rushing water through a broken dam. Angola came alive and lived up to its reputation as one of the most violent prisons in the world, especially in the 1960s, when Denver was there. If it had been the *Survivor* reality TV show, Denver would have won the million-dollar prize.

Though the stories were gory, fascinating, and sometimes inspiring, I decided they did not drive or substantially alter the story we had written. Our publisher agreed and said that just a mention of this portion of his life was sufficient to cover our hides. After a day of adjusting, and inserting a few additions where necessary, the presses rolled once more.

We laughed that someday, after Denver learned to write, he could tell the whole story.

———

One of my favorite annual events, the Cowboy Spring Gathering, came quickly after the book was put to bed. About two hundred real, live, Western cowboys and their sons traveled to my friend Rob Farrell's ranch up the Brazos River from Rocky Top to bond over a long weekend of riding, roping, sleeping in tents and teepees, and reciting cowboy poetry around the campfire. Denver had been attending the Gathering with me for quite a few years now and had really come to enjoy it. But the first time he'd been my guest at the event, he had panicked at the sight of a hundred or more white men riding horses with ropes in their hands. I'd never thought about that when I insisted he join us. But, God forgive me, there were many complexities about this simple man I stumbled over.

At this particular gathering Denver confessed that a couple of years earlier, when a friend of mine brought an African American former rodeo champion as his guest, he'd been afraid his number might be up. As it turned out, they actually knew each other—from Angola. The man had been a many-times champion of the Angola Prison Rodeo. He'd served thirty years there for bank robbery and had been imprisoned the entire length of Denver's sentence.

Suffice it to say that the two of them had *not* been happy to see each other. For the whole weekend they avoided each other as if they were strangers, though they were the only two blacks there. Denver had breathed a big sigh of relief when the man did not show up the next year and blow his cover.

We arrived back in Dallas from the Cowboy Gathering late on Sunday afternoon. Just before midnight I was awakened by a call from Denver on my cell phone. He said he had the worst headache he'd ever experienced and needed me to take him to the hospital. "Meet me at the car ASAP," I told him.

I got to my car and waited a minute or so, then tried to call him on his cell. No answer. I raced upstairs to find him leaning against the wall, trying to balance. I noticed that his lip drooped, with drool streaming down his face, and his left arm had gone limp. "You're having a stroke!" I said. I grabbed hold of him and helped all two hundred and fifty pounds of him down the stairs, through the courtyard, and into the car like he weighed nothing.

We raced at Grand Prix speed to the nearest hospital, where we bypassed paperwork and went into lifesaving mode. The doctor knew immediately that Denver had a stroke, but a quick CT scan revealed something even worse. Denver had an aneurysm—a life-or-death emergency. He needed immediate brain surgery.

Denver was sent by helicopter to another hospital about fifteen miles away, where a neurosurgeon was standing by to save his life. Once more I pushed my Range Rover to a speed that nearly hit the top on the speedometer and arrived as they were wheeling him into the operating room. The surgeon, Dr. Chan, explained to us the seriousness of his condition and what we could expect. The aneurysm was located in a difficult place to access surgically, and almost assuredly there would be some paralysis. There was a 25 percent chance he would not survive the procedure.

Dr. Chan presented Denver with that report and asked him to sign a release.

"I ain't signin nothin." Denver focused his twin laser-beam stare into the doctor's eyes.

The doctor and I stepped out into the hall, where I explained I had power of attorney for Denver's health and would sign the release. But as I signed I heard commotion in Denver's room and a nurse screaming, "No, Mr. Moore! Come back!"

I turned around as Denver ran past me in his gown at a much

faster clip than his usual snail pace, his butt exposed for all the world to see. I chased after him and caught up as he waited for the elevator, surrounded by nurses, orderlies, and Dr. Chan, all pleading in choral unison for him to calm down.

"Mr. Moore, as your doctor I must tell you there is a high probability that if you get on that elevator, you could be dead before it reaches the first floor."

"If the angel of death be knockin on my door," Denver answered, "then tell 'im to come on in. I ain't afraid to die."

Then he looked me in the eye. "Did you tell 'im I's a dangerous man and they better not be messin with me?"

"No, I did not, because that is not the truth."

"Well, I's goin home. Is you gonna take me, or is I gonna walk?"

"You don't even know where we are!"

"Don't matter. When them freight-train doors slide open, I don't never know where I is. But you can take it to the bank that I be workin my way home."

The elevator door opened. He didn't look back. I jumped in with him.

The sun was rising on a warm spring morning as the security guards waved us through our gates. We drove past blossoming redbuds and colorful blocks of spring flowers with hummingbirds hovering above like miniature helicopters.

"Take a look, Denver. Heaven might look like this, and you may see it later this morning."

Pretending not to hear me, he neither looked nor commented.

I helped him up the stairs and put him in bed. He was hungry and wanted fried chicken. I offered to fix oatmeal and eggs instead, then carried the food up to his room.

By now Aunt Vida and Carson had shown up for work and listened to my incredible tale of the last eight hours. Out of the corner of my eye, I saw Denver standing in the courtyard, fully dressed in his khakis and blue button-down. He pointed at me and gave me a come-here motion. So I came there.

"Mr. Ron," he said, getting the jump on me before I could chew his butt out for getting out of bed. "You know why I burned off from the hospital?"

"I have no clue."

"They don't like blacks."

"That's crazy, Denver. Every single person in that hospital was doing their best to save your life."

"Not everbody, 'cause they is at least one prevert that done me bad."

"I don't believe it."

"Well then, just listen. When you was out in the hall talkin to the Chinaman, I peeked under the sheet, and somebody done stuck a rubber hose up my pecker!"

"Denver, that was a catheter," I managed to say as laughter engulfed me.

"What's a catheter?" he asked, dead serious.

"That's to keep you from peeing on the Chinaman while he was cutting on your brain!"

"Now you is tellin me it was s'posed to be in there?"

"Exactly."

"Oh man, I talked real bad to all them peoples that was helpin me. Take me back, and let's take care of our bidness."

41

DENVER

Mr. Ron drove me back to the hospital, but the Chinaman had done gone. There was a whole new crowd, and we had to start all over in the emergency room like we ain't never been there. They was stickin me with so many needles—it was worse than walkin barefooted through a watermelon patch covered in goat-head sticker-burrs.

It seem like we waited a long time 'fore they wheeled me back to the operation room. I was hooked up to more lines than a moonshine still. Mr. Ron kept dozin off while we was waitin. He ain't slept in a long time. The nurses told him to go on home and rest, sayin my operation was gonna take 'bout eight hours.

Before they rolled me in, Mr. Ron laid his hands on my brain and asked God to heal me. It was a long prayer for a sleepy man, so I figured God was gonna answer.

I always believed to pray God's will, then just leave it alone and stop tellin God what and when to do it. So I gots to thinkin, since Mr. Ron already prayed for God's will to be done, let's just leave it alone. I peeked 'round the room and saw I's all alone. I figured if I was gonna burn off, this was the time to do it. So I sat straight up, unplugged myself, and walked out the door.

The security guard stopped me and said I couldn't go outside in my nightgown. I ain't proud of this, but I told him if he tried to stop me I'd shove his badge and his gun six feet up his ass, then pull the

132

trigger. He chewed on that like a plug of Beechnut for a second or two, then motioned for me to come on out the door.

I was walkin across the parkin lot, and another guard come up on a li'l 'lectric buggy and told me to get in. And I told him to go 'way 'fore they called the morgue to pick up his dead ass.

I kept on walkin, feelin purty good, not like I had no life-threatenin amerism. I come upon a freeway and decide to walk down another road instead since my black butt was hangin out the back of that nightgown.

I walk a purty good piece till I spot a Texaco fillin station and decide to go in and call Mr. Ron. And you ain't never gonna believe it, but before I even tried to make the call, he drives up as I was standin by the pumps lookin for some change on the ground. He asked me if I run out of gas. That made me laugh so hard, I figured if that bubble in my brain was gonna pop, this would be the time.

"Get in, Denver. We're going home."

42

RON

What can I say except this was possibly the most unbelievably frustrating day of my life. Who does not understand a life-or-death emergency? Only the poor wise man of Debbie's dream—now acting a fool.

How many sixty-nine-year-old black men in hospital gowns with their butt flashing in the breeze can walk a mile on one of the busiest streets in Dallas and nobody calls the police?

The hospital administrator called Vida to report that Denver had threatened two separate security guards as he made his escape. As he was now out of their jurisdiction, the administrator suggested Vida file a missing persons report. She had no idea I'd already captured the runaway.

On the way home I tried my best to reason with the most unreasonable man on the planet. He believed my prayer had healed him, but no new CT scans had been taken to prove him right.

"Mister Ron, the Chinaman told me last night that if he cut on my brain I might end up bein a dummy or paralyzed or somethin. I'd rather die than end up back in a mental hospital like I did after I gots outta the Hole."

"Denver, you have been offered the best medical advice available. You are in a life-and-death situation. Sounds to me like you are choosing death."

"Nosir, I's choosin God."

For the second time that day, I helped him into his bed and explained that there would be no catch and release. Until he fulfilled his God-ordained days on this earth, I promised to take care of him. That's what real friends do.

It was painful thinking that Denver might die. We had grown close as brothers and were settling into what I hoped would be a long life together. He was excited about learning to read and count, and maps fascinated him. Best of all, the book we had worked on for three years was just weeks away from hitting bookshelves and hopefully raising the tide for all who work with the homeless.

Denver had saved my life when depression threatened to take it. There were times in the days after Debbie's death that I wanted to join her. I prayed for God to take me. I would lie on a pile of her clothes in her closet crying for hours, unable to speak. Denver sat nearby in silence, praying I wouldn't harm myself—my kids needed me, he said, and suggested they might not survive the loss of both parents. When I wouldn't eat, Denver fed me. I owed him the same favor.

I desperately wanted him to be able to bask in his accomplishment as an author and become famous for helping change the way the world looks at the homeless. And we were close. Right now, though, what he needed was food. He was hungry, and once again he wanted fried chicken.

That didn't seem like the healthiest option, so I suggested chicken soup or maybe Chinese food, which I had finally gotten him to try. I had beaten him at his own game by using a little trickonometry to convince him to branch out. Since he couldn't read a menu, I just renamed the chicken fried rice "Mama's chicken and rice." Lately he could not get enough of it. But after today's encounter with the Chinese doctor, he was ready to remove China from the food map and snarled at the mere suggestion.

Before I left to pick up the food, I asked him to surrender his

car keys, explaining that in his condition he could die at any minute
and that he would not want that to happen while driving and take
an innocent family down with him.

"Yessir, I understand." He handed them over without any
resistance.

Thirty minutes later I returned with the soup. His car was
gone, and so was he.

43

DENVER

I knowed Mr. Ron was tryin to do the right thing. He always do. But my car be my freedom, and ain't nobody gonna take that away—Abraham Lincoln guaranteed that for us. I had another set of keys hidden, and it took me just a little bit to find 'em in the paint box in my studio. I had to make my escape 'fore he come back with the chicken soup.

"God, take me where I's needin to be" was all I could say as I closed my eyes, put my size twelve on the pedal, and pushed it all the way to the floorboard. I had no idea where I would end up or how long it would take me. I had a full tank but no wallet or money. At one point I opened my eyes and seen that the needle on the speedometer say one hundred twenty.

Next thing I knowed, I was layin on the ground with my car still runnin, in the parkin lot of a big ol' hospital. Ain't no way to 'splain it 'cept God drove me there. It took three or four nurses to get me on the stretcher. Then all of a sudden I felt real peaceful, almost like I was dreamin. It was a hot day, but they was a cool breeze blowin, and I could see it wadn't missin nary no leaves or trees.

I come to with a big bright light in my face, like I was layin on my back in a cornfield with the sun just a foot or two away. They was askin my name and where I's from.

"Denver. . . . I's Denver." Then I fell back asleep.

44

RON

An All-Points Bulletin Silver Alert for an aging black man
prone to violence in a black Jeep Cherokee was put out by all police
departments in a one-hundred-mile radius of Dallas.

Carson and my son-in-law, Matt, scoured Fort Worth and Dallas,
checking the mission, the jungle, and all known hangouts Denver
had ever mentioned. No one had seen him. Vida called every hospital in the area—no Denver Moores. As a last resort we called the
morgue, searching for an unidentified black man found dead in the
last twenty-four hours. Thank God, still nothing.

I drove out to the ranch, thinking he might have realized he
was dying and wanted to die beside Miss Debbie. After all, nearly
six years ago he'd slept on her grave in a cold rain the night we buried her. Like then, it had rained the night before, and it would be
easy to track him. But I saw no signs he had been there.

Forty-eight hours after he went missing I got a call from
Carson—Denver had been found. Carson was with him in the same
Fort Worth hospital that had sent Debbie home to die. Denver was
on life support and in need of someone to sign off on brain surgery.
His aneurysm had worsened.

"Oh boy! Here we go again."

When I arrived, Denver was strapped down to a bed in what
looked like a straitjacket after several attempts to escape. One nurse
had taken a liking to him and was able to calm him down both with

medicine and kindness. He saw me walk in and started laughing. "What you doin here?"

"Trying to deliver some chicken. It's cold now!"

He laughed. A good sign.

"Mr. Ron, I done blacked out when I burned off, and the onliest thing I remember is lookin down at the speedometer and it sayin a hundred and twenty. Hear me real good. God was drivin that car, 'cause my hands was not on the wheel! Did you hear what I say?"

The nurses and staff were glad to finally know his name, since up till then he'd been officially listed as "Unknown from Denver." They told the story of emergency room nurses finding him lying unconscious in the parking lot, car door open, engine running. He had no idea where he was, no identification, and had mumbled only "Denver" before a total blackout.

They confirmed he had an aneurysm and needed immediate brain surgery. And they were completely dumbfuzzled after I informed them of his antics over the previous several days. No one could believe he had survived his escapes. There had to be a reason God was keeping him alive.

Overhearing the conversation, Denver hollered out to the hall, "Ain't nobody gonna cut on my brain and make me somebody's dummy!"

45

DENVER

I been at that hospital maybe a week when a doctor from Houston, Texas, come to see me. He say there is only two mochines in the whole country that can fix my amerism without cuttin open my skull and messin with my brain—and one of 'em was in Fort Worth, at another hospital not too far away. I told 'im to start fixin.

You ain't gonna believe this, 'cause I told 'em not to, but they stuck another rubber hose up you know where. I still can't figure out what that rubber hose gots to do with my amerism. I got upset, and the next thing I know they is alarms goin off and nurses hollerin somethin 'bout codes. They start whoopin me with 'lectric paddles on my chest, and I pass plumb out.

Two days later I woke up. I musta been real tired. Mr. Ron was standin over my bed and say I nearly died from a heart attack, but they fixed my amerism. He say the Devil was messin with me 'cause I's just gettin over my amerism, and now I gots to have a heart operation. Oh man, all this clean livin in a millionaire's mansion is 'bout to kill me. I done spent twenty-five years on the streets and ain't never even caught no cold.

I told him I was hongry and needed a cigarette real bad. He told me the doctors say I can't never smoke no more. Well, I betcha there is more old smokers than there is old doctors. He started laughin when I told him that, but I wadn't bein funny.

Mr. Ron's friend, the country singer Dan Roberts, come to see

140

me the next day. He was my friend too. I met him at the Cowboy
Spring Gatherin at Mr. Rob Farrell's ranch. While he was visitin,
the nurse made me get up and walk. I told her I was too tired, but
she wadn't takin no for no answer. Mr. Dan walked behind me,
pushin a hat rack holdin some gluecoat they had me hooked up to.
He was holdin my nightgown 'cause he said my butt was hangin out
the back. I told him let's keep on walkin outside so I can smoke, and
I believe he was gonna do it, but 'bout that time, in walks Mr. Ron.

Don't get me wrong. I's always glad to see Mr. Ron 'cause he's a
friend, a real friend—done a lot for me. He and Miss Debbie loved-
ded me when I was unlovable. Maybe sometimes I still is. But I'm a
sixty-nine-year-old full-grown man, and a lotta times he treats me
like I'm just a boy.

46

RON

Unbelievable. The man had just spent two weeks on death row and received a miraculous eleventh-hour pardon from God, and the first thing he wants when he wakes up is a cigarette!

The doctor had told him the previous day, with me standing there as a witness, that he was never to smoke again. Denver had just looked at me and winked. I'd seen the words go in his left ear, then exit the right in a plume of smoke.

But then, Denver had never claimed to be normal or reasonable. And it would have been foolish of me to question his wisdom, since he had spoken into me some of the wisest, most life-changing words I've ever heard—words that now guided my life path. So I decided to classify his smoking under "bad judgment" and "things that are just not going to change."

"Mr. Ron, take me home." It was an order, not a request.

"The doctor said you need to spend at least two weeks here in rehab, walking every day. When you can walk up a flight of stairs without getting winded, then you can go home."

"If that's the test I gotta pass, I'll be here the rest of my life. Hear me real good—I ain't stayin nowhere that don't let me smoke. Did you hear me?"

"Yes, I heard you, but listen to me."

"Nosir, I ain't through talkin. Now, Mr. Ron, *you* listen to *me*. I been smoking since I was five years old, and this ain't no time to

142

quit. Plus, I don't like the food here. They gives me a little cup of soup that look like pee and tastes like nothin. They gives me crackers but no sardines. And they keep pumpin me full of this gluecoat stuff that I can't figure out what is s'posed to do, but I can promise you, it don't stick to your ribs. I want me some fried chicken."

"If the nurse says it's okay, I'll bring you some tomorrow."

I stopped by the grocery store and picked up a few essentials after making the nearly one-hour drive back to Dallas in traffic. When I pulled in the driveway, I saw what appeared to be his car. Surely not.

As I walked in the back door, Vida came running after me. "He's home?"

"He beat me home?" I felt like I'd been hit by a stun gun.

How did his car get back here? I wondered. We lived forty miles from the hospital where he'd had the surgery, and his car was supposedly still in the garage of the hospital where he had passed out in the parking lot.

Come to find out, earlier that day one of Denver's old buddies from the jungle had come to visit, and Denver had promised him twenty dollars to go pick up his car. You can imagine what happened from there.

For the next week, in the comfort of his own room, Denver lay in bed smoking, watching TV, and eating fried chicken. Then, seven days after his escape, he walked into the kitchen as I was cooking his breakfast and declared himself healed. No medicine, no rehab—just cigarettes, fried chicken, and Christian TV.

An hour later, in pouring rain, he pulled out of the driveway and headed to Louisiana to visit his ninety-five-year-old auntie. I scratched my head, smiled, and told Vida, "We can't make this stuff up!"

47

DENVER

A big truck, long as a boxcar on a freight train, pulled up as I was sittin on the curb smokin. Once I got well, Mr. Ron made me start smokin outside again. The driver asked me if this was the home of Mr. Ron Hall. He say he gots a thousand books to drop off.

I crushed out my cancer stick on the bottom of my shoe and stuck the butt in my pocket—I always try to leave a little for my podners in the jungle that can't afford a pack. I ask the driver if I could help 'cause it was hot 'nough to fry an egg on the sidewalk.

Mr. Ron walked outside as I was shakin my head, disbelievin what I was seein. I asked him if we write ever one of them thousand books. He just laughed and told me they was all the same. Then he asked me: "What's this 'we'? How much did you write?" That made me laugh.

We opened a box, and I'll be a son-of-a-gun, it was just like he promised. There was my name, Denver Moore, and a picture of me standin by the tracks in front of the Man's store starin back at me from the front cover of a book. Man oh man, I wished Big Mama and Uncle James could see this. And if them boys that dragged me ever learned how to read, I hoped they seen whose picture is on the cover of a book.

Mr. Ron say they be sellin that book in ever bookstore in America. I hoped everbody that never thought I'd 'mount to nothin would see

144

it in the store. I knowed they ain't gonna buy it, though. Some of
'em might even steal it!

We sat down at the kitchen table and started signin our names
in books for peoples that had really helped us. I signed so many my
hand curled up in a cramp and stuck like it was froze in a block of
ice. Mr. Ron had to help me pull my fingers back and straighten
'em out. He laughed and told me to eat a banana and get used
to it.

Looked like my luck was finally startin to change. I'd been paintin pictures for two years, and they was stacked up in the garage like
bales of hay in a barn. Mr. Ron was the onliest man that bought any.
We used to make us a trade when folks would pay us to come and
speak at they organization. He knowed I likes foldin presidents, and
he liked my paintings.

Mr. Ron had a friend named Mr. Max that was quite a talker. He
used to come and see me even if Mr. Ron wadn't gonna be here. He
say he is a art collector, and he wanted some of my pictures.

One night I found a squirrel's tail that was left over after the
bobcats ate the rest. I thought it was real purty, so I glued it on my
head—but not really my head. You see, I was lookin in the mirror
one day and I gots this idea to paint a picture of me. After I finished,
it just didn't look right since all my hair done flew the coop, so I
decided I'd glue that squirrel's tail on my head in the paintin.

Mr. Max saw that paintin and thought it was real funny—say
I look like Davy Crockett in sunglasses. Oh, I forgots to tell you I
glued on some real sunglasses over my eyes in the paintin.

"How much?" Mr. Max asked. First I thought of tellin him fifty
dollars, but I said one hundred fifty 'cause I knowed he was a rich
man. Mr. Max was the pilot of his very own airplane that he flew to
Dallas hisself from where he stay out in West Texas.

"I'll give you seventy-five," he say. 'Bout that time I looks up,
and Mr. Ron was standin behind 'im. And Mr. Ron say: "Shame on

you, Max, for tryin to beat a homeless man out of seventy-five dollars. Pay him his price and give him a tip."

Mr. Max busted a gut laughin. Then he pulled out two hundred-dollar bills and gave me both of 'em. He bought a lot more of my paintins after that. He even invited us to his home and paid me to speak at the prayer breakfast in his town.

48

RON

The first copy of our book that we took out of the box I signed to Denver. The next ones were to Regan, Carson, and Debbie's twin, Daphene. Earl and Mama got their own copies next, then Aunt Vida, who had typed the whole thing at least twenty times. Then we continued on down the line of friends and family who had played a part in Denver and Debbie's story.

After a successful book signing at River Crest Country Club in Fort Worth, we still had a pile of eight hundred books now neatly stacked like a pyramid sculpture in our living room, thanks to Aunt Vida. We'd sold books to all of our friends. The tough part of finding a real audience was ahead.

Some TCU friends told me about the Texas Book Festival, which was held annually in Austin in late October—nearly five months away. Two hundred seventy-five Texas authors would be selected from all who had written books that year. And it turned out that the chairman of the festival was a good friend of Debbie's and mine. In addition to being Debbie's Tri Delta sorority sister, she was my daughter's namesake.

What a stroke of luck! I thought as I explained to Denver how we would launch our book to the public at the festival. I logged on to the website, filled out the application, and FedExed two signed and personalized copies of our book to our friend. Then I made our Austin hotel reservations. I didn't want to get caught short with no place to stay.

Meanwhile, one of the largest Baptist churches in Fort Worth invited us to speak at their Sunday-morning service. We'd told our story a few times at churches before the book came out, but this time many had read it and wanted more of the story. Denver and I talked about who would tell what part of our story. He did not want to be responsible for remembering anything, so he instructed me, "Mr. Ron, you open 'em up, and I'll shut 'em down."

Sunday morning came quickly. I'd spent days organizing my thoughts, so I was ready. Denver would never disclose what he intended to say, so I hit the highlights of our story. After fifteen minutes my talk was coming to an end, and it was his turn. It was then that I heard a terrible yet familiar noise behind me.

Denver, sitting next to the pastor on stage, farted and began snoring loudly. I asked the congregation in a booming voice to welcome Denver to the pulpit with a rousing round of applause. That still didn't awaken him. I turned around and tapped him on the shoulder, and he jumped about a foot out of his seat with fists doubled, preparing for attack.

The audience roared with laughter as he stumbled to the pulpit, wiping the slobber off his chin with the tattered washcloth he always carried in his pocket. Trying to steady himself, he grabbed both sides of the pulpit, then told the audience, "Now, I'm gonna tell y'all the truth. I just woke up and don't really know where I'm at and what I'm s'posed to say."

I stepped up beside him and said, "You're at the Broadway Baptist Church in Fort Worth to preach a sermon."

To which he pointed at the audience and replied: "Now, I ain't no preacher, so don't be tryin to get me to preach. I'm gonna tell you the truth. I ain't nothin but an ol' ex-con, a sinner saved by grace with a message of hope for those that ain't got none." Then he moved into his familiar closing, adapted to this particular audience:

"Now I'm fixin to do somethin ain't no Baptist preacher or the Devil ever done for you. I'm fixin to cut y'all loose!"

Laughter spread throughout the congregation.

"But before I sits back down and finishes my nap, I want to leave y'all with something to think about. Whether we is rich, or whether we is poor, or somethin in between, we is all homeless, just workin our way home!"

Like a gavel, his fist pounded on the pulpit as if he were a judge pronouncing a sentence. Then he sat back down. The crowd cheered like they were slaves who had just listened to Lincoln give the Emancipation Proclamation.

49

DENVER

One mornin I walked in Mr. Ron's office and seen him cryin. I ain't really seen him cry since the first few years after Miss Debbie passed. I knowed he'd spent a lot of time worryin 'bout the book, tryin to figure how we was gonna get rid of that pile in the livin room. I turned 'round, tryin to slip out and let the man be.

"Denver, we got rejected by the Texas Book Festival," he say, holdin up the letter. He show me where it was signed by Miss Debbie's friend and even the first cousin of Mr. Ron's son-in-law. They wrote him a note sayin there was no place in their festival for a book like ours.

Since this was the onliest book I knowed 'cept the Bible, I couldn't really figure out what kinda books they was lookin for. The onliest thing I could come up with is maybe they didn't think folks would like to read 'bout poor homeless niggas that is ex-cons.

I commenced to scoldin Mr. Ron like he was a little boy, tellin him we didn't write this book for book festivals or TV shows, so we didn't need to put no faith in those. He looked at me kinda funny, like he didn't like what I was sayin. But then I reminded him who we did write this book for, and that was Miss Debbie. And even more important, we wrote it for God, 'cause it was really His story.

Then I stared him down and told him very serious to never— and I meant *never*—ask nobody to do nothin for our book, 'cause

we was gonna give it to over to God and let Him take care of His
bidness.

I believe He did, 'cause a few weeks later things started heatin
up. Mr. Ron even ordered more books, so then we gots a pile of 'em
in our house nearly tall as me. Ever day we put a few in the trunk
of his car and sell 'em at white ladies' Bible studies and book clubs.
Seemed like ever day we was goin to another rich white lady's house
to tell our story. Lord have mercy, I ain't never worked so hard since
I left the plantation.

Folks started tellin us everwhere we go that we was gonna be
on the *Oprah Winfrey Show*. 'Cept Mr. Ron say she ain't called. Now,
I knowed she's a rich sister, but I ain't never seen her show. I overheard some ladies at one of the Bible studies sayin she done a lot for
our race. If you ask me, I ain't done nothin 'cept to bring it down.
Fellas like me don't get on no TV shows 'less it's *America's Most
Wanted*. I don't sing no blues, dance no jigs, can't throw or catch no
balls. All I done for so long is sit by a Dumpster and wiggle my toes.

A few times back on the plantation, I remember playin a little
baseball, 'cept we never had no bats or balls. We used a tree limb
and the green apples that fell from bois d'arc trees. You ever seen
one of them? Don't never take no bite.

When you hit one of them bois d'arc apples with a limb, mostly
it blowed up like a grenade on a war show. Ever once and a while
one make it all the way to the swamp, and we'd just let it be 'cause
the gators'd take your arm off if you reached for it. I'd seen a one-
arm man when I was a boy. That was 'nough for me.

That crazy man on TV that played with gators finally got killed,
and not by no gator. They say he got poked by some kinda fish with
a sharp stinger. I was sad to hear 'bout it 'cause I liked him a lot, but
Big Mama always told us chilrens that if you mess with the bull, you
gonna get the horns.

One day Mr. Ron hire some folk from up North that don't talk like us to teach me how to talk like them on a TV show. I couldn't understand them and they couldn't understand me. But hour after hour they tried to make me talk like some college-educated white man. But I is what I is—that's the way God made me, and I'm proud of that. They ran me purty hot, and I walked out and told 'em where they could stick their TV talkin.

Sure 'nough, we gets invited to be on a TV show in Boston. I ain't never been there and don't plan on goin, but they say to just show up at a TV station in Dallas. So we did. They was confusin me, tellin me not to look at no cameras but look at the man askin the questions that wadn't even in the room.

Some lady sticked her head in the door and counted backwards, and then I heard, "Live from Boston." The man say a few words about two unlikely best friends that wrote theyselves a book, and then I heard him say, "Mister Moore, tell us about your book."

There was a picture of the man askin the question on a little bitty TV screen that I couldn't really see 'cause I forgots my glasses. They was a lady on the other side of the glass wavin her arms at us to hurry up. That was a little flabbergastin. I's just tryin to figure out who I was talkin to and what I was gonna say, when all of a sudden Mr. Ron was startin to answer my question.

I push him back, look straight in the camera, point my finger, and say: "I'm gonna tell y'all the truth. I don't read, and I don't write, so I didn't write that book, and I ain't even read it. Now, what's your next question?"

50

RON

We pulled into the parking garage of the Worthington Renaissance Hotel in downtown Fort Worth. Denver reminded me that he used to sleep on the steel grate covering the sidewalk because it blew hot exhaust air in the winter. I reminded him that I used to see the homeless there nearly every morning and sometimes would call the police and even the mayor complaining about the trash on our streets. He laughed as he pulled out a handmade cardboard sign from the back seat and held it where I could read his phonetic writing:

"So," I asked, "what is your plan to end homelessness?" He flipped the sign over and erupted into a coughing belly laugh.

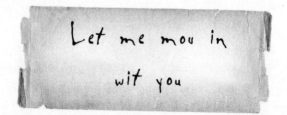

"What do you thinks, Mr. Ron? You thinks I can make some more of these and sell 'em to the homeless for a dollar or two?"

Today was special. We were on our way to a banquet in the grand ballroom where Denver was going to be honored as Philanthropist of the Year because of his fund-raising efforts for the Union Gospel Mission. More than ten million dollars had been raised since Debbie's death, and her dream mission he'd spoken about at her funeral was now nearing completion.

As we entered the lobby, I asked if he remembered this place from his years on the streets. He remembered the outside, but he'd never set foot in the lobby, with its soaring fifty-foot ceilings, contemporary art, and furniture. I found it strange that he'd slept on the sidewalk outside the lobby but had never entered to even use the restroom or seek shelter from a storm.

"It's open to the public," I told him.

"Mr. Ron, the homeless ain't no public. They is invisible trash everybody includin you wants hauled off in a Dumpster."

"Don't you think I've changed?"

"Yessir, you sure have!"

Not long after that, in front of more than eight hundred of Fort Worth's movers and shakers, Denver received his award—along with a standing ovation. He told the audience, "For many years, some of y'all thought I was trash on y'all's streets." He met my eyes as he spoke those words, then looked out over the audience to continue. "But did y'all know that God is in the recyclin bidness of turning trash into treasure? I wants to thank all of y'all for this reward, and God bless you."

———

The next morning our security guard called and said a woman was at the gate who had driven from Tennessee to meet the man of

Debbie's dream. Denver scratched his head at that, wondering why some white lady would drive that far just to shake his hand. But it seemed he was becoming somewhat of a rock star now that several TV and radio talk shows had us as guests.

Fan mail was delivered almost daily from across the country. Collectors started wanting his art and signed photographs of him with it. Even our middle-aged African American lady letter carrier, who previously had thought Denver was just a toothless—he seldom wore his teeth at home—illiterate homeless man living on our property, started taking an interest in our new celebrity.

Another morning Vida informed him that several ladies from another town were driving to Dallas that afternoon to meet him and to buy some of his art. She asked that he not leave before they got there. He had a bad habit of going to the grocery store or filling station, and after a couple of wrong turns he'd be lost. Sometimes it would be hours before he returned from a normal five-minute trip.

In fact, a few weeks earlier he had called my cell phone and said: "I'm lost. Can you come find me?" I laughed and told him I'd quit playing hide-and-seek when I was a kid. Then I tried to explain that if he was really lost, I had no way to find him. But he pointed out that when little kids play hide-and-seek, somebody always finds them.

"Okay, where do you think you are?" I asked. As expected, he had no idea. So I asked, "What kind of signs do you see that might give an indication of your location?"

"They's a sign nailed to a fence post here that I believe say 'Dr. Pepper.'"

"Well, keep driving until you see a store or filling station, then call me from there."

Five minutes later he called and handed the phone to a cashier in an Exxon station. "Tell Mr. Ron where I is."

"Durant, Oklahoma," she said. I asked her to point him back toward Dallas.

At least that time he called. But he also had a bad habit of not answering his cell phone when he knew he was lost or possibly in trouble—like the day when, despite Vida's request, he had disappeared. The ladies who had made the appointment arrived, and she spent two hours giving them all a tour of our home and Denver's studio. She apologized to them over and over, even telling them the story about him winding up lost in Durant, Oklahoma.

Like almost everyone else, these ladies wanted to buy paintings, but only from the master himself. Finally they had to leave, but before they did they scheduled another visit.

Some time later we saw Denver drive up. I met him in the driveway and expressed my disappointment that he had embarrassed Vida and disappointed fans of our book. He made a sad face but said nothing.

"So where have you been?" I asked. He could tell I was peeved.

"Mr. Ron, I went to the eye doctor to get me some glasses, and the lady deleted my eyes!"

"Well, it looks to me like you still have both of them."

"I might have 'em, but I sure couldn't see nothin outta 'em!"

51

DENVER

Mr. Ron was real good at tryin to hold me 'countable. But let me tell you, he ain't no perfect person hisself. At first, I let a lotta things slide, like him sleepin in on Sunday mornins. I wadn't even sure that was a sin, though, since him and me was spendin a awful lot of time in churches anyway. But we wadn't worshipin, just tellin our story. So that still bother me some.

But the number one thing that bothered me 'bout Mr. Ron was the way he treat his daddy. It's a precious thing for a man to grow up with a daddy in the house as long as he don't hit you or your mama. I wished BB hadn't got killed. He was nice to me. I still ain't sure what happened to my momma.

His daddy did got a lotta hell in 'im, and like I told Mr. Ron, sometimes you just gotta bless the hell outta folks like that. Me and Mr. Earl didn't start off too good 'cause he didn't like black folk that didn't have no jobs. But we was purty tight now, even though Mr. Ron ran him hot for tellin everbody in our book that his daddy drank a lotta whiskey.

Ever time I told Mr. Ron somethin, he be wantin to know if I hear it from God or if it's just me talkin. I try and tell him the truth, but I don't always know myself. Me and him do a fair amount of prayin over our book, hopin folks'll be more like Miss Debbie.

We was out speakin one time, and the fella that introduce us told the crowd the world needed more Denvers. Man, I nearly jumped out of my seat, but I stayed down. When it got my turn to speak, I told 'em there is a million Denvers. What the world really need was more Miss Debbies.

———

One night Mr. Ron cooked everthing I likes to eat. I had to teach him how to cook like Big Mama—fried chicken, turnip and collard greens cooked in hog fat, and creamed potatoes with white gravy. After we cleaned it all up, he made banana puddin with vanilla cookies—he called 'em wafers. That meal reminded me of the night the warden sat me in the Ol' Sparky and threatened to pull the lever. I sat there all night long thinkin what would be my last meal if I was on death row—they feed you good the night 'fore they kill you. Well, what I come up with was what Mr. Ron made that night.

After supper Mr. Ron wanted to talk bidness. First, though it wadn't the first time he told me, he say he want me to quit callin him Mr. Ron—"Drop the Mister," he say. I heard what the man was sayin, but you just can't go against who you is as a person. That's respect. Most of his friends and Miss Debbie called him Ronnie Ray. Sometimes when I joke 'round, that's what I call him too.

But then he wanted to talk 'bout a letter the mail lady delivered from the IRS. I figured I must be gettin important, 'cause I ain't never in my whole life got no letters from the IRS.

Mr. Ron read it to me, and they be askin for 'bout half the money Mr. Nelson sent me for the book and the money Mr. Ron paid me for speakin at churches and guardin his art. He say they don't know 'bout the art I was sellin, but as an American citizen I needed to pay 'em some of that too. In fact, he told me he done got me an appointment with a lawyer and 'countant and he was gonna take me the next day.

That kinda run me hot and spoiled that last little bit of his banana puddin. I told him to hear me real good. My peoples was slaves, and they ain't never got paid nothin. And now that I'm the first one in my family to ever get a check, he was tellin me I gots to give half of it to the gov'ment, that ain't never done nothin for me or my kin—no schoolin, no welfare, nothin.

Mr. Ron tried to tell me they gave us our freedom. I looked him straight in the eye and say: "Freedom? Man, don't you be talkin to me 'bout no freedom. I had to hop a freight train for freedom. I had to serve ten years in Angola, workin daylight to midnight with no pay for my freedom. And I done spent twenty-five years on the streets and hobo jungles costin the gov'ment nothin. And you tellin me I's got to give 'em half? I just ain't gonna do it. Uncle Sam can take that to the bank.

"Now listen good. If I give it to the gov'ment, I don't know who they gonna give it to. I know lots of folk in Louisiana and in the hood that could use—I mean need—half my money. So if anybody gonna gets my money, it's 'cause I gave it to 'em to bless 'em and help 'em outta the hole they is in."

Mr. Ron say he agreed with me, but he say the IRS don't care 'bout nobody. And if I don't pay they gonna put me back in prison, and that would be a black eye on Miss Debbie and our book.

I told him I'd talk to Miss Debbie 'bout that. He looked at me real funny. He knowed I still talked to her, and sometimes she pay me a visit. I didn't always tell 'im everthing, though. A man's gotta keep a little somethin back 'cause if you tell everthing you knows, you ain't got nothin else to say.

But I had to school Mr. Ron 'bout prison. You see, a man my age that ain't violent will get a good job like shinin the warden's shoes and makin his coffee. Plus, you gets three hots and a cot and ain't gotta pay no taxes. Now that's a good retirement plan, since I ain't got none.

52

RON

Denver made some great points about knowing who needed money that his taxes would not benefit. I applauded his heart and vision for helping those who had crossed his path and left a memorable impression. On the Fourth of July, for instance, he took a carload of kids from the projects and spent more than two hundred of his "foldin presidents" on fireworks. He came home with a big smile on his face and tales of kids who had never seen a fireworks show.

His heart was in the right place, and his aversion to paying taxes was not a selfish thing. A lot of money had crossed his hands, and the only thing he'd bought for himself was a gold cross on a chain. A young lady at the cell phone store said he had helped her out of a jam after she helped him replace countless lost phones. Denver told me about buying some toys for a little white boy whose single mom was a friend of the mail lady. He felt sorry for him since he didn't have a father. He knew that empty feeling, and it brought him back to memories of the few short months he got to spend with his dad.

One of Denver's biggest giveaways came at a luncheon where we were invited to tell our story and raise a little money for Debbie's mission. It was hosted by a group of very wealthy philanthropic women at the very posh, very exclusive Dallas Country Club.

Concerned that his paintings were not selling well, he took about fifteen and put one on every table. From the podium, he charmed the crowd with his wisdom and funny tales of life on the streets. He closed with a song and got a standing ovation. Then he really started working his magic.

"Y'all was prob'ly wondering what that painting was doin on your table. Well, I'm gonna tell y'all the truth. I been paintin pictures for 'bout three years, and ain't many of 'em sold. So this mornin I was thinkin I'd just start givin 'em away. Did all you ladies hear what I said? So I done give one to each table as a blessin. Now it's up to y'all to decide who at your table gets to take my blessin home. Now listen to me real good. Them pictures ain't for sale, so don't be tryin to buy 'em. But, if any of you rich ladies wanna *bless me*, then I'd be blessed to accept it."

Fifteen minutes later, his blessings totaled more than three thousand dollars.

Riding home he started laughing and reminding me how slick he used to be at getting a free meal on the streets. Some caring man who passed him would give him a dollar and he'd buy a hamburger, eat half, then wrap up the rest and put it in the trash. When a rich lady would walk by, he'd start digging in the trash, pick up his burger, and time it just right so she would see him take a bite. He said no respectable white lady was going to let a man eat out of the trash, so it worked nearly every time. By the end of the day he'd have enough for another burger plus a half-pint.

"Mr. Ron, I's a little shame-faced that I got slick with them ladies today, but I'm gonna bless someone that really needs it with they money. You heard what I said, didn't you?"

53

DENVER

We was at some fancy Dallas country club, and I overheard one of them rich ladies tell Mr. Ron 'bout somethin she read on her computer 'bout the president that got shot a long time ago. She say she was gonna load it down and drop it off at the mansion. What she say made my skin crawl, and ever hair on my body stand straight up like the time we crossed paths with the Devil in Hershalee's house.

Wadn't long after we got home the lady pulled up in the driveway in a big ol' foreign car that look like a Rolls Royce to me, though I ain't sure I ever seen one. I could hear her in the next room talkin to Mr. Ron. They didn't know I be listenin. She was sayin some lady was givin a deathbed confession 'bout bein in Mr. Murchison's big house (where I use to stay) the night 'fore the president got killed in Dallas. I already knowed all this 'cause I heard spirits talkin 'bout bringin down the gov'ment in the big lodge room when I first move in.

After she left, Mr. Ron asked me to come to his office. He had somethin he thought I'd be interested in hearin. Lordy, I wish she hadn't brung this up 'cause a lotta folks died from waggin they tongues. I already told Mr. Ron that.

He started readin lots of pages and showin me videos on his computer like I didn't know nothin. I could feel the heat risin in my head, and it was heatin the screw in my amerism. I stared him down and told him real strong that he could stop all that readin right now

'cause I'd already told him 'bout all this stuff years ago on the night the front doorknob nearly electrocuted him.

He figured it might be the same information and figured I'd like to know. Well, I didn't want to know, and I wadn't gonna be like no rabbit in the briar patch and get tangled up in the mess. I didn't never want to have another conbersation 'bout it. I said this before so hear me real good. Everbody that's supposed to be dead . . . ain't dead yet.

54

RON

What a stroke of luck when talk-show host Tavis Smiley called
and invited us to be on his show in Hollywood. Our book had been
struggling to find an audience. With exposure to one of the largest audiences on TV, hopefully book sales would take off and more
money would roll in for Debbie's mission.

Denver was like a kid in a candy store in sunny Hollywood.
Just outside our hotel, we walked and stepped on the star of every
famous African American we could find, adding only Elvis to the
stops.

"Mr. Ron, do this one say B. B. King?" That was his favorite. We
stopped for a photo of him kneeling by B. B.'s star near Hollywood
and Vine.

On the day of the show, Denver started getting a little skitzy
as he flashed back to his last TV appearance on the morning talk
show in Boston. But a tour of the studio and a rehearsal seemed to
relax him a bit, even though it was our first time in a full-blown
Hollywood studio.

He complained the lights hurt his eyes and wanted to wear his
shades. "You're not Ray Charles," I said.

Then he complained the lights hurt his "amerism," so he
wanted to wear his bowler hat. I laughed. "And you are not Charlie
Chaplin."

He told me: "Chaplains don't wear no hats, least not the one at

the mission. They wears black shirts with white collars." He obviously had never heard of Charlie.

Everything was fine until we got to the makeup room. A beautiful African American woman introduced herself as Shelia and offered to put a cape on him to keep the makeup off his shirt.

"Makeup?" He looked at me with a suspicious, cocked-eye scowl. "Real mens don't wear no makeup," he told her with a look like he was fixing to burn off.

She had read our book and began talking to him about struggles in her life. Her daddy, Charles, was the brother of Medgar Evers, the civil rights activist who was murdered in Mississippi by the KKK when she was a young girl. Denver knew Medgar's story well and had also heard of her father, also a longtime civil rights activist. They shared memories of their childhood in the South surrounded by racial prejudice and hatred. Before he even realized it, the dark powder had been brushed across his face.

"Break a leg," she said, smiling. A curious, maybe questioning frown served as his response.

We stood in the wings as the producer gave us the five-minute countdown. "Mr. Ron, I'm 'bout to puke," he said and made a mad dash for the bathroom. I stood outside the door to make sure he didn't burn off for a smoke. There was a rumbling going on inside, and a producer shouted: "Ron and Denver, move to the set. One minute and counting."

"Denver, we gotta go," I hollered through the door as he made his exit with a face of death in a pale shade of purple.

Tavis was live, cameras rolling, making our introduction. And then Denver, in his unique fashion, casually strolled onto the set as if he had all day to get there. Not a soul in the studio or the millions of viewers watching the show would have ever had an inkling of the drama behind the curtains. He spoke with confidence about his changed life, adding dashes of humor about God's recycling business. Pride filled my soul as I imagined Debbie watching from a perch above the balcony.

That evening Denver made arrangements to visit his daughter Tracy for the first time since she was born in the early '60s. I asked if I could go. His answer was an emphatic no. He said it could be life-threatening for a rich white man to go into the projects where she lived.

Early the next morning, I was having breakfast alone in the hotel coffee shop when I saw him get out of a taxi in the same clothes he'd been wearing the night before. I met him in the lobby and invited him to join me. Man oh man, did he have a story to tell about a family reunion and a narrow escape from gunfire and gang wars. Twelve hours after the fact, he could finally laugh about it.

Our *Tavis Smiley Show* appearance opened bigger doors for us than we'd ever dreamed. It wasn't long before TV and radio stations began calling in search of my friend, who was such a fascinating guest. He'd even won over the mail lady, who'd stopped dropping the mail into our mailbox at the curb and opted for a more personal delivery. She would park her mail truck on the street, walk to the back door, and peer in to see who was sitting at the kitchen table. Often she would come in without knocking, then sit and talk to Aunt Vida. But I'm sure she was secretly hoping for a brief encounter with the famous one.

55

Denver

Ain't no doubt 'bout it; Tracy's my daughter. She look just like me—got the Moore nose and laugh. She never knowed I was homeless. Her mama didn't talk too much 'bout me—for good reason, 'cause I done her wrong. Like Mr. Ron when we was writin our book, Tracy ask too many questions, but we had a real nice time. She act like we been best friends for years, just huggin me and tellin me she was glad to have her daddy home. I gots to meet my teenage grandchilrens I didn't even know I had, and we played some video games and listened to rap. Them chilrens called me PawPaw and made me laugh a lot. And of course I blessed 'em with a little somethin.

'Bout the time I was gonna burn off, it sounded like firecrackers outside the front door. My daughter say all the screamin and hollerin was gang activity, and most of the shots was prob'ly bein fired in the air. They was a time, when I was a gangbanger livin on these same streets, that I'da walked out that door and challenged 'em all. But to tell you the truth, I'm too old for that kinda BS. So I closed all the curtains and slept on the couch, worryin 'bout my family havin to live like that. Come daylight I hightailed it out of there, back to Hollywood and Dallas.

Lotta folk seen me on Mr. Tavis Smiley's show, and that was beginnin to be a problem. I had to start hidin from the mail lady, who wanted to be handin me the mail instead of leavin it in the box

167

or givin it to Miss Vida. She was bein a little too friendly for my taste, always wantin to have a conbersation.

One day she showed up at the kitchen door after work and invited me to come to her friend's house. Miss Vida done told her I ain't comfor'ble ridin in a car with ladies, even sisters. But she convinced me to follow her to some white lady's apartment 'round the corner where she lived with her young son. As it turned out, they was real nice. They treated me like a friend, and I enjoyed playin with the boy. That was the first white boy I ever played with since I was 'bout eight or nine years old.

The Man's nephew, Bobby, and I used to ride bicycles together after his daddy bought me one for pickin fifty pounds of scrap cotton. That's the little pieces left behind when all the pickers is done. It took me two seasons to gather fifty pounds. Bobby helped me 'cause he wanted a podner to ride bikes with.

One day I rode up to his house, and he asked me if I wanted to play KKK. I didn't really know what that was. But when we opened a door in the barn, there was a whole lotta white sheets hangin with holes cut out for the eyes. We put 'em on and grabbed a couple of crosses and turned 'em upside down and made 'em swords, then commenced to sword fightin.

Next thing we knowed, Bobby's mama was standin there watchin us. The fun was over when she seen my little black feet stickin outta the bottom of that white sheet. She started whoopin my butt and chased me off the property hollerin, "You better not tell nobody, or your little black bo-hiney's gonna get in trouble and your family's gonna be lookin for another place to live!"

I kept my mouth shut, but I never got to play with Bobby no more. Mr. Ron is the onliest person I ever told that to.

On the way home from that lady's house, Mr. Ron's mama's Jeep he gave me just shut down, so I left it on the road and walked back to the house. That wadn't the first time it done that, but I made sure it was the last 'cause I give it to our maid. She and I was purty tight—friendly, you know, nothin more. I used to give her a little extra for washin my clothes, cleanin my room, and helpin me keep things lookin good in the studio for customers.

Mr. Ron loaned me his skillionaire's Mercedes while he went huntin with some of his cowboy buddies. To tell you the truth, I didn't like drivin no Mercedes. But I was drivin it by a used-car lot not far from the house, and I seen the car of my dreams just sittin there like it had my name written all over it! The white man in that lot say he ain't never sold a car to no Mercedes-drivin authors, and he ain't never seen no blacks 'cept pushers pay cash for no white Escalade.

This ain't nothin but the truth. I ain't drove my new car 'bout a mile when I gots pulled over by the po-lice for rollin through a stop sign. They ask me to get out while they search my car. I knowed what time it was. The white po-liceman was jealous and figured the onliest way a black man could be drivin a white Escalade was from sellin drugs, so he was gonna try and ruin my happy day. He asked me where I work, and I told him I's an author and ain't got no job. He run my name through his computer and didn't find out 'bout no author bidness, but he seen I gots a warrant for my arrest for a unpaid ticket.

This was perfect timin to pay my ticket 'cause Mr. Ron was off huntin in Mexico. I could go cool my heels in jail, workin this off my record without him ever knowin. It only costed me one night.

Miss Vida knowed what happened 'cause I missed a 'pointment with a lawyer and a 'countant she set up while Mr. Ron was gone. He kept talkin about taxes and a will. I wadn't interested in neither one—'specially not no wills, 'cause that means I'll be dyin. It bad luck to talk 'bout death and dyin.

So I asked Miss Vida if she thought I was dyin, since I done had my stroke and amerism. She laugh and say: "Denver, you're like a cat with nine lives. You haven't even lived half."

Well, Miss Vida done lots for me, so I felt real bad I made her look bad to the lawyer. She may be Mr. Ron's auntie, but she's a real friend to me. Sometimes when I's feelin down, she and I sits at the kitchen table and talks for hours till I gets to feelin better. The difference in talkin to her and Mr. Ron is he always try to talk me outta my feelins, but Miss Vida just listen while I talk myself back to normal. And she sells my paintins, boxes 'em up and ships 'em, and won't take nothin for it. Believe me, I tried. I love the lady, 'cept I ain't told her that 'cause I don't want nobody—no white lady or any other body—to confuse what kinda love I's feelin. So I don't say nothin, and I avoids that word.

That night I started havin chest pains real bad, so I drove myself to the hospital and spent a couple days there restin. The doctor—not the Chinaman, but another dark-skinned doctor from a foreign country, not Africa—say I need to have a bypass 'fore too long. I told 'im I can't do nothin till I check with Mr. Ron, 'cause I heard him say we gots places to go.

56

RON

After a twelve-hour drive across all of New Mexico and half of Texas, I arrived back home in Dallas with a six-by-six bull elk head and four ice chests full of meat in the back of my pickup. Denver was nowhere to be found. That was not unusual except he hadn't answered his cell phone in a few days. It was lying dead as a doornail next to his unmade bed. Well, that was not unusual either, but it still caused me to worry, as I'd not seen him in a week.

The next morning my phone rang. I didn't recognize the number and nearly didn't answer because I was tired of winning free vacations to anywhere I chose. Luckily, it was Denver. He said he was in the hospital but had "just been discounted" and needed to be picked up.

I asked if he meant discharged.

"What's the differment?" he asked.

He looked a little thinner and forced a weaker-than-normal laugh, but said they couldn't find anything wrong. He was glad to see me, even missed me, he said. As we drove home catching up on small talk like the two bobcat kittens, I told him about being on top of a mountain in northern New Mexico aiming my rifle at a huge elk when my cell phone started ringing just before I pulled the trigger. My hunting guide, Rob, had ripped me apart for bringing a cell phone, but I didn't remember bringing it and for sure didn't think it worked in the mountains. But when I answered, I was glad I did.

On the line was a Pastor Dave Bechtel in Richland, Washington. He had just finished our book and wanted us to tell our story on Sunday at his church.

"Wow, you guys are a long way from Texas," I said to him. "How did you find out about our book?"

He told me one of his church members, Don Paddock, had a sister in Syracuse, New York, who'd seen our book on the new-release table at the public library and checked it out because she liked the cover. After reading it she'd called her brother in Washington to recommend he read it. After finding the only copy of our book at a Barnes & Noble store shelved under "Black History," he read it and passed it along to Pastor Dave. They were offering two airplane tickets, some home-cooked food, and new friends dying to hear more of our story.

"Is that where we seen the president?" Denver asked.

"Nosir, that's a different Washington."

Pastor Dave wanted to make sure Denver could make the trip, and if not they'd wait until he could. In our few short months of being coauthors, that request came every single time an invitation was extended. "What am I? Chopped liver?" I asked Denver, who found it curious every rich man wanted to meet a homeless man and every homeless man wanted to meet a rich one!

A few days later we boarded the first leg of our flight. It was clear in Dallas, but weather was expected at other stops. The first stop was the city of Denver, where a light snow had fallen. Denver wanted to take a taxi into town to visit his namesake. However, time between connections to Seattle was short, so I promised to bring him back another time, then did my best to hurry him along.

Of course a bathroom stop was needed, so I finished quickly then waited outside the door for another ten or so minutes. Time was getting shorter—moving toward critical. I looked for Denver's shoes with their cutout heels under the stall doors and found him on the last commode, asleep.

Denver had only one speed—slow. As we walked toward our gate, he became irritated that I was out in front trying to hurry him along, so he stopped dead in his tracks and motioned with his finger for me to come back to him.

"See all them airplanes sittin out there on the concrete?"

"Yes, but now they are calling our name to board *our* plane immediately! We've gotta run!"

Not budging, he said, "Well, if we miss the one we s'posed to be on, we'll just hop on one of them other ones!"

I tried quickly to explain that it did not work that way—that we were about to be stranded in Denver and miss our event. But he was not through explaining that it worked that way on freight trains and buses. "If you stand 'round long enough," he insisted, "another one'll come by in a hour or so." Then he went on to school me on travel. "If we gets on one of them airplanes out there and stays on it long enough, I'll betcha one day we will gets to where we wanna be."

It was the equivalent of a Holy Ghost miracle that we walked on our plane as the door was closing.

57

DENVER

We landed in Washington, the state. That's what Mr. Ron say, but I couldn't figure out why we gots two Washingtons and why the president don't stay in this one. Some ladies at the airport say they seen me on the TV and ask for my autograph. I told 'em I wadn't no B. B. King, but they didn't seem to care.

Some real nice folk done paid our way out there so we could speak at they church. I didn't really have too much to say, so I started singin, and when I finished the whole place stood on they feet and clapped. Musta been a thousand or more, standin like they was at Miss Debbie's service. I told 'em straight up I wadn't no preacher, but some fella kept hollerin out, "Preach on, brother."

After we finish speakin and singin, folks was waitin in a long line, wantin to shake our hands. Then a little bitty white fella, about six or seven, steps up and hands me a bright-red toy fire truck. He was like a little man in his suit and tie and told me his mama read to him from our book that I growed up so poor I didn't never have no toys when I was his age, so he told his mama he was gonna give me his favorite fire truck. That was sacrificial. It made tears run down my cheeks. Ain't nobody never done nothin like that for me.

His mama started talkin and tellin me and Mr. Ron that when he growed up, the first book she wanted him to read was *Same Kind of Different as Me*. I looked over at Mr. Ron and told him, "Let's go home and write this boy a book he can read right now."

174

When we gots back to Dallas, we started writin that book. Well, Mr. Ron did the writin, and I painted the pictures for it, 'cept he called 'em illustrations. Miss Vida had a real nice wood stand made for my fire truck and even put a glass box over it so everbody could see it without touchin. It stays in the big livin room and sits right next to all them high-dollar pictures and statues. That's one of the most importantly possessions I got—more precious to me than my new Escalade.

I likes little chilrens, 'specially Mr. Ron's granddaughters. He invited me to the lake to take a ride on his big ol' boat with him and the grandbabies. It gots two bedrooms 'bout the size of a jail cell and two itty bitty bathrooms that ain't big enough for a big man like me to be able to take care of his bidness. You know what I mean. I seen it before, but I wadn't hankerin for no rides.

Mr. Ron ain't knowed much about black folk not likin no water 'less it come outta the hose in the front yard. And for sure, they ain't gonna step in no water that they can't touch the bottom and still see they belly button.

When we gots to the lake, I told Mr. Ron real strong that I wadn't gonna be gettin on his boat even if he gave me a winnin lotto ticket. Now, what good is a winnin lotto ticket gonna do for a man that drownded on a boat and can't spend it?

So I sat on the dock with a fishin pole, watchin the bobber, and started kinda dreamin without bein asleep. I was back in Red River Parish on the plantation. I could see cotton ready for the pickin in the fields near where I was sittin barefooted in my overalls on the riverbank with a cane pole, watchin a cork bobbin. I just sat there dreamin and reflectin for a few hours till the sun set and lit up the lake like glory struck it. That made me start praisin God and bein thankful to be seein and doin things I never thought possible. God done really blessed me.

58

RON

It was maybe the most exciting call I'd ever received. Former first lady Barbara Bush called to invite Denver and me to speak at her Celebration of Reading fund-raiser in Dallas. She said our book had become one of her all-time favorites and she had bought cases of them to send to her friends.

The event was held at the Myerson Symphony Center. Denver and I spoke to an audience filled with millionaires and political superstars, including the former president George and first lady Barbara Bush. After the event we were invited to sit at the head table with the distinguished parents of the sitting president, George W. Bush. Denver was wearing his bowler hat, and Mrs. Bush very nicely asked him to remove it, telling him that "gentlemen don't wear hats at seated dinners."

"Yes'm," he said, then he stood and walked toward the front door. We all assumed he was checking his hat. But he never came back. Mrs. Bush asked the Secret Service to look for him, and they asked the Dallas Police Department to assist. For two hours at least thirty officers and Secret Service looked for the man of Debbie's dream, who had simply vanished like a Russian spy.

Denver and I had a seven o'clock flight the next morning to Charlotte, North Carolina. We were slated to speak at a citywide fund-raiser for the homeless. Nearly a thousand people would be attending, and every one of them was anxiously awaiting the arrival of the dream man. But at the moment I wasn't sure I ever wanted to see that dream man again.

It was past midnight when I crawled in bed with a knot in my stomach the size of a six-foot, two-hundred-fifty-pound former homeless man called Suicide who was causing me to think about the same. Embarrassment and anger coursed through every vein in my body, and I felt like I was going to puke. All the effort I had put into bringing about a change in Denver's life seemed in one glorious night to have been wasted.

If ever I wanted to release my catch, this would have been the night I tossed it back in the river like a gar and never looked back.

59

DENVER

That first Bush lady run me hot. She say it's a rule that a man can't wear no hat at the supper table. Well, if the rule don't line up with the circumstances, it ain't a very good rule. Cold air was blowin down on my amerism, and that screw felt like it was gonna come out my bald head or my eyeball, covered in ice. I'll betcha a hundred foldin presidents she never had no amerism.

I ain't gonna lie to you. I was glad she sacked me out 'bout my hat 'cause I wadn't wantin to sit there with no presidents and first ladies worryin 'bout which fork or what spoon to eat my soup or chicken with. Mr. Ron spends lots of time tryin to teach me good manners, and I knows it's a good thing to be sayin "yes ma'am" and "no ma'am," but the big deal white folk makes 'bout knives, forks, and napkins don't make no sense to me. In fact, when Mr. Ron ain't 'round, I use my fingers and eats outta the pots so I don't have to wash no dishes.

I walked most of the way home that night. Then, 'bout three in the mornin, a bus come by and the driver ask if I wanna hop on. I had blisters on my toes from new shoes and didn't have no money, so the driver let me ride free. I told him I'd been havin supper with the president and first lady and I got lost. He look at me like I was crazy. He was a young white man and wadn't scared of me. I told him I 'preciated that.

Mr. Ron was sure 'nough surprised to see me sittin at the breakfast table, waitin for him to drive us to the airport. I was still in the same suit I worn last night, but my bag was packed. I started laughin when I seen him walk in, but he didn't think nothin was funny.

60

RON

Denver buckled his seatbelt and began snoring louder than a freight train at a school crossing before we even left the gate. I elbowed him at least a dozen or more times with no results. In fact, an anesthesiologist sitting across the aisle commented that he'd never seen surgery patients sleep more deeply. The flight attendants and people around us began laughing, and I couldn't help telling them our story. I'll take Las Vegas odds that Denver's snoring sold more than ten books.

Kathy Izard, chairman of the Charlotte event, picked us up at the airport and drove us to a barbecue place to meet the other committee members. It's a real Southern thing, a competition of sorts, for every city and state to have their own secret recipe for the rubs and sauce. No matter where we travel in the South, the first stop is usually at a local rib joint. Sometimes it's just a shack.

While we ate, I spun the tale of Denver's disappearance the evening before. We were all laughing about that when one of the ladies spotted him about a block away, walking away from us. Just moments before, he had excused himself to use the restroom. I joked that he preferred to pee in the woods, adding that we might or might not see him again until we left on Sunday. That realization switched the mood from frivolity to panic, and Kathy jogged down the street to retrieve him.

Kathy came up with the idea to have volunteers tail him like

180

a suspect in a bank robbery. And that worked pretty well until the next morning, when we were slated to be interviewed on NPR. We arrived at the station in plenty of time for a get-acquainted coffee with the host, followed by a tour of the studio. We turned a corner, and suddenly the host realized Denver was missing.

We traced our steps back through the studio. No Denver—and now we were ten minutes from going live for an hour-long interview. Producers were taken off the job to search the outdoor plaza and surrounding blocks. Still no Denver. I had to go on alone.

The show began with an apology from the host, who stated that in his thirty-year history in the radio business, he had never had anything like this occur. So the interview proceeded with my telling the tale of last night's nightmare in Dallas and trying to explain my friend, why I tolerated such behavior, and why I loved this man of Debbie's dream.

Forty-five minutes into the one-hour interview, Denver strolled in like he was thirty minutes early, with time on his hands. He asked for a cup of coffee. Then he casually put on his headphones and explained how the simple urge to have a cigarette had caused him to lose his way.

It started when he slipped out the back for a smoke and remembered that his lighter had been taken by the airport security. He hadn't wanted to ask the white businessmen that passed him for a light, so he'd begun searching for a homeless man. He spotted one who was enjoying a smoke and bummed a light. Then he sat down, a conversation began, and he totally forgot where he was or what he was supposed to be doing.

The host told me afterward that Denver's late arrival had given our story great credibility and that our interview had been one of the most memorable of his career.

It was the best of times and sometimes the worst of times, but as I step back a moment to reflect on our friendship, I must ask forgiveness for my occasional impatience and even anger at my skitzy brother, the one who so easily and conveniently could slip between the personalities of the apostle Paul and Harry Houdini.

Lord, help me celebrate every moment with this glorious human you created so uniquely, the man of Debbie's dream that you threw me together with so that we could save each other.

61

DENVER

Charlotte is a real nice town, full of nice folks that treated me real good. You ain't gonna believe this, but Billy Graham's sister came to our party. He be my favorite white preacher.

I figured God meant us to be there, 'cause I met a fella downtown sittin on the curb and I asked him for a light. The man been sleepin on the streets for four or five years. He told me Charlotte ain't got no place for homeless peoples to sleep at nights—don't matter the weather, rain or snow.

Before Miss Kathy take us back to the airplane, I asked her if she would take care of that bidness. She told me that after Mr. Ron and I spoke to what looked like half the city, the folk done wrote lots of big checks, and they was gonna use that money to build a place where that man and others could spend the night. That made me real proud, and I knowed it would make Miss Debbie proud. To me, it was what carryin Miss Debbie's torch was all about. As we was gettin out of her car, Miss Kathy made me promise to come back and speak at the dedication.

Our airplane ain't no more landed in Dallas when Mr. Ron say we gotta get on another one and go to Atlanta. I always wanted to go there. I heard Dr. King used to preach there till he got killed.

That caused me to remember when we was in Washington for the president's big dance party after he got elected. Mr. Ron showed me where Dr. King gave his speech 'bout his dream. I stood on

183

those steps in front of Mr. Lincoln sittin in a big chair, and I had big tears in my eyes 'cause I was standin on the very same spot as Dr. King. I wished I'd been smart enough to figure out how to get there to hear 'im, but our man's plantation wadn't connected to the rest of the world.

We spoke at a place they said was the World Congress Center. It sure looked big enough to hold the whole world. But before we did that, I got myself out to Dr. King's and Miss Coretta's graves and spent an hour or so sittin aside 'em. I didn't talk 'cause he couldn't listen, but I prayed so he could hear me thank him for what he done for me and my peoples. Big Mama taught me that Mr. Lincoln set us free, but I never knowed any coloreds that felt they was free till Dr. King had his dream.

Somebody told me it was that speech got him killed, and there's some folk believe the Klan paid that white man to do it. Don't know if that be true, but I knows the Klan's mean enough for that.

You prob'ly ain't gonna believe this, but I ain't scared of no KKK. But I do worry what they'd do to my family if I caused somethin to come down on 'em like an eye for an eye or a tooth for a tooth. I can't figure out why nobody never does nothin to them white-hooded monsters. If they do, the news don't never report it. Maybe them news people is scared.

Now I knowed I shouldn't have said that, 'cause now I travel 'round tellin folk 'bout Miss Debbie's dream, and Mr. Ron tell me to be careful how I act and what I say. He calls it 'countability and responsibilimy. I sure don't wanna do nothin that's gonna embarrass her. She was my angel—my stubborn angel.

62

RON

The Atlanta blessing, as Denver and I chose to call it, started with one book bought by a woman named Jill Bee. In June of 2006 she went to our first book signing at a Barnes & Noble near our home and stood in a long, hot line to get her book. After she read it, she sent it to a friend in Atlanta, and it got passed around until it landed in the hands of David Smith.

David, an ordinary man with an extraordinary vision, served on the board of Trinity Community Ministries, a homeless mission in Atlanta. After reading our book, as the story goes, he set up a meeting with his banker. He asked the banker to read it and decide what he was willing to do—or not to do—for the homeless in Atlanta.

A week later David dropped by the banker's office, and there was a check made out to Trinity for twenty-five thousand dollars. The wheels in David's brain started spinning as he asked himself, "If one book brings in a twenty-five-thousand-dollar donation, what will five hundred books produce?"

Shortly thereafter he called and asked Denver and me to come to Atlanta and speak at his church. I thanked him but explained that we were looking to make a larger impact than just one church. He replied, "How about if I rent the Georgia World Congress Center and fill it as a fund-raiser for the homeless in Atlanta?"

The plan was put in place, and a few months later Denver and I arrived in Atlanta. Over a two-day period we visited many homeless

shelters and passed out hundreds of new designer shirts provided by
my friend Mike Ryan.

The situation on the streets in that city was bad and growing
worse by the day. We were invited to meet with city leaders in a
large downtown conference room to discuss what was going on.
For the first hour we listened to a presentation of a ten-year plan
to end homelessness in the city. When the speaker finished and the
applause silenced, Denver raised his hand.

"Mind if I ask y'all a question?"

"Not at all, Denver. We would appreciate hearing what you
have to say," the speaker replied very enthusiastically.

"Why is it gonna take y'all ten years to solve this problem in
your city?"

The speaker began to explain it had taken a year and hundreds
of thousands of dollars to do the study. Now that it was finished, a
staff had to be hired, land acquired, buildings built, and so on. After
five or six years, hopefully, some results would be evident, and after
ten years homelessness would be a thing of the past.

"How many homeless y'all got in this town?" Denver asked.

"We have six thousand homeless who sleep in overnight shelters or on the streets."

"How many churches y'all got?"

A gentleman spoke up, saying, "We have more than six thousand, five hundred churches in the city and suburbs."

Denver replied: "So ever church takes 'em one. Somebody ain't
gettin none. Do that, and we'll take care of this problem in thirty
days."

His plan was brilliant. Think about it. If every church in America
took in just one homeless person and was responsible for that person's housing, transportation, job, health care, and most importantly
spiritual growth, homelessness for the most part would no longer
exist.

Why churches and not the government? In Denver's view, churches offered something a government simply could not give— love. On many occasions he and I had talked about his years on the streets. Honestly, he could not remember anything the government had done to help him get out of homelessness. He was very clear that a roof over your head in bad weather and a full belly might keep you alive, but only love can change lives. And love is something churches have—or at least should have—in abundance.

After our speech in Atlanta, CNN anchor T. J. Holmes set up an interview with Denver and me at the World Congress Center. Denver found it fascinating, almost unbelievable, that a young black man could be a real, live news reporter in the South. He came alive for his young friend and in the process captivated a nation.

Sixteen segments of our interview aired that weekend, and by Monday our email server had crashed, with more than six thousand hits in a matter of hours. Most of those were speaking requests that would take us months just to read. A few days later we signed with a Los Angeles talent and speaking agent for five thousand dollars each per speech.

The Atlanta blessing took us to a newer, higher level. Life as Denver and I had known it was about to change.

63

Mr. David Smith done bought most of the pictures I ain't
already sold. He paid good money, no hagglin, all foldin presidents.
But there was a catch. We had to carry Miss Debbie's torch over to
his hometown of Knoxville, Tennessee, and speak at a fund-raiser
for the homeless there.

I hadn't met many mayors of towns 'cause many mayors never
wanted to meet me. I don't blame 'em. But this Knoxville mayor,
Mr. Bill Haslam, and his wife, Crissy, invited us to sit with them
at they table at the fund-raiser. Mr. Ron told me Mr. Bill was fixin
to become the next governor of Tennessee. Oh Lordy, I wished he
ain't told me that, 'cause it prob'ly mean I couldn't wear no hat at
the supper table.

I didn't tell nobody 'bout the time the first lady wanted to blow
up my hat, but there is another reason I wore it besides my amerism.
Since I'm kinda superskitious, I didn't really talk about it. But just
so everbody don't think I'm just a crazy man, listen up: my hatband
has a rock in it that come off the hill where Jesus died.

I gots a friend—Mr. Ron's too—that done walked hisself up
on Mount Calvary and picked up a couple of rocks and put 'em in
his pocket. When Mr. O. S. Hawkins got home, he give me one of
them rocks. It looked kinda red to me, and I wondered if that was
the blood of Jesus. At first I was kinda skitzy 'bout blood and dyin,
but I remember the Bible say Jesus is the rock and I's covered by

his blood. I ain't very smart, but I figure if I put the rock in my hat and my hat covers my head, then I got 'em both covered—rock and blood.

So now you knows why I didn't never take off my hat 'cept to sleep and shower. If somebody ask me to take it off, I just 'scuse myself and burn off.

When I sat at the table with the mayor's wife, she done asked me a lotta questions. She seem to me to be spiritually like Miss Debbie. What she found out is I gots the same answer for nearly ever question, and all my answers come from the Holy Bible. I done heard the Bible more'n most preachers.

Now, I ain't say "read."

I say "heard."

A homeless man is made to listen to a Bible story ever time he be hongry. That's the rule in the missions. I mean breakfast, dinner, and supper—three times a day. And when I was in Angola, only the inmates that went to church on Sunday got the day off.

There was only one brother in the Bucket of Blood cell block where I was incarcerated that could read, and he had a King James Bible he read to us. Soon as he quit readin, the guards would holler down from the walk, "Back to work." So the brother read under a big oak tree all Sunday long—sunup to sundown. Ever so often we'd stop and all sing "That Ol' Ship of Zion." In the ten years I was there, he read the Bible from Genesis to Rebelacious seven times.

One of the answers I gave Miss Crissy seemed to cause her to do some thinkin, so she asked me, "Denver, if you've never been to school and don't read and write, how do you know so much about the Bible?"

I thought 'bout it for a bit, then say, "Well, the Lord knowed I was never gonna get no smarts or schoolin, so he overconfiscated me with a photospastic memory!"

64

RON

Dinner at a historic hilltop home cantilevered over the Tennessee River with the Knoxville mayor and his wife was one of our most memorable and blessed evenings ever. It's where I made a conscious effort to record and remember all the pearls that flowed through Denver's pearly whites—Denverisms, I tagged them. When Denver answered the mayor's wife about how he knew so much about the Bible, I asked if he meant that God gave him an extra measure, possibly overcompensating him, with a photographic memory.

"That's just what I told the lady," he said, as if those were his exact words.

Knoxville blessed us in many ways. David Smith bought at least a thousand more books and used them to raise hundreds of thousands of dollars for the homeless in his hometown. My part of the royalties from all those books helps keep Debbie's mission in Fort Worth afloat. David had a great vision to repeat this in every major city across America.

Denver asked if he had to go to each and every one of all those cities. He claimed I was working him three-quarters to death, and he pleaded for a break after more than two hundred events in the last couple of years.

Knoxville turned out to be a double blessing. It's where we met Anne Neilson and her husband, Clark, face-to-face. An artist from Charlotte, North Carolina, Anne had a vision to use her painting as a way to give back. Over the phone before the event, we'd talked about blending art and philanthropy, and she'd sent me one of her first angel paintings. She'd donated another to the mission there. These masterfully done works on canvas spawned two books and a line of products that still bless the homeless coast-to-coast. Our friendship became a collaboration to change the way the world sees "God's people," as Debbie called them. Through the lenses of God, let them become visible.

———

While Denver and I had been traveling all over the country speaking, the mail lady at home had been busy too. A deluge of letters from readers who had read *Same Kind of Different as Me* and been inspired to make a difference filled our mailbox. Those were the inspiration for our second book, fueled by a network of readers like Barbara Bush, David Smith, Kathy Izard, and Anne Neilson.

Denver and I spent a few months again with Lynn Vincent, crafting the stories of hope and healing, but we were stumped at the end on what to name it. Our publisher set up a conference call that would last as long as needed to come up with a title. Recalling the hours we'd spent titling the first book, *Same Kind of Different as Me,* I assumed this process would take a while.

On the morning of the call, I was sitting in my office waiting for all participants to join, when Denver walked in. My phone was on speaker as the last caller joined.

Denver asked, "What is you doin this mornin?"

"Well, I'm on a conference call with our publisher to choose a title for our new book, because they don't like the one I suggested."

"What difference do it make?" he asked, very matter-of-fact.

Everyone on the call heard his question, and the chief editor blurted out, "What did Denver just say?"

"What difference do it make?"

"That's it!"

"That's what?"

"The title for the new book!"

A few days later, I received a call from my high school English teacher. She had just celebrated her ninetieth birthday and claimed my book was her best present ever. She said it had been her dream that one of her students would someday write a *New York Times* bestseller, and I was the first to accomplish that. But then she went on to scold me about my incorrect use of the King's English in the title, pointing out that she had taught me better.

"It should have been *Same Kind of Different as I*," she scolded. "I hope that if you plan on writing more books you will use better grammar."

I thanked her and ended our conversation by saying I hoped she would read our new book.

"What is the title?" she asked.

"What Difference Do It Make?"

65

Travelin 'round the country, Mr. Ron was always pullin out maps and teachin me 'bout jography. One day he tell me we was fixin to fly to Florida. He say they call it the gator state. That just tell me he don't really know as much as he think he do, 'cause I's purty sure we gots more gators in Louisiana than all the whole world put together—Florida included.

In fact, I'll betcha if y'all give me a test, I'd be smarter'n a fourth grader. I knowed all my ABCs and lots of two-tums. Mr. Ron calls that 'rithmetic, but when he tells me two times one is two and two times two is four, I just calls it knowin my two-tums.

Lord have mercy, we showed up in Florida and a blonde movie-star-lookin white lady picked us up in a white-on-white some-kinda-fancy convertible with the top down. The sun was so big and hot in Florida, you could fry a pork chop on her hood. Hear me real good—I wadn't lookin to get no tan, and for sure I don't like folk starin at me like I's a dirty spot on a new white shirt. I ain't been that uncomfor'ble since Miss Debbie picked me up off the streets and took me to that religious retreat with all them white ladies in her white-on-white SUV.

Remember how I say Miss Debbie was the bossiest lady I ever run into, black or white? Well, Miss Debbie done met her match. Miss Carmen Brown could talk to a corn patch and make it lay flat and never shut up. I kept tryin to tell her I wadn't comfor'ble in no

convertibles with no tops down, and the lady wanted to know if I
need a sweater. What I need was a bus to take me to her show. The
lady was just too young to understand 'bout crossin color bound-
aries. They is some white folk that gets fightin mad 'bout crossin.

Miss Carmen, she was a radio personality. She read our book
and flew us down there on an airplane to be on her show. But first
she gotta drag me all over town to take my picture with Mr. This and
Miss That, Pastor Who and Lady What, and even the newspaper.

We was all sittin at a resterunt by the ocean, and it look real
familiar. I say to Mr. Ron, "I thought you told me you is a bidness-
man." He say he used to be but he give it up to raise a teenager. I
didn't know nothin 'bout that. Then he laugh and say he was kiddin.
But I was serious. I wanted to know if he was such a good bidness-
man that knew how to be a millionaire, why didn't he take care of
our bidness that last time we was here so we didn't have to waste
time comin back. I's getting tired of all this travelin.

"Denver, this is our first time to come to Florida together."

I know he purty smart, but I figured he forgot, so I reminded
him. "I remember just a week or so ago we was sittin right here
havin a meal and lookin out at the ocean."

"Denver, that was California. So your geography lesson for today
is that we are now in Florida on the opposite side of America, three
thousand miles away."

Three thousand miles? That seem to me like all the way to
the moon and back. It didn't make no sense. "Mr. Ron, is you
tryin to tell me that Florida done gone out and got theyselves an
ocean too?"

Well, I finally got over that ride in the convertible, and it wadn't
long before me and Miss Carmen got to be good friends. I sang a
song for her at her church, and next thing I knowed, she was flyin
me out to Nashville by myself to make a record. Well, not really
makin my own record, but singin on one with a famous singer

named Chris Tomlin. That man is a star, and he treated me like I was B. B. King.

Now, I ain't gonna lie to you. That was the first time I flew on a plane by myself, and I missed a couple of flights. They was callin my name over the loudspeakers, but I just couldn't walk that fast. Like I said before, I done lived my whole life with nowhere to go and plenty of time to get there. I always figured it was like a bus—if you waits long enough, another one'd be goin your way. But between you and me, I finally figured out why Mr. Ron was always rushin me to the gates.

66

RON

Every week, like Olympians, Denver and I carried Debbie's torch to cities such as Atlanta, Chicago, Nashville, Tulsa, and Houston. We traveled throughout the Bible Belt and the heartland of America. And our message, Makin a Difference, was always the same: honor Debbie's memory and tell her story, our story, at fundraisers for the homeless, some weeks as many as five. At a few of those events, Denver surprised the audience with an impromptu song. Word spread, and soon, by request, Denver was singing and sometimes playing the piano every time we stepped on a stage. We were like a band playing one-night gigs.

None of these events were a walk in the park for either of us. The more tired Denver became, the more he burned off or conveniently got lost in the smoke plumes of his cigarettes. And the more he got lost, the more time I spent searching alleys and side streets for him. In a matter of one month, smoking caused Denver to miss two flights. By the second one, I suspected he'd hid, so I made him pay for his own bus ticket back to Dallas. The bus was more his speed—slow. He claimed to have enjoyed both trips because, as he said, "there wadn't no rushin like at the airports."

We were crossing the Skyway Bridge across Tampa Bay with radio host Carmen Brown in her white convertible with the top down when my phone rang. "Is this the Ron Hall who wrote *Same Kind of Different as Me?*"

Mark Clayman, a Hollywood producer who was looking for his next project after *The Pursuit of Happyness*, was on the line. A friend in Dallas had given a copy of our book to a friend of hers in Los Angeles, and a few days later Mark had read it. In a matter of minutes we struck a deal for an option on our book. In a matter of weeks, he and a producer from Dallas, Brad Reeves, had commissioned a screenplay and attached Samuel L. Jackson to star as Denver. Our dreams were starting to come true as the two producers shopped for the right studio deal.

From Florida we went to New York. After radio and TV appearances, we had a luncheon hosted by the executives at Barnes & Noble that Denver almost missed. Thank goodness his cell phone was charged and in his pocket, because he wandered off and forgot the name and location of the hotel where we were staying. He went to the front desk of several in the neighborhood looking for me, with no luck. Finally he called, and in the nick of time I retrieved him a few blocks away at a Starbucks.

New York was way too crowded and confusing for Denver. His neck ached from looking up at tall buildings—the Empire State Building hurt the most, he said. There were too many hotels, and they all looked alike. He wanted to go home. So I put him on a plane back to Dallas and I stayed for a few more days of art meetings. Although the Murchison art was basically all sold by that time, I wanted to keep current on what was happening in the art world and to catch up with my old business partner, Michael.

The smell of freshly mown grass and the warm air of a Dallas summer evening welcomed me back home as I drove into our driveway. Walking to the house, I heard soul music and laughter not too far away. At first I thought it was our neighbors having a party, but they lived hundreds of yards away. Passing from the kitchen to the big, glass-walled living room, the music and laughter intensified, and I heard splashing in the pool.

I walked through the open glass doors just as Denver shouted like an announcer for an opening act, "Ladies and gentlemen, meet the famous Mr. Ronnie Ray Hall."

He served me a plate of dry-rub pork ribs, a slice of white bread, and an ice-cold beer. And I met his friends—the ones who didn't burn off when they saw me walking their way. I sat down next to a very pretty woman and her young daughter, who with a big smile said this was better than a birthday party. The woman was a former resident of the mission who had graduated from the program and was now living on her own with a good job. Thankful for the opportunity to start life over, she had started volunteering at the mission. A young man, Steve, was also a graduate of the program. He now owned a truck and was in the moving business. His hobby was street preaching with Denver on the streets around the mission.

Later that night, after the beer ran out and the party ended, Denver told me he'd decided to share his blessings with some of his homeboys and girls from the jungle and the mission. He had bought a case of beer and enough ribs to feed a football team, though according to him only seven or eight people had showed up.

Seriously? I'd seen seven or eight hightail it out of there when they saw me walking through the door. He blamed the error on the head count on his two-tums. No matter. I applauded his benevolence.

These kinds of stories are what mission work is all about. It's what Denver and I hope and pray—that our book inspires a generation to pick up Debbie's torch and share their blessings.

67

DENVER

I ain't never seen a buildin so tall it poked a hole in the clouds
and made it sprinkle on my head like my auntie did with a broomstick back on the plantation when she played 'round with black
magic. We tried to take a ride up to the top, but they say the clouds
was blockin the view. That's the same way I felt 'bout those mountains in Colorado the first time I ever seen 'em.

Who was it decided that New York City is so fine that everbody
gotta go there? Somebody say it be called the Big Apple but I didn't
see nary a one. I know lots of folk thinks I's a crazy man, but let me
tell you—I seen more crazies there in three days than most folks see
in they whole life.

There was one fella wearin a cowboy hat and boots and ridin
on top of a bicycle with just one wheel, and he was all naked 'cept
his red bikini bottom that showed off his manhood. You ain't never
gonna see that kinda crazy in Texas, 'cause even though he was
white, a real cowboy just might throw a noose 'round his neck and
drag 'im and his one-wheel bicycle behind a hoss.

Me and Mr. Ron had gotten real comfor'ble with each other and
was spendin nearly all our time together now. We gone way beyond
friends—we likes to laugh and tell folk we is brothers by a different
mother. He didn't say so, but I figured he needed a little time to hisself to see his friends while we was there, so I come on back home.

I was walkin and lookin 'round that big ol' house and swimmin pool and gots to thinkin it was a shame to just let it all go to waste. I knowed some folks that would 'preciate a little swim in a place other than the public Water Gardens in downtown Fort Worth. The po-lice will arrest you for swimming there. I know, 'cause I used to bathe in there, then spend the night in jail. Anyway, with Mr. Ron bein gone, I decided to throw a little party for some folk that don't never get shown no love.

God don't give us no credit for lovin those that's easy to love, but we just might get us a crown for lovin the unlovables. I sure wadn't 'spectin it, but I was glad Mr. Ron got to come to the party. My friends was surprised a millionaire would treat 'em all so nice— just like they was regular folks.

I told Mr. Ron that he prob'ly wadn't gonna believe it, but I didn't drink a drop of that beer. I bought it for my guests. And he say somethin then that I ain't never gonna forget: "Of course I believe you. Denver, I trust you, even with my life."

Did you hear what I just told you? Ain't nobody never say that to me. I feels the same 'bout him, 'cept I ain't never told him.

After the party I was talkin to Mr. Ron and he agreed with me that this was lesson number two. If we is gonna change the world, we gots to start right here in our own backyard. And lovin the unlovables is the answer. That was the first time I remembers the man ever thinkin I was right.

68

RON

Two weeks later, while I was out on a date, Denver started having chest pains again and couldn't breathe. He left a message on my phone, but I had turned it off while in a movie theater. It caught him by surprise when he was relaxing with a cigarette on the back porch. Miraculously, he was able to drive himself to the hospital—he knew the way by heart! By the time I got there it was a full-blown heart attack, and he was on life support, awaiting the bypass surgery he'd not gotten the last time this happened.

Three days later the doctors took a vein from his leg and repaired his heart. He came through just fine, but his first words were—you guessed it—that he wanted a cigarette. Same song, second verse, but more likely a never-ending verse. By hook or by crook he found his way to a bench by the outside entrance and bummed a cigarette from another patient.

I drove up just as he crushed the butt on the sole of his hospital-issued house shoes. He smiled and gave me a wink as he slipped the butt in his pocket like he had outsmarted the doctors.

We were sent home with a bottle of pills so small that Denver said they looked like white BBs. I set the bottle on the kitchen table and laid out one for the first night. He was supposed to take it with food, and we decided supper would be the best time.

For three days he followed doctors' orders with the exception of smoking. On the fourth day, he didn't show up at suppertime and his medicine bottle was empty. No luck getting him to answer his phone.

By the time supper was on the table, I had a call from the police—not just any officer, but one who had read our book and recognized Denver. He had been driving like a drunk and gotten pulled over. He was barely coherent.

After determining that he had overdosed and was not drunk, the officer said he would wait there with him until we picked him and his car up. Luckily he was just fifteen minutes away. Vida came with me so I could drive him home safely.

On the way I asked Denver, "What happened?"

He slurred like a slow-talking drunk. "Mr. Ron, I was takin one of them little white BBs ever day, and I couldn't tell I was gettin no better. I figured since they was so tiny, maybe I should take the rest of the bottle and see if that'd heal me faster so I can go see my auntie in Louisiana. She's nearly a hundred, you know, and ain't got long to live. So I kicked back them pills and I decides to head off to Louisiana, but I didn't get far from the house when all of sudden I starts goin blind—I mean Ray Charles kinda blind. So I pull over and go to sleep. The officer woke me up sayin that somebody called 911 on me for drunk drivin. But you know I don't do no drinkin no more since Miss Debbie sacked me out."

I'd stopped listening. *The whole bottle?* As fast as my fingers could dial, I got his doctor on the phone. He told us not to waste a single second getting to the emergency room. A quick blood test shocked the doctor and every medical person in ears' reach. There were no records of anyone surviving this great an overdose of the medicine he had gulped down like sprinkles on ice cream.

Back in the hospital for his overdose, he developed an infection, and the heart operation had to be repeated. The Devil was messing with him sure enough. But Denver was skilled—actually, the best I'd ever witnessed—in battling enemies. Luckily we were on a break from speaking events.

It took more than a week in the hospital to get him straightened out and to bring him back from the brink of death. I started calling him Lazarus. Vida told him the cat was on life number eight. That caused a dangerous, possibly life-threatening, belly laugh.

69

Denver

Lots of folks just can't understand how I could take such a lickin and keep on tickin. Listen to me real good—God wadn't through with me yet. Just like all the doctors that told Miss Debbie she was gonna die a long time 'fore she did—God wadn't finished with her neither.

It seem to me like I was in the hospital a long time for eatin too many of them little BBs. It was good to be back home. But I been wonderin 'bout my auntie in Louisiana. She ain't got no phone—never did. Can you believe that? Let me tell you, if you drive down to Louisiana right now and get off the blacktop, I'll betcha you ain't gonna find many phones in houses on dirt roads.

I knowed I was s'posed to be lettin my heart be restin, but to tell you the truth, I couldn't rest till I seen if my auntie be all right and take her a little blessin so she can buy some cigarettes. They done got too expensive for her little check. Can you believe it costed me more to smoke now than it did to buy gas for my Escalade?

After Mr. Ron was sleepin I slipped off real quiet so he couldn't hear my tires cracklin on the gravel. It took me a while to figure out how he always knowed when I slipped off at night, but now I knew. I rolled all the windows down 'cause the fresh air feel good after the smell of the hospital—plus, I wanted the wind to keep me awake.

It didn't work too good. Rollin 'bout ninety-five in my Escalade

204

with the windows down, I started noddin off. And you ain't gonna believe this, but it's the Lord's truth that right at that same time my hat blowed clean off my head and out the window. That wadn't no regular hat. It was the one anointed with a rock in the hatband that come off Mount Calvary. But now it was after midnight, and I couldn't walk with my leg all swol' up, so I decided to just let it go.

I seen a po-lice doin a U-turn, and the next thing I knows his lights is flashin and he is pullin me over. I didn't think I'd done nothin till he tell me I was drivin nearly a hundred miles an hour. He shined his big ol' flashlight, lookin 'round in my car. And the next thing I knowed, he starts hollerin for me to get out with my hands up and not touch the gun.

I thought the man was jokin till he shined the light on my pellet gun that was sittin on the seat next to me. He blowed up like it was a Saturday-night special. He kept on hollerin, "Get outta the car." I told the man very calmly that I couldn't walk 'cause I just got outta the hospital and I gots stitches from my knee to my balls.

'Fore I knowed it, he opened the door, grabbed me by the collar, and dragged me out on the pavement. That white boy began hittin me with his stick, then kicked me in the sore leg and make the stitches open up and bleed like a stuck hog. He called for backups and kept his revolver pointed 'tween my eyes.

"Pull the trigger," I told him, and I meant it, 'cause he done run me hot.

It took both of 'em to cuff me 'cause I's a scrappy nigga when you come after me with that kinda bull. Them white boys throwed me in a cell and slammed the door with my leg bleedin through my britches and down into my shoe till it was sloshin.

I was layin in the cell thinkin 'bout my hat that blowed out the window and that rock with the blood on it. The Bible say Jesus is the rock, so I believe since my rock come off the hill where he was killed, it was spiritually protectin.

Think about it. Ain't nobody done nothin bad to me in a long time, ever since I was wearin my hat. So I thinks the Devil stole it when I dozed off at the wheel.

Like I always say, if the Devil ain't messin with you, he's already got you.

70

Ron

At 6:30 A.M. I was awakened from a sound sleep by my ringing phone. I didn't recognize the number and usually don't answer unknown numbers. But since it was so early and a Texas number, my curiosity was aroused. On the line was an East Texas sheriff looking for Mr. Ron Hall, who wrote the book.

"That's me. What can I do for you?"

"First let me say that I and several of my deputies have read your book and really enjoyed it. Now, that being said, I'm sorry to report that Denver Moore was arrested around midnight for resisting arrest."

"Resisting arrest? He is supposed to be here in bed recovering from heart surgery. How could that even be possible?"

The arresting officers, according to the sheriff, were two of the only ones on the force who had not read our book, so they had deduced (by racial profiling, I assume) that Denver was a pusher with something to hide.

He went on to tell me it had started as a speeding violation that went south after the officer noticed a gun in the passenger seat. As it turns out, it was a pellet pistol Denver had bought to shoot rats in our garage—nothing illegal. However, I knew he carried it in full sight when he cruised the hood around the Stop Six carwash looking for people to bless or convert. It made him feel safer to have it sitting on the seat when gangbangers approached his Escalade thinking he was a drug dealer.

The sheriff went into full apology mode as he described the brutal arrest, adding that he was dropping all charges. He said Denver was free to go and suggested he go to the hospital and have his leg checked out. I offered to come get him and asked him to put Denver on the phone.

"Mr. Ron, I ain't leavin my car in this racist town. I'm drivin home as soon as I hang up."

I heard the gravel crackle as he drove in less than two hours later. He was in shock from the trauma and the loss of blood and wanted to sleep. He dropped his pants, and I saw burst stitches and an open wound oozing blood. Instead of putting him in bed I rushed him to the emergency room. Sure enough, his leg wound was severely infected. He spent the next three weeks confined to a wheelchair in a rehab hospital.

The whole arrest was disturbing to me. Denver swore he'd been calm and courteous up to the point that the officer grabbed his collar and jerked him out of the car and to the ground.

"Mr. Ron, I tried to tell the man I couldn't walk 'cause I'd just had heart surgery. He told me he didn't care what I had and by the law I just needed to get myself outta the car with my hands in the air. I was tryin to tell him a law ain't a very good law if it don't line up with the circumstances. But I never got them words outta my mouth 'fore he jerked me down."

That sounded like police brutality to me, and we talked about filing charges against the arresting officer. Denver requested that I hold off—he wanted a few days to think about it. We prayed for wisdom.

72

DENVER

Them white boys run me hotter than a Rolex in a pawn shop. In fact, I didn't cool down till I was coolin my heels in the rehab hospital. I was tired then. Didn't even think of burnin off.

Mr. Ron was plenty hot hisself and thinkin 'bout filin charges 'bout po-lice brutality—puttin them white boys in jail and lettin 'em see what happens to white cops that abuse a brother. But let me say this—if I ain't been drivin ninety-five in a fifty-five, I'd be sippin sweet tea with my auntie instead of bein laid up in a jail cell. So let's get real. I done brought that on myself. The white boy was doin his job. I ain't defending him for hittin me with his stick and kickin my leg, but a black fella racing through his town past midnight in a white Escalade is cause for concern. I coulda been runnin from the law. Or he coulda been jealous he ain't got no Escalade.

"That Escalade's been causing you a lot of problems," Mr. Ron told me. But listen to me real good—I got ever right to drive a white Escalade just like any other person with the money to pay for it. And the po-lice ain't got no right to stop me just 'cause that's the car I likes.

I told Mr. Ron that we was too busy carryin Miss Debbie's torch to be fightin with the po-lice. I figured the best thing for me to do was stop breakin the law.

Them folks at rehab treated me real good. I signed lots of books for the nurses, and they made sure they was always a sugar cookie on the plate by my bed. My friend Miss Cindy come by nearly ever day. I met her at Starbucks with Mr. Ron—she's an artist, a rich white lady, a lot like Miss Debbie. She brung me lots of art supplies, and we drawed and painted together.

72

RON

Rehab was good for Denver, and he was good for rehab. It let him know how many people loved him—nurses, staff, and friends. The hospital, thirty miles northeast of our home, was not in a convenient place, so every visitor had to make an effort to show their concern for him. It was not uncommon for friends, especially Fort Worth friends, to drive fifty miles or more. A few, like Cindy from our Starbucks and cowboys like Roy Gene, Rob, Dan, and Randy, whom he'd met at the Spring Gathering, drove a hundred miles.

Now, it's one thing to stop by and say howdy when passing by in the neighborhood or to sit and talk at a Starbucks sidewalk table. But driving long distance just to show you care is something different. Visitors during Denver's three-week stay showed truly sacrificial love, and he was amazed by it all. So was I.

Even more love came to Denver in 2008 when the State of Texas honored him by declaring Denver Moore Day in the House Chamber of the state capitol in Austin. State representative Susan Lewis had met with the governor to give him our book and tell him our story. A few days later he'd signed the proclamation, and we stood in awe on the speaker's podium in front of hundreds of elected officials as the Speaker of the House banged his gavel and read the proclamation aloud.

After the ceremony Governor Rick Perry invited us for a private meeting in his walnut-paneled office. He wanted to hear Denver's perspective on homelessness. Sitting in front of the century-old desk that had served many a governor, Denver poignantly spoke of his twenty-five years on the streets, when no one ever asked his name. "I was invisible 'cept when I had to take care of bidness, like whoo-pin up on those that mistreated the weak and scared ones. White folk and blacks too was scared to look me in the eye."

The governor was surprised to hear Denver say that he felt government was not the solution to homelessness. Denver shared once more how, after those twenty-five years on the streets, Miss Debbie had been the first person to see through all his anger and confusion and show him the love of Christ. And only then had he begun to change. "Mister Mayor," he said, "love is the only solution."

It was obvious the governor had never met anyone like Denver, and he was fascinated by his homegrown perspective on life and homelessness. It was especially eye-opening for him to hear the Denverism, "We is all homeless, just workin our way home." As a Christian, he admitted he'd never thought about that simple truth.

The governor's assistant opened the door and reminded him of his next meeting, now overdue, with guests waiting in the foyer. Governor Perry asked Denver if he would be willing to stand behind him, lay his hands on his back, and pray that he would have wisdom in his dealings with the homeless problem in Texas.

Denver stood and slowly moved behind him. I joined them. "Lord, this is a good mayor that love you and want the right thing for your peoples. I prays for this mayor, that you gives him more insight than eyesight so he won't be regrettin no hindsight. Lord, this mayor know he ain't the only customer you got. That's why he be workin for all the peoples—rich, poor, or somewhere in between. Help this mayor not to judge peoples like me 'less he know they heart and what cause 'em to jump track and get throwed off in life. In your precious name we pray. Amen."

We all hugged, and then the assistant led us out of the secured office area. I wanted to laugh, but I held it in because first I wanted to tell Denver how proud I was of him and to bless him for having the courage to stand, lay hands on, and pray for such a powerful yet humble man.

However, there was a slight problem, I said as we were walking to the car. "Denver, that was not the mayor."

"What was he?"

"The governor," I answered.

He stopped, squinted one eye, and cocked his head in his classic thought pattern before asking, "Well, Mr. Ron, what be the differ-ment? Did I pro-mote him or de-mote him?"

73

DENVER

The last time we come here we didn't get to go inside. But this time Mr. Ron said we was gonna do more than go inside. We was gonna sit down and eat with the president of the U-nited States and his whole family.

The night 'fore that dinner, me and Mr. Ron had us a long talk 'bout manners and stuff like wearing my new hat inside the president's house, so I left it back in the hotel—it ain't got no rock like the other. I done learned Miss Barbara don't like nobody wearing no hats or shades at her table.

Since I be knowin Mr. Ron, I gots to ride in a few limousines, all black. Today, some fellas with wires in they ears picked us up in a blue one—first blue limo I ever seen. Can't nobody just drive up to the White House. You gots to go through a lotta gates and show your ID and your invitation a lotta times to mens in uniforms with machine guns—and you know them guns is loaded with real bullets.

We was walkin up the steps past marines standing stiff as a pine stump on both sides, and they didn't blink or smile. Mr. Ron said we was standin in the room where dimpamats and kings wait to see the president. You can't just walk in his office like I do Mr. Ron's.

Another man in a blue suit with a wire in his ear done put us on an elevator just big enough for two, maybe three peoples, unless they is as big as me. The man say this is the president's own private elevator, where he can sneak away up to his bedroom and watch baseball on the TV. The man say Mr. Bush still love the Rangers but don't own 'em no more.

Miss Barbara Bush and Miss Laura Bush was there when the door opened, and they gave us both a hug. I never met Miss Laura before, but I'd seen her on the TV enough that I was purty sure it was her. They was a couple more folks that wrote books there. We was all gonna speak that night for Miss Barbara at some fancy concert building they call the sympathy center.

She took us all 'round that big house, but 'bout the onliest room I remember 'sides the president's office is the Lincoln Bedroom. You ain't never in your life gonna see more gold in one room than where Mr. Lincoln and his wife slept—gold rug, gold curtains, gold chairs, gold covers on the bed. It reminded me of Mr. Murchison's fancy bedroom, where I used to sleep 'fore I moved into the guest house. I was wishin I had my shades.

Next stop was the president's office. Miss Laura Bush showed us his desk and said it was the same desk where President Lincoln hisself sat and signed the Emancipation Proclamation that set my peoples free all them years ago, 'fore I was born. I wanted to cry, 'cept I didn't want to look a fool in front of all them fancy white folks. But hear me good—I was proud to touch that desk for my great-granddaddy and great-grandmama, that was bought-and-sold slaves Mr. Lincoln set free.

I heard Miss Laura say, "Hi, sweetheart." I turned 'round and there he was—Mr. George W. Bush, the president of the whole U-nited States of America. That man walked right up to me like he knowed who I was and stuck out his hand to shake and say, "Denver Moore, what an honor to meet you, sir."

I took one shoe and stepped on my other big toe to make sure I wadn't dreamin. I can't remember what I said 'cause it was like I was in another fella's body. For sure, I was disbelievin that the most powerful and famous man in the whole world knowed my name and acted like he knowed me. I even thought 'bout paying my taxes since he knowed who I was.

Shakin his hand felt like a lotta history done passed through our hands. I remembered when a colored man couldn't ride no buses or drink outta no fountains 'less they say colored. I remembered the Klan draggin and hangin folks like me all across the South and callin us niggers. Now here I was standin with the president—a free man, a changed man, and all 'cause of the love of a white lady named Miss Debbie.

A Bible verse came to mind I wanted to share with the president, but he moved on to shake hands with a war hero, Mr. Marcus Luttrell. Since I didn't get to tell Mr. Bush, I'm gonna tell you. God say *all* things is possible. Did you hear me? What do *A-L-L* spell? That don't spell or mean *some*. That mean *all*. And I just seen that happen.

A black man like me, 'cept he was wearin a bowtie and suit like I wore to the nawguration, come into the room and say, "Lunch is ready."

I ain't lyin—I ain't never seen so many knives, forks, spoons, and glasses. They even had a sign with my name on it by my plate, and the two Bush first ladies sat beside me. I could read their names. I was proud of that. But to tell you the truth, sittin between them two fancy white ladies made me a little skitzy. I wadn't too much interested in eatin 'cause I likes to take my teeth out when I eats, and I knowed that would embarrass Mr. Ron.

We been sittin and talkin 'bout two or three hours with no end in sight. Really, I was just answerin their questions—and was runnin outta answers! I'd done looked at more plates with food too purty to eat that I pushed 'round to look like I was eatin. I didn't know what any of it was, but it sure wadn't no pork chops, mashed potatoes, or greens. I needed a smoke, and I needed to pee, but I couldn't figure out how to do either one.

Ding, ding, ding. I hit my knife on the water glass to get folks' attention. I'm fixin to call this meetin to an end!

74

RON

Denver was getting fidgety, but I was proud that he had conducted himself like a gentleman with decent manners for more than two hours. After all, I knew it had to be stressful sitting between the first lady, Laura Bush, and the former first lady, Barbara Bush, who was making sure he practiced his reading every day. After all, that's why we were there!

I was at the other end of the table between Neil Bush and Doro Bush. President Bush had excused himself just before lunch when a Secret Service agent whispered in his ear about an emergency phone call in the Oval Office. Former president Bush sat to my left with Anita Perry, Governor Perry's wife, along with a couple of dignitaries and four other authors. I've never been so proud to be in a room, and I was justing thinking about how proud I was of Denver—and how thankful I was that he'd conducted himself as a gentleman, with not a hint of an embarrassing moment like the last time we ate with the Bushes in Dallas.

A loud banging on glass interrupted my conversation with Doro. It was Denver getting our attention. Oh boy!

The first lady asked for the attention of all the guests. "I think Denver would like to say something."

"Yes, ma'am, I sure do. First, I'd like to say y'all gots a real nice house here. I'll bet y'all is mighty proud of it."

"Oh, Denver, it's not our house. It's your house too."

"Ain't my house. I ain't never had no house," he said with a big smile.

"You know what I mean, Denver," she said so sweetly. "It belongs to all the citizens and taxpayers of the United States."

"I ain't never paid no taxes, neither! But that's not why I banged on the glass for. What I really would like to do is go 'round this table and thank all y'all by name for what y'all done for me and Mr. Ron and our book. But to tell y'all the truth, I can't remember none of y'all's names 'cause all you Bushes look alike. In fact, I'm gonna tell y'all the truth. All white folks look alike to me!"

Everyone at the table roared except me. I cupped my hands around my face and shook my head, unsure if I should join in the laughter or cry.

Shortly after the laughter died down, Denver was taken out on the balcony overlooking the Washington Monument, where he lit up a smoke.

An hour later it was time to return to the hotel and dress for our speaking event at the Strathmore Symphony Center. We exited through a marine honor guard, who saluted us like heads of state. As the limo pulled away from the White House, Denver began laughing hysterically.

"What's so dang funny?" I asked, reminding him he had just embarrassed the tar out of me in front of the whole Bush family and guests.

"Mr. Ron," he said, catching his breath. "I done gone from livin in the bushes to eatin *with* the Bushes! God bless America, this is a great country."

"Yes, it is," I said, my spell of anger broken by laughter over his brilliant observation.

"Them Bushes treated us like we was real somebodies."

"Yes, they did."

"But you and I both know that we ain't nothin but a couple of ol' nobodies." Then he paused before getting serious. "But we was both loved by a real somebody. She done give meanin to our lives."

75

A few months later somethin else very disbelievable happened.
I figured I was one of the first black people to visit the White House,
but Mr. Ron said I was very wrong. It's just I ain't never knowed or
heard 'bout no black folk goin there 'cept Dr. King.

But then one mornin I woke up, and the man on the TV say we
gots our first black president, Mr. Barack Obama. I asked God to
protect him from the Klan 'cause I figured they was gonna try and
do him wrong.

That was one of the first days I ever remember bein proud of
my race. Ever since that white man kill Dr. King, seems like nobody
on the news never talk about the good things we do. It's always a
black fella shot somebody, a black fella jacked a car, a black fella
robbed a fillin station. But today a white man on the TV was sayin
a black man was our president. Now, you listen to me—it has been
written and the ink is dried and the pages is turned over. Ever day
carries its own miracle.

I asked Mr. Ron if we was goin to Mr. Obama's party like we
did with President Bush. He say we won't be gettin no invitation
'cause President Bush done give him a job in the State Department
when he was in office and he didn't vote for Mr. Obama. I didn't
tell nobody, 'cause people of my race won't understand, but four
years ago I done voted for the first time in my life, and I voted for

President Bush. I respects a man that treats a homeless man just like he treats a millionaire.

Mr. Ron and me didn't never talk 'bout no politics. Not really. But I gots a lot of time on my hands to think 'bout stuff like God and what was good for our country, and I talks 'bout that to Mr. Ron and a lotta fellas. You might not believe this, but most homeless folk thinks education is good and jobs is good—though most of 'em, includin me, ain't never had both. And you ain't gonna find many brothers that believes the way I do, but everbody that ever knowed me knows how I feel 'bout this. I thinks welfare is bad. Little girls shouldn't be getting paid for havin babies, and folk don't need to get a paycheck for doin nothin. That just ain't right.

76

RON

The dream we had of making our book into a movie was becoming a nightmare. Many people were now involved, mostly lawyers. Mark Clayman and Brad Reeves had worked for two years and invested a lot of money, but no major studio was willing to take the risk.

About that time I received a call more shocking than our movie failure. My art partner in New York City called to say that Larry Salander, a dealer we had millions invested with, was on live television being handcuffed and escorted out of his gallery. He'd been charged with stealing one hundred twenty million dollars from his investors. Several million of that was ours.

Denver walked into my office as I logged on the Internet to watch the live coverage. The media were calling him the "Madoff of the art world" and suggesting that no investors would recover a cent.

"Mr. Ronnie Ray, you look like you done lost your best friend."

"Denver, I'm broke. Someone stole all my money." My hands shook on the keyboard and my heart pounded. I didn't want to meet Denver's eyes for fear of him seeing me cry.

"You ain't broke," he said kindly, like it was the gospel truth. "I gots plenty of money, and I wouldn't have nothin if you ain't written that book and taught me to paint. Look at me," he ordered. "You can have it all. You hear me? I said *all*."

"That's extremely generous of you," I told him, "but it doesn't work that way. That's your money. You earned it."

"Nosir. Now, you listen to me. All your money and possessions can't really be possessed—they possesses *you*." He said it like a preacher pounding on the pulpit to bring home a point.

"Now, God don't make no mistakes. You lost your money for a reason that only God knows. But what God do know is that you been takin care of me for a lotta years, and I ain't never paid nothin for nothin—not for no cars 'cept my Escalade, not for no rent, not for no groceries, not for no airplane trips and hotels. You has paid for everthing the whole time I been knowin you. Now it's my turn to take care of you."

Now I really was in danger of crying. "I love you, man. Remember when we were walking the streets years ago and you were schooling me about helping people? You said that in order to really help somebody who's in the ditch, you gotta crawl down in the hole with them. And when they are strong enough to crawl out on your back, then you really helped them. It just occurred to me, Denver—I may have to crawl out on your back." He smiled, and I smiled back.

He laughed. "Now you gonna know what I told you another time. Remember this? You knows you really gots somethin when you can thank God for nothin—and then he'll give you everthing. So hear me real good. Now that you gots nothin, you needs to start thankin him for that—and I mean right now. Did you hear me?"

I heard him, believe me.

Now, I had no intention of letting Denver take care of me financially. Though I was in shock, I realized I still had assets and no debt, so I immediately canceled my pity party. Yes, Salander had stolen the money, a lot of it, I'd marked for retirement. But I still had enough cash to pay bills for a year or two. I also owned a ranch and a valuable art collection that soon would be going on the market or auction block. With God's help, I would find a way to make the money back. But I also knew Denver was serious. Just a few weeks earlier, the owner of a favorite restaurant, Antonio's, where Denver and I had eaten hundreds of times, confided in Denver that his business was not doing so well. The next day Luciano called to tell me that Denver had offered *him* all his money.

"He meant it," Luciano said. "Denver told me, 'Lucci, I gots plenty of money, and you can have it all. I done run outta people to bless and still gots a lot. You been my friend, my only Eye-talian friend, and now I wants to bless you.'"

Luciano didn't take his money, either, but we both appreciated the generosity of our remarkable friend.

Salander was sentenced to eighteen years in prison, but I didn't get my money back. It was all gone. It's funny—a few weeks before he was arrested I'd gotten a letter from Salander praising me for the work Denver and I were doing for the homeless. In his closing sentence he thanked me for trusting him with my investment.

77

DENVER

Them was some rough days for Mr. Ron. First, he lost all his hard-earned money, then he lost his daddy a few days later.

Mr. Ron took his daddy's dyin purty hard. When me and Mr. Ron first got to be knowin each other, him and his daddy wadn't on very good terms. Then his daddy got sick and Mr. Ron had to start takin care of him. That's when me and his daddy started gettin tight. His mama was my friend too. But just like her son, she didn't allow no smokin in her house.

When Mr. Ron was off workin, I used to sit on the front porch smokin cigars with Mr. Earl and listen to him tellin war stories and braggin on his son. The man give me the pocketknife that he carried in the war—he was a hero, won a medal. It's sure 'nough one of the specialist things I ever owned.

Mr. Ballentine was the first white man I ever went to his burial. Now Miss Vida gonna drive me over to Fort Worth to pay my respects to Mr. Earl. I remember when I wouldn't get in the car with no white ladies, but that was before Miss Debbie. Now I done been in a white convertible with a white, blonde lady radio star, so I was comfor'ble with Miss Vida.

Now let me tell you, Miss Vida is one of the nicest ladies I ever knowed, but she talked too much and trusted everybody like they was her preacher or her Sunday school teacher. Did you hear what I just said? I had to sit her down and tell her that everbody that smiles

224

at you ain't necessarily your friend and everbody that frowns ain't necessarily your enemy. She say that was confusin and didn't seem to know what I's talkin 'bout. So I told her they is some folk been smiling at me to sign some papers 'bout bidness stuff that I can't really read.

Listen to me. Everbody's bidness ain't nobody's bidness, and if everbody know your bidness, you ain't gots no bidness! I ain't gots lots of smarts, but I gots instincts that I done talked too much 'bout my bidness and somebody's up to no good. I gotta figures all that out.

$$78$$

RON

Life was getting better. The old saying "the harder I work, the luckier I get" was true. Art deals began coming my way again as I set aside my writing cap and dusted off my art dealer's hat. The collection Debbie and I had built over the years had grown in value, and some of my best paintings sold easier than snow cones on a hot day.

Denver and I began spending more time at the ranch. Denver fished and painted. I began a new hobby. The neighbor who built the Brazos de Dios arch for Debbie's cemetery taught me to weld and helped me fashion my cardboard models into large out-door sculptures. Denver helped me put the finishing touches on one that stood over ten feet tall. He wondered what it was, and I explained it was just an abstract design like relationships and friendships—it's what you make of it. Before heading back to Dallas that evening, we decided to name it "Celebration" as a symbol of our friendship.

It was just after eight in the morning the next day when I answered the door and signed the receipt for an unexpected certi-fied letter. Certified letters from lawyers are rare in my world, so my curiosity was piqued. Movie stuff, I guessed.

The envelope was taped shut, so I went to the kitchen to get a small knife and sliced through the tape and glue.

Dear Mr. Hall,

Upon receipt of this letter, you are hereby ordered to cease and desist all formal or informal contact, conversations, or correspondence with Mr. Denver Moore. You are under orders that any and all attempts to contact Mr. Moore will be made through his legal representative, Mr. , Esq.

Any violation of this order will result in the immediate issuance and enforcement of a restraining order and subsequent arrest.

Very truly yours,
Mr. , Esq.

Vida walked in the kitchen to put her lunch in the refrigerator. "Sit down and read this," I said as I handed her the letter.

"Has Denver gone crazy?"

"Sounds like it. Is his car out there?"

"Yes."

"Do me a favor. Go to his bedroom and ask him to come to the kitchen. I am forbidden to contact him!"

She gave an incredulous laugh. "What in the world is going on?"

A few minutes later Denver walked in. "What's for breakfast?" he asked, as if we were still at the ranch.

"Here, read this." I handed him the letter. He looked it over and said, "You know I can't read."

"That's not the truth. You read for Mrs. Bush, and I see you reading the newspaper every morning."

"I sure do, 'cause you made me practice."

"Okay, so sit here and let's practice reading this letter."

He got the "Dear Mr. Hall" with no problem. Then, frustrated, he pushed it back to me and asked me to read it to him. As I did, he began looking at me as if I were the crazy one, and his face stayed frozen that way until the end.

He pushed back on the table as he straightened up. "Mr. Ronnie Ray, I didn't send that letter, and I didn't ask nobody to send it. But I'm gonna tell you the truth, you and Miss Vida gots a friendly enemy. Did you hear what I say?

"Think 'bout it, Mr. Ron. Why in the world would I send such a letter when I lives in your house free and goes with you everwhere you go and gets paid for it?" He started laughing like the whole thing was funny. "But listen to me—I ain't gonna lie. I knowed you was gonna be gettin some kinda letter 'fore too long 'bout not touching none of my money or my car."

"You know I've never touched any of your money except to give it to you, and the only cars I ever touched were the three I gave you."

"I knows that, but listen to me real good—your friendly enemy claim they overheard a conbersation 'tween you and Miss Vida 'bout y'all's secret plan to steal *all* my money and my Cadillac too!" I couldn't help but laugh, which brought his nonsense to a standstill.

"Denver," I said after the laughter helped me calm down and realize someone was messing with his mind. "You once told me years ago you never trusted anybody. I feel like after the last few years together that might have changed. Do you remember telling me, after you drove all Regan's worldly goods to Colorado, that I was the first person who ever trusted you? So now you're telling me you have finally found someone you believe is trustworthy, and it's not me?"

"Well, let me say they caused me to get a little skitzy. You know, like I used to be. Listen to me, Mr. Ron. The bad make it bad for the good, and the good gots to suffer for the bad."

He dropped his head without a word for several seconds before looking up and locking eyes with mine. "Somebody be makin it bad for you. You and Miss Vida is too trustin, and y'all needs to quit allowin all these folk you don't really know in our house, 'cause one of 'em say they is gonna teach me 'bout bidness—but by listenin to that letter, it seem like they be wantin to take over my bidness."

Truthfully, I felt sorry for him, knowing his pride in his accomplishments and his desire to move toward independence had gotten tangled up with the secret desires of a person who had their own interest at heart—not his. Maybe I was foolish to believe that everyone who met him wanted the best for Denver.

Our conversation switched back to breakfast. Over grits and eggs, we talked about what the future looked like. He told me someday he would like his own place in the country. I reminded him he had it already at Rocky Top. "Too far in the country," he said with a smile. He loved the small tract house in Haltom City I grew up in and wondered if he might be able to buy it now that my dad was gone. "Absolutely," I told him, but it was nearly an hour's drive and I explained for our business and travel schedule it would be better to find something closer to me.

The next morning at breakfast, Denver told me he'd gone to see the lawyer. "I walked past the lady at the front desk and went straight to his office and throwed the letter down on his desk. I told the man to not be sending no more letters to you. Then I fired him. But to tell you the truth, I never did hire him. Not really."

I worried that possibly his schizophrenia or bipolar disease or whatever was acting up. I knew he was not drinking. Maybe he was still hearing voices from ghosts, since I knew it was impossible for anyone to have overheard a conversation that had never taken place about me stealing his Cadillac!

Lupe, the former resident, had been kidnapped in the 1980s, so our home was equipped with a high-tech camera system that covered the entire property. When we moved in, we'd disabled it because it was constantly going off, mostly triggered by animals. Hoping to crack the case, if indeed there was one, we fired up the system for the next several months. But most of the things we captured on video were bobcats and Denver smoking in the woods, by the pool, and every other place where the camera focused.

I never did find out the whole story about that letter. Vida did a little snooping around with no success. It was a mystery about how Denver got connected with that lawyer in the first place, and the subject eventually disappeared like smoke after the fire. But whatever lack of trust Denver may have experienced during those "skitzy" moments had apparently been resolved. We were able to move on with our lives and our many adventures.

79

DENVER

We been on a lotta airplanes but never on no private jets till Mr. Disney come knockin. Some folks sent a whole jet that had only six chairs—ever one of 'em recliners. We was flyin out to some place to meet a man named Mr. Netter who was makin a movie 'bout waterin some elephants. I ain't never seen no elephants for real, but years ago I gots hired on a day-labor job to clean up they poop when the circus left town. Did you know one elephant can poop a number-nine washtub full in a day?

Mr. Ron say the other fellas tryin to make our movie didn't have no luck. That reminded me what Mr. Ron's daddy say 'bout our book. One day when Mr. Earl and me was sittin on the front porch, I heard him ask, "Who in the world is gonna read a book 'bout some black homeless ex-con and a white-man art seller?" Maybe he was right and that's why nobody wanted to make our movie.

But now Mr. Gil Netter and Mr. Brad was flyin us out somewhere 'cause Mr. Netter read our book and liked it and maybe would make the movie. He already made another movie Mr. Ron took me to see called *The Blind Side*. I liked it 'cause it was 'bout a young homeless boy, a real nice fella—not like me. One day he was walkin down the road back to the hood when a nice white lady like Miss Debbie pick him up and bring him home to live with her family. The boy was a good football player, went to college, and became famous. We need more young black mens to act like him. I heard lotta folks went to see that movie.

But even Stevie Wonder could see the differment in that movie and our book. For one thing, I was not a nice man. How do you think I got the name Suicide? And I don't play no sports, 'less you call wigglin your toes by a Dumpster a sport. But I did have a base-ball bat—still do, and I knows how to use it. Ask Mr. Ron 'bout that! So I ain't gonna hold no grudge if folks don't wanna make our movie. Maybe I needs to start actin a little nicer.

Mr. Ron and I spent two days sittin in the hot sun, watchin 'em shoot a scene for the elephant movie of a fella jumpin on a train. They'd back up that train, blow the whistle, and do it all over four or five times. I didn't understand why they done the same thing over and over, always hollerin action and cut. As many trains I hopped, I coulda jumped on it and got it right the first time, and we coulda gone back to the motel and cooled off.

They was some fellas there that was talkin to us like we was gonna be the next big stars. Then, a few days later, Mr. Ron was readin me a contract they was purposin. They was gonna be payin me fifty thousand dollars for my life rights and another fifty thou-sand to fly 'round town to town talkin 'bout it like Mr. Ron and me was already doin.

For the last couple of years, folks been payin us five thousand dollars ever time we get on a stage. Who woulda ever thought a black sharecropper with no education would be gettin paid five thousand dollars just to say a few words and sing 'em a song?

And who woulda ever dreamed that some fella like me would get his life made into a movie?

80

RON

It was the most important meeting of our career as authors. Contracts were spread all across the large table in our living room. Movie lawyers were gathered there, awaiting the star of our show, Mr. Denver Moore. In just a matter of hours, he and I would be under contract with one of the biggest studios in Hollywood. That is, if I could manage to find him. But true to his reputation as the modern-day Houdini, he'd pulled another disappearing act.

That morning at the breakfast table, Denver and I had talked about how important this meeting was. I had asked him to be showered and dressed nicely and ready for the start of the meeting at one o'clock that afternoon. Actually, the meeting didn't start until two, but I always padded it an hour or so. I had even set an alarm in his phone to remind him and asked that he not leave the house all day until they left.

He had definitely left the house.

We made small talk for an hour, then went over the contract, which I signed. Vida went searching for Denver because he was not answering his phone. Finally, at four that afternoon, everyone left to catch their planes, never having met the first black Houdini—or gotten his signature.

I was as mad as I've ever been. I told Vida the only acceptable excuse was death.

Around six that evening, Denver arrived back home alive and well. I was waiting in the kitchen drinking my second glass of wine with the intent of finishing off the whole bottle by myself.

"Where have you been?" I demanded. He started laughing. "This is not funny!" I said, staring him down for once.

"Fort Worth," he answered. I reminded him that I'd asked him not to leave all day, but he said he'd had an appointment in Fort Worth to get his eyes deleted, and then he couldn't see how to drive home.

"Sounds to me like you got your brain deleted for missing the most important meeting of our lives. Did you forget accountability and responsibility?"

He shrugged and said that before going to the eye doctor he had met with his lawyer about movie business.

A year or so earlier, I had told Denver he needed a lawyer he could trust because he was going to need lots of advice other than mine. He'd been through several since then, because he did not take advice well. But now he was saying that his new lawyer, whom I'd not met, knew somebody who made a movie and never got paid. The lawyer had advised him to get everything up front because movie studios seldom pay authors on the back side. I'd heard the same thing and realized that, though his timing was off that day, he had made a wise decision to seek counsel. I was listening.

"Mr. Ron, you know how when we go speak, you always open us up and I shut 'em down? On this movie bidness, it's time to switch. I's gonna open us up, and you shut 'em down. What that means is I take the up-front and you gets the back. My lawyer tell me I prob'ly ain't gonna live long enough to see no back-end money."

"Sounds kinda like eating the hog the Man gave you for Christmas," I said. "You get the rooter and I get the tooter!" We laughed so hard we had to pull out his oxygen tank.

A few weeks later we had a deal using his newly found business acumen and, per the contract, we would get our money up front. A year later the whole thing blew up, and we were back to ground zero, starting all over again.

81

DENVER

Man, I had to change my cell phone number again. My phone be ringin day and night with folk wantin to get in on this movie bidness. I done spent my whole life never tellin nobody nothin 'bout my bidness—but if I's bein honest, I ain't really never had no bidness til now and I done let the cat outta the bag.

I never knowed makin a book and movie would cause this much trouble. It even caused me to think better thoughts 'bout the cotton fields and simple dirt-road life before cell phones, lawyers, 'countants, and contracts.

Ever since I met Miss Debbie, folk been thinkin they know what's best for me. But listen to me real good—homeless is freedom, real freedom. That don't mean I be wantin to go back to that Dumpster in the jungle. I even sleep in a bed now and gots a maid that washes my clothes and changes my sheets. I showers ever day and gots plenty of clothes, nice ones, to wear from the White House to the cathouse. Well, not the cathouse—I'm just messin with you 'bout that. But what I'm tryin to say is the more things you gots, the more trouble you gots too.

I remember the time when me and Mr. Ron was just getting to know each other. He pulled out a big ol' ring full of keys and laid 'em on the table. I took a good long look at all them keys, maybe twenty-five or thirty of 'em, then asked him if he owned something that fit ever one of 'em. It took him a bit, but he say he 'spect he did.

Then I asked him if he owned them or did they own him? That kinda throwed him off, but I was serious, 'cause at that time I ain't never owned nothing.

Now I gots a key ring with a few keys, and all this stuff seem to be causin me some problems. Folk see me drivin my Escalade and they thinks I gots a lot of money—and they is right. But it seem to me some of 'em is runnin game on me.

Mr. Ron be tellin me he want what is best for me, and I needs to figure all that out. Lord have mercy. If you asked me, bidness ain't all it's cracked up to be.

82

RON

Vida resigned her all-work-no-pay job as Denver's art dealer a couple of years back. His paintings were selling very well at a local gallery next door to his favorite restaurant, Bubba's Fried Chicken. It was owned by one of his big fans, Caroline Crockett. She had an idea to do a joint art show for Denver and me with a book signing by both of us at her gallery.

Only a few people knew I was making large outdoor sculptures. The idea had been born in Italy, where I'd escaped to grieve and write. I'd found that writing was laborious and painful, and so during my burnouts I would craft with scissors and colored paper small designs I hoped one day to make. Making art was fun and became my therapy—much better than antidepressants.

The last big art deal I had completed before I stepped away to care for Debbie involved a sixteen-ton sculpture by Alexander Calder known as *Eagle*. It sat in front of the tallest building in downtown Fort Worth, but was owned by Canadians. In a highly secret transaction, my partners and I had purchased it from a failed bank and, in a carefully orchestrated move under the cover of darkness, removed it from its perch. A year later, it sold to the former president of Microsoft for a downtown sculpture garden in Seattle. So, when I started attempting sculpture after Debbie's death, Calder became my inspiration. In my friend Julio's beautiful fifteenth-century studio overlooking Florence, I began making maquettes—small preliminary models—of modern Calderesque sculptures. My friends jokingly referred to them as Halders.

Back at Rocky Top, I had started work on the actual pieces, learning the craft as I worked. My helper and I welded, shaped, and painted enough metal to cover a quarter acre of my horse pasture at Rocky Top, but sales had been few. When Caroline offered both Denver and me our first shows—together—I hoped the sales would allow my horses to get their pasture back.

On a pleasant, cloudless fall evening, hundreds of people lined the sidewalk for our opening night. We signed books, shook hands, and posed for countless photos of what some patrons were overheard calling us—the ultimate odd couple.

When the cheese board was empty and the last drop of wine poured, we tallied up the results. Denver had sold twenty-eight paintings—every single one he'd brought. I had sold zero. Even Denver felt sorry for me and offered to buy one of my pieces. I refused and offered to give him any one of his choice. He didn't want any!

As Caroline was about to hand Denver his check, he instructed her to send all the money to homeless kids in Haiti that were suffering from the recent earthquake.

83

DENVER

Oh Lordy, I done met another bossy white lady. Miss Caroline
say a lotta folk be wantin my pictures. The woman call me ever day,
wantin to come pick up some more. What Mr. Ron taught me to
do to make me stop drinkin was gonna cause me to start drinkin
again!

Naw, I'm just messin with you. I'm gonna keep my promise to
Miss Debbie till the day I die.

Mr. Ron was doin real good in his art business again. Stackin
foldin presidents, I 'spect. I'm glad he didn't let the Devil get the best
of 'im. But while he was away on a bidness trip, the Devil done got
the best of me. Now I had a little problem, and Miss Vida helped me
out of a sticky jam. I was layin up in my bed in the guest house on
my breathin mochine when I fell asleep and dropped my cigarette
on the bedsheets. They caught fire like I'd poured gasoline on 'em.
Even the leg on my britches was burnin as I runned into the crapper
to grab a bucket.

By the time the fire department come, I done got the fire out
with a mop bucket, but the whole place was smoked up and smellin
like a ghetto barbecue joint.

Miss Vida kept her cool, but she say Mr. Ron was liable to be
smokin hot hisself if he find out, 'cause there ain't 'sposed to be no
smokin indoors, never. She knowed I knowed that, but that lady just
smiled and say don't worry. She call the painters and some folks that

240

brought big mochines that sucked the smoke outta the furniture. It took a whole week and costed ten thousand dollars. That was the first bill I ever paid to live in that mansion. I had to sleep in the kitchen on a cot 'cause the big Murchison house where I used to stay done sold to some folks who is makin it look like new. Lord have mercy, I coulda burned Miss Lupe's glass house to the ground, and Mr. Ron woulda been homeless hisself.

The man no sooner parked his car in the driveway when he be wigglin his nose like he smell a little smoke. Miss Vida wadn't gonna tell him. But he saw me sittin in the kitchen and asked me if they had been a fire and I wadn't gonna lie to the man. He was real nice 'bout it all, but he told me if I ever smoked inside the house again, the 'state managers might just 'vict us, and we'd both be lookin for another place to stay. That would be a shame for me to cause all that mess. We been livin here 'bout ten years, and I tried to obey that no smoking rule. But I ain't had no success.

I thought about it. He was right. And I knowed they wadn't a snowball's chance in you-know-where that I was gonna quit smokin, inside or outside. He laughed and told me if he saw any more smoke, I'd better be on fire! We'd done a little talkin 'bout my future, so maybe it was time to make a change. Now I gots plenty of money, so I asked Mr. Ron to help me buy a little house for myself. I really liked his daddy's house, but he say it's too far.

It wadn't but a day or two later he say he found me somethin close by and wanted to show it to me. A real nice little house, he say.

84

RON

Less than two miles from the Murchison estate, we parked in front of a small, white, postwar frame house on the market for eighty-nine thousand dollars—a relative bargain.

Denver, barely paying attention to any details, passed quickly through the house and out the back door without asking any questions. The small tool shed in the backyard brought a smile to his face and was a big selling point. It was nearly like the one where he used to smoke with my father before Earl passed away last year. There was an old-fashioned clothesline with pins still on it that reminded him of the one Big Mama had strung between two oak trees.

"Where you do the washing?" he asked.

The lady holding the open house thought he was asking her to do his washing and answered, "I'm just a real estate agent; I'm sure you can find someone to do it."

"Who gonna mow the yard?" was his next question directed toward her as he looked down at the ankle-high grass.

"It will be your choice to hire someone or do it yourself," the agent responded.

He opened the door to the shed, disturbing a small hornet nest as the agent backed away. "I don't see no mower, and I didn't see no bed or no couch in the house."

"Those would be the buyer's responsibility," she told him.

I chimed in and asked about the monthly bills—electricity, water, and gas.

"Less than two hundred a month," she said, "depending on use."

"But I ain't never paid no bills," Denver said, "and I thought water was free. That's why it's the onliest drink I orders in a resterunt. How is I s'posed to handle all that?"

"Vida can help," I assured him.

"How much are the real-estate taxes?" I asked next. And before she could answer, he interrupted. "I ain't paying *no* taxes."

The agent could tell he was no normal homebuyer. "I'm sorry to inform you, but that is not an option. If you don't pay the taxes every year and continue to pay them as long as you own the property, the city will take your property away from you and sell it to the highest bidder on the courthouse steps."

Denver looked at me as if she had just pulled a .357 revolver, pointed it directly at his head, and driven off in his Escalade. He turned to me, eye cocked, and asked quietly, "Is that white lady crazy?"

"No, Denver. She's telling the truth."

He fixed me with a Clint Eastwood stare and said: "There's fixin to be a big problem, Mr. Ron. 'Cause if that kinda stuff happen to me, I'm liable to go to the courthouse and open up a big ol' can of whoop-ass on the whole place! I don't think I needs to be buyin me no real estate."

85

DENVER

It don't make no sense to me that if I pays cash for a house, I still gotta pay the gov'ment ever year just to keep somethin I already own. That ain't right. So I told Mr. Ron to take me to a motel, and he did.

Right near our house we found me a smokin suite at the Comfort Suites motel for a thousand dollars a month. I gots a bed, a couch, two chairs, two TVs, and a kitchen. They say they'd clean my room ever day and I'd get free breakfast, but I told 'em I gots that at Mr. Ron's, so they give me free lunch instead.

It wadn't long till me and the night manager became podners and he let me in the kitchen any time I was hongry. Best part— wadn't nobody chewin me out for smokin in bed. I could smoke three packs a day if I want to and nobody gonna say nothin. I pays for that privledge.

Ain't nothin changed after that, not really, 'cept I slept and smoked at the motel. The rest of the time I be paintin and hangin at Mr. Ron's, waitin for him to cook some fried chicken and greens. He was my family. Still is and always will be.

———

It wadn't long after that my daughter Tracy and her family come here from Los Angeles. My podner at the motel got 'em a room by

244

me and I paid for they whole trip. That's the least a daddy can do for his daughter. Took 'em three days ridin the train to get here, and they was hongry 'cause they only packed enough food for two days. So our friend Luciano and Mr. Ron throwed a big party at Luciano's resterunt for my whole family. Miss Vida and Mr. Ron's kids come too. The Moores, ever single one that I ever knowed, is large peoples like Big Mama, and they 'bout cleaned out the kitchen.

That girl of mine gots a lotta forgiveness in her heart. I only seen her once when she was born and then I burned off 'cause I wadn't ready to be no daddy—never was till now.

She gots a brother, name's Thomas, born on the same day in the same hospital by 'nother mama. That's when I was hidin from the Fort Worth law in Los Angeles. I knowed I was goin to the hospital to see one baby. But, oh Lordy, when I gots there, they was two.

I got another son by 'nother mama. He servin a life sentence in California for killin a undercover officer in a bad drug deal. But he say it was an accident, and I believe him. He's real smart and done wrote a book—Mr. Ron read it to me and he say my son got talent.

I don't believe that boy'd be in prison if I'da stuck 'round and been a daddy. That's what real mens do. Sometime I sit out on the porch and think 'bout what my life mighta been like if I'd met Miss Debbie 'fore I jumped track and got so throwed off.

86

RON

Denver was having breathing problems when I knocked on his door at the motel to pick him up. This was not a paid event for us, just making a personal appearance as a favor at an uptown charity fund-raiser. He was coughing hard and asked if I'd let him slide tonight. His health was getting worrisome to me.

I almost turned around to go home, since I had grown to believe an invitation to a homeless fund-raiser meant they wanted the star of our show, Denver—and if his sidekick showed up, that was okay too. But I was dressed for the semi-formal affair, so why not go?

———

"Hi. Remember me?" I asked, fighting to hold my position in a moving crowd of attractive people.

"Yes, I heard your book is a *New York Times* bestseller," she stopped and replied. In that moment the crowd dispersed as if a movie director had ordered it, leaving us alone together. I was mesmerized and strangely found breathing to be difficult.

Beth Walker and I chatted for the next thirty minutes. She had lots of questions about Denver and the book. She had not actually read it, but her Bible club was discussing it and she knew the story. I offered to get her a copy signed by both of us and have a mutual friend deliver it.

"That would be nice," she said. Then she waved to her date, who obviously had been searching for her. As I watched her walk away, I couldn't help thinking I was glad I had not gone back home—I even wished she'd been my date.

I had met Beth briefly four years prior when she and a date were invited by my girlfriend at the time to join us for an evening together. The ladies modeled for the same agency and frequently were on set together. I had enjoyed her company, but we'd both been in relationships at the time and hadn't really connected. Now I was unencumbered, and for the next several days I couldn't help wondering if she was in a serious relationship. I asked a friend to find out.

As promised, I had the book delivered by a mutual friend, who later reported back to me that Beth's current dating relationship was on life support and that she was about to pull the plug.

Interesting.

Beth was a very busy fashion model whose photo appeared frequently in the magazines and newspapers I read on a daily basis. As I thumbed through pages, passing over feature articles in search of more photos of the auburn-haired, fair-skinned beauty, I surprised myself by dreaming of someday having a wife like her.

I'd thought I'd never be interested in marrying again. Now I wasn't so sure. There was something really special about Beth.

Just a few months later, Denver and I were having dinner on the patio at Luciano's with the mutual friend who had delivered the book. This time she informed me that Beth had ended her relationship, retired from modeling, and moved back to Charleston, South Carolina, to live with her family.

"You should call her." Her words seemed to float in the air as sugarplums danced in my head. The friend took a photo of Denver and me and sent a text to Beth: "Guess who I'm having dinner with?"

The meal went on, and at one point I began talking about my

upcoming travel plans. Denver had been diagnosed with chronic obstructive pulmonary disease (COPD), no doubt due to his lifetime smoking habit. And because of his need for daily oxygen, which he breathed between puffs of cigarette smoke, his doctor had banned him from air travel. That meant I'd be doing upcoming speaking trips on my own. But as my financial situation improved, I had joined an exclusive travel club and had begun planning some trips for fun.

As I spoke of the exotic locations that were my options, I commented that it would be nice to have a travel companion—*other than Denver*, I thought to myself, as he was sitting next to me. Our mutual friend pounced on that. "Why don't you ask Beth to go with you?"

Well, why not? Grabbing my phone, I fired off a text. "Hey Beth, this is Ron Hall. You are a person of interest to me. Would you like to be my guest on a trip to Cabo San Lucas, Nantucket, and Martha's Vineyard?"

"Is this a drunk text?" she replied.

"No," I texted back.

"Then I would suggest if you want to ask me for a date, you should call me rather than text me."

I was only slightly embarrassed at her show of class and my lack of it as I quickly dialed her number. After twenty-five years of modeling, she was bored. That night she was sitting on the couch with her parents watching *Dancing with the Stars*.

She said she was interested in the trip I was proposing, but what I thought might cinch the deal was she would have her own bedroom and there would be four other couples with us. Still, she needed to think about it.

"While you are thinking, here is my credit card number and security code. Charge a full fare to Cabo. If at any time you are uncomfortable, I'll put you on the next plane back to Charleston with no hard feelings."

The next morning I boarded a seven o'clock flight to Los Angeles, where I was to speak at a fund-raiser for the downtown Gospel Mission. It was one of the first events Denver had not attended with me—a strange feeling. By noon, however, I was on Skid Row in LA, interacting with the homeless population. While praying with a middle-aged man who had been on the streets for twenty years, suddenly my phone began ringing. I opened my eyes and saw the name *Beth Walker* light up across my screen.

"Excuse me, buddy," I said, stopping the prayer and stepping away to take the call.

Beth was calling with great news. She had bought her ticket to Cabo and was excited to meet me there in three weeks. But instantly I decided I couldn't wait that long to see her.

"While I have you on the phone, would you also like to go to Paris with me?"

"Paris, Texas?" she asked.

"No, Paris, France. And the same deal—my credit card, and of course your own bedroom."

"When are you going to Paris?"

"Tomorrow."

"I can't go to Paris tomorrow."

"When can you go?"

There was a pause as she considered the offer. "Day after tomorrow!"

"Let's do it!"

Three days later we met at London's Heathrow Airport and took the Channel Tunnel to Paris. To help her be more comfortable about spending a week in a foreign country with a man she had never even held hands with, I also invited the friend who had suggested I call her.

———

My choice of a trip to Paris was a calculated one. I knew the city like a tour guide, having been there more than a hundred times in my twenty-five-years in the art business. I was able to give both women the scratch-and-sniff tour of Paris and surrounding areas, including Versailles and Monet's home in Giverny.

Four days into our trip, on the way back to Paris from Giverny, I dared to be so bold as to place my hand on top of hers in the back seat of our chauffeur-driven limo. The feeling for me was pure magic.

That night at the Moulin Rouge, we shared our first very brief kiss and held hands on the steps of the Sacré-Coeur Cathedral overlooking the city. The kiss alone sent a large enough electrical charge through my body to power the whole City of Lights for a night.

After a merry-go-round ride at the base of the Eiffel Tower, we returned to our beautiful seventeenth-century apartment on the Ile Saint-Louis near Notre Dame—courtesy of my new travel club. Sitting on the sofa with a view of the lighted cathedral and the city, I made her an offer I hoped she would not be able to refuse.

"Give me ninety days to shock and awe you," I proposed. "I'll show you the world and give you a get-out-of-jail-free card you can use at any time along the way if you have had enough of me."

The next morning we changed her flight. She would return with me to New York and then on to Dallas to meet Denver and the rest of my family.

———

Vida, my children, and most of my friends were surprised to hear I'd been smitten so quickly. Up until now I'd never mentioned Beth's name, thinking she was the impossible dream. But now it was looking more possible, and I could barely contain my excitement.

For the next two months, Beth and I jetted in and out of Dallas and Charleston, both of us getting to know each other's friends and families. Denver took an instant liking to her and would sit and talk with her for hours, telling stories and talking about God. He was impressed that twenty years earlier she had been baptized at Prestonwood Baptist, a church he and I had spoken at and attended frequently.

The final leg of our ninety-day first date was a three-week grand tour of Italy. We started in Rome, then motored up the Amalfi Coast and on to Tuscany. We even stayed in the ancestral home of da Vinci's model for the *Mona Lisa*—now a vineyard. And we ended the trip with a week's stay at the Villa d'Este on Lake Como.

Sitting at dinner on the last night of our trip, I was feeling melancholy, stumbling with my words and wondering where this adventure was going—or was it ending? We were talking about the *Same Kind of Different as Me* movie and speculating who should play me, Debbie, and Denver. "Denzel Washington and George Clooney were Debbie's two favorites," I said, "so why not them?"

"Don't turn around," Beth told me. "George Clooney is sitting at the table behind us." My reflex went ahead of my ears, and my head turned like a toy doll head on a swivel. My swift disobedience caused her face to flush, matching the red of her hair, and after a moment to process, she managed a quiet giggle. Regaining my decorum, I let Mr. Clooney dine with his date without sneaking a photo or autograph request.

Our conversation turned to our return flights the next day— mine to New York City and hers to Charleston. "When will I be able to see you again?" I asked.

"When do you want to see me again?" she responded.

"Every day for the rest of my life," I said, trying to express my growing love without having the nerve to voice it.

"Well, if that's what you want, why don't you call American Airlines and tell them to change my flight!"

87

DENVER

I ain't seen that man so happy since back when Miss Debbie was alive. For nearly ten years, I been the first face he see ever mornin and the last he see ever night. Maybe it was time he had someone purtier to look at.

That wadn't all. With all these mochines and pills keepin me alive, I was thinkin I be workin my way home 'fore too long. And the man is a caretaker. He need somebody else to take care of.

I told Mr. Ron I didn't think I had long to live. He asked me if I wanted to be buried next to Miss Debbie at the ranch. But I don't like talkin 'bout dyin and buryin. I's skitzy 'bout that kinda talk.

When I cross over, God gonna take my motor and junk the body so they ain't no use to dig another hole—just toss me in the closest junkyard. I heard they ain't no showers in heaven, so God just takes the spirit. He don't need no funky-smellin bodies to stink up paradise.

———

Mr. Ron had dated a few ladies before now. They was one I thought he might get serious 'bout and live the rest of his life with, and I was fine with that. But Miss Beth, she somethin special. That lady waked up with a smile ever mornin, and me and her could sit and talk like we's old friends. I figured Mr. Ron done found him a woman he couldn't live without.

That's a good thing when a man can find a good woman. I ain't never found me none of those, and listen to me real good—I ain't lookin for one.

Since I becomes rich they is a few womens tryin to use a little trickonometry on me. But listen to me—you can't fool an old fool. Do you think for one minute that after seventy-four years of freedom, I'm gonna let some woman trick me into marryin her? Just ain't no way that gonna happen.

That's the reason I still dress like a hobo most of the time. Sometimes I wear a baseball cap turned 'round backwards like a gangbanger. Think 'bout it. If I be dressin in a sharkskin suit with gator shoes and a gold Rolex, I'd have a Mardi Gras–long parade of sisters followin my Escalade. The way I dress, ever sister thinks I be drivin Mr. Ron's car.

Now that's the way you use trickonometry.

———

Now that I stays the night in the Comfort Suites, I gots more freedom. Ain't no security guards sayin "Bye, Denver" when I leaves and "Hi, Denver" when I rolls back in the gate. And best of all, they ain't no "No Smokin" signs.

Freedom be a good thing. My peoples had to fight and die for it. I never thought much 'bout it when I was a little boy. In fact, I never really gave it much thought at all till I hopped that first train. And now I'm gonna be honest with you. I don't sleep good, so I likes to take me a ride ever night. Now, I ain't sure if I is actually breakin the law when white po-lice stop niggas like me drivin white Escalades through they towns past midnight. 'Cept they was one brother that stopped me, and I'll be a lyin son of a fool if he ain't 'bout the onliest one that wrote me a ticket.

I ain't never really thought 'bout this till I heard Mr. Ron tellin his chilrens, "Nothing good happens past midnight." But seem to me, nearly ever night when I takes a ride in my Escalade, I gets pulled over. It's always somethin—crossin the line, rollin stop, too fast, too slow, wrong side of the road. I ain't never had such trouble in the three cars Mr. Ron gave me.

Let me tell you, when I traded him some paintins for his dream-sicle yellow '47 Chevy pickup, the po-lice would stop me just to look at the truck. It was sure 'nough a showstopper—leather seats, an ol' timey sun visor, and a stick shift. When I'd show 'em the chrome V-8 under the hood with a four-barrel carburetor, them officers'd take off they shades, shake they heads, and give me a high five.

I drove that truck to Louisiana once, and a brother wouldn't let me leave till I sold it to 'im. The fella paid me a lotta foldin presidents. He was my auntie's neighbor down the road in Cedar Grove. I stuck the cash in my shoes and rode the bus back to Dallas.

Now let me tell you the real problem. I believes nearly ever po-lice officer in Texas done read our book. A lotta times when I show 'em my driving license, they want my autograph. Some of 'em want me to get Mr. Ron on the phone just to talk to him. That's how he know I ain't doin much sleepin at the motel.

88

RON

Denver was transitioning. Every time I'd walk in the kitchen he'd be sitting there reading, or at least attempting to read, the Bible. And without fail he'd tell me he loved me. Two weeks before, he'd actually mouthed those words. That was the first time I'd heard them from him, and it happened while I was trying to sleep in a chair in his hospital room. He must have said it without thinking, because he caught himself and muttered, casting his eyes down and away, "I wadn't never gonna say that again."

I had been trying to fall asleep while visualizing the night he moved into our Dallas home when his words broke the silence.

"I love you too, Denver." Nothing else was spoken for at least twenty minutes.

He broke the silence with: "Mr. Ron, I ain't never done nothin for you 'cept cause problems. Why you been so nice to me when you didn't have to?" I sat up and looked into his eyes, which pierced the darkness of the room.

"You changed my life and gave me a gift money can't buy. You gave me true friendship. I remember hearing you say at the dedication of the cemetery at Rocky Top that you'd asked God to let you trade places with Miss Debbie and let her stay on earth. I believe you would do the same for me today if I were in her shoes."

"Yessir, I sure would."

Back home, I shared that moment with Vida. Tears rolled down

her face as she told me he'd said the very same thing to her. I wondered if his time was short and he was truly working his way back
home. But I had no fear his "I love you" was an omen he'd warned
me about years ago when he moved in with me, though his hesitation after delivery indicated it disturbed him.

A couple of days after he was dismissed from the hospital and
I drove him back to the motel, Denver hadn't come by the house. I
began to worry and called repeatedly. No answer. I drove to the motel
and talked to the manager, who told me he had simply disappeared.

We checked his room. Everything was the way it was supposed
to be. His medicines were all sitting on the nightstand by his bed.
Nothing seemed out of the ordinary.

As Beth and I drove back into my driveway, though, his car was
in the garage and he was sitting in the kitchen. He told us he'd spent
one night in Louisiana with his auntie and another at Rocky Top in
the cemetery, sitting on the big rock under the giant, leaning oak
tree and praying with Miss Debbie.

Beth asked why he hadn't stayed in his barn apartment. "It's so
cozy and beautiful," she said. He told her he had not gone there to
rest. He'd gone to say good-bye.

That night around midnight, he called to say he was having
difficulty breathing again and asked if I would take him to the hospital. After two hours in the emergency room, the doctors could
find nothing wrong except he wasn't using his oxygen and breathing machine.

Oh, and they suggested he stop smoking! That was a miracle I
didn't really expect to see.

I suspected cancer and asked if they would keep him overnight.
After several more tests, thankfully, no cancer was present. Waiting
for the results, I kept flashing back to Debbie in the blue recliners of chemo rooms being poisoned to near death and praying that
Denver would be spared that agony.

But the doctor's report made no sense to me. *How can a man smoke so much for so many years,* I wondered, *and have no trace of cancer in his body?* Then, reflecting on the badly scarred body I'd seen so many times in emergency rooms all over Texas, I realized cancer had been the least of his worries. Years before we met, he had survived numerous gunshots, stabbings, and deeply carved prison tattoos. Maybe, like the cat, he really was on his ninth life.

But I remembered him telling me on so many occasions, when I felt it was near the end for Debbie, that God was not finished with her yet. I believed the same for him. What was there left to do?

As I sat by Denver's bed while he slept, I listened to a recording of the song I'd heard him sing hundreds of times on stage at the end of his talks. It was called "Lord, I'm Tired."

89

DENVER

In my whole life, I never remember sayin them three words, "I love you." But I told Mr. Ron I loved him, even gave 'im a hug. Mr. Ron is the onliest man I ever hugged or let hug me. And he is the onliest man that ever seen tears in my eyes. So now you know I ain't really so tough or bad as I pretended to be.

I guess that's the kinda stuff that happens when you lets someone gets close. That's why, until Miss Debbie, I never got close to nobody or let nobody get close to me 'cept Big Mama. It's just too painful when you lose someone that was your everthing—a tragible you can't never shake. It's like your skin. You takes it to the grave, then it turn back into dust—ashes to ashes, dust to dust.

Since I left Mr. Ron's, I been existin in the disaster of doin no good when I needed to be livin in the beauty of blessin others. I ain't been doin no speakin, singin, or nothin else. The man was my earthly rock, and without him I was kinda drifting. But listen to me real good, God knows I been mixin it up, and now I'm gonna turn it over to Him and let Him fix it up.

The Lord reminded me this morning that it's the things you gives away for nothin that you gets to keep forever. So I guess it's time for me to do some givin. I know they is still some folk I needs to bless.

9 0

RON

Just past two in the morning, the ringing phone awakened me from a drug-induced sleep. I was trying to turn the corner on a bout with the flu and a hacking cough that had kept me awake for several nights.

"Is this Ron Hall?"

"Yes."

"Sorry to waken you at this hour, sir, but this is Officer Jones in Godley, Texas, and we have Denver stopped on the side of the road out here on the Cleburne highway."

"What's the problem?"

"Someone called 911 to report a drunk driver in a white Escalade, and they followed him until we pulled him over."

"He's not been drinking these days, but he does get dizzy. He's got some health problems."

Then, admitting he'd recognized Denver from reading the book, he asked if I'd come pick him up. He didn't want to arrest a man who probably just got his meds mixed up or else didn't take them.

I explained that I couldn't drive until my medicine wore off and suggested that the officers take Denver to a motel. I'd give them my credit card and come pick him up in the morning. He agreed that was the best solution and hung up.

I had a hard time sleeping after that. I kept thinking of the disconnect between Denver's long-time heroic stage presence and the current reality of putting people's lives in danger from his late-night dizzy driving. Looking back, I could see how his accountability and responsibility had taken a nosedive after his heart attack, and now that he was living on his own I suspected some dementia. Heavy doses of medicine taken in the wrong amounts at the wrong times were no doubt taking a toll on him and others. The dream man had become a law-enforcement nightmare.

Feeling better the next morning, I walked into the kitchen to find Denver sitting at the breakfast table reading the paper. I started shaking my head, and he started laughing.

"I thought you were spending the night in a motel."

"So did them white boys, but I used a little trickonometry on 'em and watched out the window till they drove off, then I burned off."

I asked him to tell me what had happened, knowing that problems like that always started with a wrong turn. The best he could remember, he'd been driving out to Rocky Top to pay Miss Debbie a visit and seen a sign pointing toward Godley. He wondered if maybe God used to live there and decided to take a look. However, since he didn't start his voyage until after midnight, he got a little sleepy. The next thing he knew, lights were flashing and he was getting pulled over.

"But the place where you got stopped was nowhere near the ranch. You must have taken a wrong turn."

"I sure did!" he said, pausing. "I ain't gots no idea how I found my way home. I just got here a few minutes ago."

"Denver, I'm worried about you and your health. I've talked to your doctors. Your memory is not as good as it once was. They have given you medicine for that, but you need to take it the way it is written on the bottle—no more, no less."

"I gots so many medicines, ain't 'nough hours in the day to get 'em all down."

"Would you consider moving back home with us? We can help you take them on time. Your bedroom is just like you left it, except it has a fresh coat of paint. You should know. You paid for it—after you set it on fire."

That made him laugh, but he quickly grew serious. "Mr. Ron, funny you say that. I think I might be workin my way home right now."

"Well, your earthly home is right up those stairs," I said, pointing the way.

He nodded.

"Beth and I are going to Costa Rica for a week," I told him. "Hopefully we will get engaged there."

"What's that?"

"I'm gonna ask her to marry me."

"That's good, Mr. Ron. That's real good. She love you, and you needs somebody 'sides me to look after."

"I want you to be my best man."

"Whatcha mean?"

"Stand up with me at my wedding—if she'll marry me!"

9 2

DENVER

Mr. Ron asked me to move back in the house while he was goin to get enraged in Costa Rica. I wondered where that might be. It didn't sound like Texas. Mr. Ron even told me I could smoke out on the porch—but not in the house. The man's real smart 'cause he knowed I's gonna smoke somewhere.

I knows he be worried 'bout me, but I ain't scared to die. I just don't wanna take nobody else with me. And I know he's scared 'bout that, but I believe Miss Debbie still be protectin me, and she's gonna do that till God take me home. The Bible say that to die is gain, and I sure am looking forward to that.

You know Miss Vida done had a heart attack, too, and was in the same hospital where I had mine. That lady don't even smoke. I hoped I didn't cause that. I's still feelin real bad that I cussed her one time and accused her of bein dishonest. I knowed the Devil made me do that 'cause if he ain't messin with me, he done got me. I took her some flowers, red roses, and asked her to forgive me. She told me she done forgot 'bout that and never believed for one second I really meant it.

I knowed Mr. Ron gonna be proud when he come back, though. I ain't done no midnight ridin the whole week he and Miss Beth been gone.

Mr. Max come to see me while I was there at the house by myself. He say he was gonna buy more pictures till he found out my prices had gone up from two hundred to eight hundred dollars. I told him I'd buy his back for four and sell 'em again! He laugh real hard, then tells me I's the same kinda different as him.

———

A few days later Mr. Ron and Miss Beth come home, and Miss Beth was wearing a real purty ring with a big smile on her face. "We are getting married," she told me, "and I'm so happy you are going to be Ron's best man." Then she and Mr. Ron give me a hug. We ain't never done much huggin—me and Mr. Ron or nobody. Now seems like we was doin it all the time.

I don't know 'bout you, but I don't like the way that sounds—being a man's best man, 'cause I'm a real man and don't want to belong to any other mens. Maybe he didn't 'splain that to me just right. I s'pose it's a white thing, 'cause ain't no brother gonna stand for that kinda talk.

Where they gots enraged was a jungle full of monkeys. Miss Beth showed me the pictures of her kissing Mr. Ron, and they was a hundred monkeys in the trees behind 'em.

I think that's the way Africa is s'posed to look. But I ain't gots no desire to go there. Don't really want to stay back in Louisiana neither. I's real fond of Texas now. I gots my own place at Rocky Top, a cowboy hat and boots, and I had my picture made on Miss Debbie's horse. I figure that gonna make me a real Texan. They ain't many black cowboys, you know.

9 2

RON

By now, the manager of the Comfort Suites was my friend. Denver moved back into his room there after we returned from Costa Rica, and the manager kept me informed on his comings and goings and who was coming to see him.

He and the local police did their best to keep Denver, who was now their favorite—or let's say most interesting—citizen, from his midnight rides. Regardless of the weather, they would sit outside the front door and smoke and chat with him every night until he got sleepy. For the most part, it was working to keep him off the roads.

Then one morning the manager called to let me know that the previous evening Denver had packed up and left. The problem began when the manager had taken the night off and had not given a proper briefing to a new girl who was working the front desk. A routine invoice for Denver's weekly rent had been left under his door, so he went to pay it. The girl had no idea who he was, so she asked for his ID and credit card. Denver said nothing in response, just moved out.

Of course, he was not answering his phone. I visited every motel within a one-mile radius searching for him. No luck. The police who knew him well and liked him helped me search for his car while on their beat. Two days later, he was spotted about two miles away at an all-suite motel. The police told me it was a few steps below the Comfort Suites, and they warned Denver to use caution coming and going. From their observations, his mental illness and/ or dementia seemed to be getting worse. I agreed.

I found Denver at his new motel and sat him down for a heart-to-heart talk. He'd lost his phone in the move and was real glad to see me. I thought it might be in his Escalade, so I dialed the number and the phone rang from the crack between the seats. His beautiful car now looked like a junk dealer's truck, piled with odds and ends he'd picked up off curbs or bought at flea markets, hoping to sell for a profit. He had hundreds of thousands in the bank, yet he had slipped back into a mindset of poverty.

We talked about his driving and the numerous calls I was getting day and night from police. I told him the police had suggested he stop driving before someone got killed, including him. He looked at me like I was a crazy man. I offered to hire him a driver like a movie star and reiterated my offer for him to move back into his old room. But he wasn't having any of it.

"My keys and my car is my freedom. Ain't nobody never gonna take 'em away, and we ain't gonna be talkin 'bout this no more— period, end of subject."

"Denver, think about Miss Debbie and her legacy and your legacy. Please prayerfully consider the things we've talked about. One terrible accident could forever alter or destroy the tremendous impact you and she have had on millions of people, your fans all across America and in many foreign countries. As your brother, I'm asking, is your freedom worth that?"

He got real mellow and said he was sorry for causing so many people so many problems. He knew the local police were his friends and had let him slide on way too many violations. They'd checked on him every night. And they worried about his health, since there had been several 911 calls from front-desk managers in the last several months. It was the same symptom every time. He was unable to breathe.

We talked about kids and grandkids, his and mine. He was hoping to see his again and very fond of all mine—he enjoyed playing
with them at family gatherings. He laughed about his own and how
after two weeks of feeding them and buying out the mall he was
going to have to start painting more pictures.

When I got up to leave, he looked away to avoid eye contact,
and when he turned back around there were tears in his eyes. "I love
you, man," he whispered softly. "You is a good man, and I'm gonna
make myself a better man too."

93

Luciano knocked on my door, dressed up fancy in a black suit. That made me remember he was s'posed to pick me up and drive me out to the weddin. I sure hated to tell the man, but I didn't got no air left in my lungs, and my oxygen done run out last night. To me it feel like an elephant was sittin on my chest. I couldn't catch no air for breathin—just enough to light up a smoke.

I know it's gonna hurt Mr. Ron and Miss Beth for me not to show up at they weddin, but I was thinkin I just might die on that stage, and I ain't want to ruin they special day. But accordin to the weatherman, a tornado just might do that. I told Luciano to let me slide today and I'd take them to his resterunt when they come home after the weddin.

Till I met Miss Debbie and Mr. Ron, I ain't never been to no weddin. But let me tell you, when white folk gets married, they throws a party like when the president gets nawgurated and dances with his wife all by hisself. Then when the bride and groom is through dancin, everbody gotta do it.

The first time I ever had to do that was at Mr. Carson's weddin. All Miss Debbie's and Miss Regan's friends kept askin me to dance. I sweated plumb through my suit out there, like I'd been bathin in the downtown Water Gardens where I used to take a bath. My feet swol' up like a copperhead snakebite. I had to take that pocketknife

267

Mr. Ron's daddy give me and cut the heels outta my brand-new shoes so I didn't have to be a barefootin it home.

To tell you the truth, today I didn't feel like doin no dancin, and white ladies don't take no for no answer. Mr. Ron knowed that after my amerism, stroke, heart attacks, and rotten lungs, I ain't needin to be too far from no hospital. In fact, I better go there right now and get me some more breathin mochines.

It didn't got nothin to do with bein no best man. Mr. Carson could do that just fine.

94

RON

The Devil was indeed messing with us. Two weeks before our wedding, the whole county where our wedding would be held was on fire. It was the largest and fastest-moving brush fire anyone could remember in this part of Texas. The Harbor resort and chapel, where our wedding ceremony would take place and our guests would be staying, was surrounded by the inferno. The entire resort was just minutes away from being transformed into a pile of smoking embers.

Miraculously, a shift in the wind spared it, but a week of tornados, heavy rains, washed-out roads, and high winds quickly took the place of raging wildfires. With both drastically different emergencies miraculously over, it finally appeared it would be smooth sailing for our nautical-themed wedding.

With the smell of smoke hanging heavy in the air, May 20 arrived. The weatherman had forecast a beautiful, sunny day. Instead, we awoke to dark clouds, heavy rains, and a damaging hailstorm. Beth and I spent the morning on our knees in prayer. But by noon the sun shone gloriously over the Harbor, and by the wedding hour it was the most beautiful day of the year.

I was fulfilling one of Debbie's last instructions—to marry anyone I choose whenever I was ready. She'd had the same talk with Regan and Carson, who'd beat me to the punch and were both married already. Now it was my turn.

The ceremony in the white-rose decorated chapel went off without a hitch except for the notable absence of my best man. I understood and had the very same concerns he'd expressed to Luciano. I was blessed to have both Carson and Regan stand with me instead. I knew it wasn't easy for them. Of course, they wished their mom was still alive and this day would not be necessary, but God had bigger plans for Debbie that we will never know until we join her in heaven.

But enter the Devil once more as Aunt Vida fell while exiting the chapel and suffered a compound fracture of her right arm. An ambulance took her away. She wanted Denver to know, so we got him on the phone to pray for her. I'd never heard him speak so softly.

Our reception went off flawlessly on a warm, honeysuckle-scented night under a clear, starry West-Texas sky. Children chased each other and wrestled on soft, green grass that streaked beautiful white dresses and little-boy suits. Family and friends dressed in festive finery gathered around us as Beth and I enjoyed our first dance—a choreographed salsa. Afterward, the crowd raised mock score paddles—a lighthearted tribute to the TV show she'd been watching with her parents when I called for our first date just eleven months earlier. The "judges" gave us all tens!

A spectacular twenty-minute, Fourth-of-July-style fireworks show capped the evening. Then it was anchors away as Beth and I left the Harbor on our boat, *Toulouse with Monet*, for a honeymoon in St. Barths.

95

DENVER

Like I done promised Luciano, I invited Miss Beth and Mr. Ron for supper at Luciano's resterunt after they gots home from they honeymoon. I even wore the suit I wore when I ate lunch at the White House. Luciano's place and the Waffle House was 'bout the only places I's comfor'ble eatin without Mr. Ron. I been eatin there with Luciano for nearly ten years and ain't never wore no suit before, but what I figured out is that peoples who dress up at resterunts seem to get treated better than the folks who comes there lookin funky. Other than Mr. Ron, Luciano was 'bout my best friend. He think it's funny that I gots the same thing ever time—spaghetti and meatballs.

The waiter, Sergio, come up and didn't even look at me, just say, "One spaghetti and meatballs," then he started laughin. Mr. Ron was lookin the menu over real good. Then he smile and say, "Denver, I'm excited to be letting you buy my meal for the first time." Then he wanted to know how much I was willin to spend. I didn't really care. The man ain't never let me pay for nothin before, so I figured it's my time to pay.

Miss Beth always ordered soup and salad. That don't cost much. Mr. Ron gots a big bone full of marrow he called "buco" or somethin like that. He offered me a taste, and I'll be horse-whipped if that wadn't the same thing we used to eat from the hog. I wished I'd known that a few years ago, 'fore I got hooked on meatballs.

271

Though I can read a little bit, for sure I can't read no Eye-talian. So to tell you the truth, when I looked at the menu, all I could figure out is "balls." They ain't but one of them on the menu.

Another waiter, Gonzolo, bring me the check. I pick it up and look, then I look again, and one more time before I call Gonzolo back over and ask him what do it say?

"Ninety-four," he say.

"Dollars?" I asked.

I gots no idea Eye-talian food costed so much. I could eat for six dollars at Waffle House with free water. When I looked in my bill-fold, I was shocked like with a bolt of lightnin that they was only a twenty-dollar bill in there. I had to ask Mr. Ron to loan me the rest, 'cept he didn't got no cash, so he put it on his credit card and laughed so hard he nearly choked.

The Lord wake me up 'bout midnight and say, "Denver, go home."

I asked Him, "Does you mean heaven, Lord?"

He say, "No. Louisiana."

Now, He didn't say it, but I knowed He meant this was the last time I'd be goin there. I already been there on my own two or three times since the weddin, but that was just me wantin to go, not the Lord tellin me to.

The next mornin I walked in Pearlie May's ol' shotgun house she lived in since she was a little girl. It was freezin cold outside, and she had her a big wood fire blazin in the potbelly stove. By now she be pushin a hundred or more. And the first thing she say is, "Denver, come look at my new commode." She been sayin the same thing for the last few years, ever since me and Mr. Ron come here together the first time to pay her a visit. She didn't gots no real bathroom; the commode just sit on the floor in the corner of her bedroom. Commodes is a mighty precious thing to folk that done lived they whole lives usin a outdoor johnny or slop jar—'specially on a cold mornin like that one.

Pearlie May wadn't her normal silly self that day. She say her chilrens was makin her go to a gov'ment old folks' home 'cause she couldn't walk and see very good no more. She was concerned 'bout who was gonna feed the ol' dog she kept chained to the front-yard tree, guardin that big pile of Natural Light cans that Mr. Ron say looks like the great pyramids of Egypt—you know, where the Bible is from. She been savin them cans for years for her retirement.

On down the road, I passed the Grand Bayou Social Club and stopped across the street on the very spot where I watched BB get stabbed when I was just a boy. If I squinted my eyes, I could almost remember what he look like, but I can't remember if I look like him or he look like me. I wished I knowed where he was buried. I'd go pay him a visit. I decided to check 'round Big Mama's grave and see.

Down the blacktop a mile or so behind the church, I found Big Mama's grave. I pull the weeds and scraped the dried mud off her small stone. It say she born in 1900 and died in '42. Uncle James and Aunt Etha was buried three or four stones over. They both hopped aboard that ol' Ship of Zion in '45. If the Lord mean what I thinks He mean, I be rejoicin with them soon. I loveded 'em, 'specially Uncle James and Big Mama.

96

RON

Beth and I awakened to a cold morning rain pelting the glass walls of the bedroom. I put on my robe and walked into the kitchen to make Beth a latte. And there was Denver, sitting at the kitchen table. He heard me push through the swinging doors and began laughing before I could say a word. "Mr. Ron, you is lookin at a walkin dead man." He emphasized the last few words like a carpenter pounding with a hammer.

"So, Mr. Walking Dead Man, how am I so lucky to be talking to you?"

He went on and on about his day in Louisiana and all the places he'd visited, even Pearlie May's commode. "She so proud of that." I laughed as he spoke. He'd passed out blessings to her and to his hundred-and-three-year-old auntie in Cedar Grove before heading back to Dallas.

It had been past midnight when he left Cedar Grove after smoking a whole pack of cigarettes with his auntie. "Do you believe that ol' woman still smoke like a chimney and ain't got *no* lick of cancer or even a cough? But that ain't what I was wantin to tell you. Somethin happen on my way home from Lousiana."

About an hour or so later on the interstate, apparently, he had fallen asleep at the wheel. The next thing he knew, he was crossing the median and locking eyes with the driver of an eighteen-wheeler hurtling in his direction. The trucker honked and swerved to avoid

274

him, and Denver ended up in the ditch on the wrong side of the road. Traffic going both ways had come to a stop—rubbernecking like there had been a wreck. I guess in a way there had been.

A young man who had seen the whole thing ran up to his Escalade and knocked on the window. "Are you all right?" he asked.

Denver rolled down his window and said he was fine. The man later said that Denver didn't seem to understand what the big commotion was all about. "I did," Denver told me, "but I was in some kind of state."

The young man then told him he'd come within a hair of colliding head-on with that eighteen-wheeler. "The red one that just pulled over on the shoulder," he said, pointing.

"Yeah, I seen 'im right before I was gonna hit 'im," Denver told the man. "And you prob'ly ain't gonna believe this, but there was a spiritual bein sittin next to me, and she done took the wheel and got me outta that jam."

The stranger shook his head. "Well, I can tell you for sure it wasn't Jesus, because I saw Him jump out of your car right before impact. He thought you were tryin to kill Him!"

Denver slapped the table as he told that story and laughed so hard that I went to the garage and got his oxygen bottle. "Miss Debbie taked the wheel, she sure did," he said as I placed the plastic hose in his nose.

Knowing Debbie, and knowing him and all he had survived just since he moved in with me ten years before, I didn't doubt him even for a moment. "Thank you, Miss Debbie," I said out loud. Denver just nodded yes and kept nodding until a peace came over him.

———

I was concerned about Denver that morning. His breathing was sporadic and strained. I felt his pulse. His heart was racing. The

thought crossed my mind he just might die right there at the breakfast table. But his stubborn angel, Debbie, had obviously saved him
again for a reason. There were things that needed to be said.

I made him a vanilla latte with extra sugar, followed by his
favorite breakfast—yellow grits and bacon, buttermilk biscuits with
grape jelly, and soft-scrambled eggs.

"Why you never let me cook you no breakfast?" he asked.

"Because I don't like sardines and greens over my oatmeal."

My answer ignited another oxygen-deprived, very weak laugh.
I told him I needed him to stop being funny, as I did not want him
to die laughing like Mr. Ballentine.

He looked gaunt and pale, with his beautiful brown skin sink-
ing and searching for cavities to fall into. I knew he was working his
way home, but I wanted him to be looking good when he arrived.

Denver's breathing gradually stabilized over the next three
hours as we reminisced about the years we'd spent under the same
roof since Debbie went to heaven. We paid tribute to the highs,
barely mentioning the lows. At one point I went and fetched a scrap-
book Vida had made, and we began turning the pages of our lives
together.

Vida had been keeping count and had told me that together
we had done about four hundred events, including book clubs and
signings, Bible studies and Sunday school classes, radio and TV,
schools and colleges, missions and corporate conventions. Denver
nodded when I told him that. "Mr. Ronnie Ray, you done worked
me three-quarters to death, and unfiltered Pall Malls is responsible
for the rest."

"What was your favorite place we visited?"

Without much thought he answered, "I didn't like Mexico." I
reminded him we had never been to Mexico together, but we had been
to New Mexico. "What's the differment?" His chief complaint about
Santa Fe was that he never saw any blacks; plus, the architecture

and food made him feel like he was in a foreign country. "Wadn't like Louisiana or Texas," he complained.

Not surprisingly, Los Angeles had been his favorite stop. There he'd been able to reconnect with his daughter and get his picture made on B. B. King's star on the Hollywood Walk of Fame. Other than that, all the cities had seemed more or less alike to him except New York City, where he'd gotten lost. He'd asked how the earth could support the weight of all those tall buildings. He'd concluded there must not be any swamps under them like in Louisiana.

Denver never asked my favorite cities, but there were many I wanted to revisit. When we were there to work, we'd never gotten too far from the hotel and the homeless missions. At least I hadn't. I don't know where all Denver wandered off to!

We reminisced about David Smith in Atlanta, who had bought a lot of his art and ten thousand of our books, and about Kathy Izard in Charlotte, who had listened when he told her the city needed to build a place for the homeless to sleep. He was sad that his health had prevented him from going to see the new Moore Place for the homeless in Charlotte.

And he laughed telling me how I had talked bad to some good people over in College Station. "Mr. Ron, you spanked and embarrassed the whole town, tellin 'em they pride for they football team done blinded 'em from seein how rotten and nasty they treated the homeless." I'll admit to that, but the end result was one of the finest and most beautiful homeless shelters in America, where clients were now treated with the same respect and dignity as the football team.

"Miss Debbie's dream mission still be the best one in the whole country," he said with a big smile. The fund-raising he did for her mission was what earned him the Philanthropist of the Year award.

We laughed together at the planes he'd missed and the times he'd burned off from the hospital over a particular rubber hose violating his private parts. His aneurysm, now fondly referred to as his amerism by him and all our friends, had caused more sticky situations than a birthday party for three-year-olds. The most embarrassing to me had been the time he walked out of that private dinner with George and Barbara Bush because Mrs. Bush asked him to remove his hat at the table. He'd refused and left because he was convinced that it kept his amerism warm and he couldn't eat with a cold amerism.

Denver was happy to know he helped me mend a lifelong loathing of my father, and together we had enjoyed his last few years of his life. I'd learned to love a former racist, and my father had learned to love Denver. In his final responsible decision on earth, Earl had become a believer and worked his own way home. We will all rejoice together one day soon.

Then Denver said something surprising. He told me God had struck him with color blindness and he no longer saw a white man when he looked at me. He just saw a friend. That may be the best thing he ever told me.

"Denver, you've been my best friend and my professor for nearly fourteen years. I admire how you have stayed true to yourself. You did not let me make you into someone I thought you should be. You held fast to the person God created you to be." His head was bowed as he continued to slowly turn the pages, but he offered no comment and apparently was not ready to speak.

"You've taught me so much, shaped my thoughts, tamed my arrogance, and changed my life. You've taught me to serve and not to judge. You've taught me to love those who are often not lovable or capable of returning the love. You made me see that I did not really own my possessions; they were owning me."

I forced myself to stop talking, wanting to hear from him.

"Now it's your turn. I'm just wondering, what have I taught you?"

Never quick to answer, he moved his head slowly up and down in an affirmative motion. I imagined he was gleaning the best from a long list. Slowly and deliberately, he rolled his tongue around in his mouth and across his smooth teeth as he pondered life lessons from our years and travels together.

"Yessir, you sure 'nough taught me somethin." He raised his head to reveal a soft smile. I was relieved to hear that. For a minute, I'd begun to believe he couldn't think of anything!

"Tell me, what did I teach you?"

"Mr. Ron . . ." He began as always with a slow, deliberate enunciation of each word. "You taught me the differment 'tween a taco and that long, rolled-up thing with cheese that sits next to it on the Mexican plate, covered in brown gravy."

"Do you mean an enchilada?"

He slammed his hand on the tabletop like an auctioneer's gavel indicating Sold.

"That's it! You taught me the differment 'tween a taco and a enchilada!"

97

DENVER

Ain't no way to tell you what it be like when you can't catch no air. I gots big green bottles of oxygen and breathin mochines on both side of the bed, and with both of 'em turned on full power, I still can't catch no air. I was shakin, callin out to the Lord. I knowed I was workin my way back home, but they is a couple of stops I needs to make on the way to do some blessins. It took all my strength to pick up that phone.

"Mr. Ron, I thinks I'm dyin, and I needs for you to take me to the hospital in my car."

"Denver, if you really think you're dying, call 911. Then hang tight. I'll be there in five or ten minutes."

I grab a shirt and was walkin toward my car, and the next time I come to, the ambulance drivers had me laid out on the carpet of the motel lobby floor, blowin in my mouth. And Mr. Ron was standin over me, hollerin: "Hang on, Denver! God isn't finished with you yet."

I reached in my pocket and handed him my keys and asked him to put my car in his garage and don't let nobody come near it 'cept him. I grabbed his arm and pulled him close enough to hear me whisper. I didn't want nobody standin 'round in that lobby to hear what I needed to tell him.

"They is money and my worldly goods hidden in there," I told him as the ambulance drivers was loadin me up. Then they hit me with something powerful, and I was a goner.

280

98

Ron

It was late when Beth and I arrived home from a dinner party with friends. We had become very popular dinner guests because we always fed the crowd with great stories of our marvelous adventures with Denver.

We got ready for bed, and I was just about to doze off when the phone rang. It was Denver in a panic. He told me he thought he was dying.

I threw on jeans and a shirt that I buttoned in the car. I got there just seconds after the paramedics. I wanted to ride in the ambulance with him, but he needed me to do something more important. The paramedics told me which hospital they would be taking him to—the usual, Baylor Medical Center in Plano.

I found Denver's car, which just months ago was clean, though it smelled a little smoky, but now smelled like a Dumpster behind a fast-food restaurant. Though the night air was chilly, I drove it home with all the windows down and parked it in my garage. I took Beth's car to the hospital, driving like I was competing in a race against time.

Denver looked painfully thin, pale and near death, hooked up to what appeared to be every machine in the building. After a couple of intense hours, several doctors, and a full set of CT scans, the attending physician reported to me they could find nothing wrong—or at least nothing new. What had happened tonight was no different from the countless other times he'd been there with the same symptoms—he simply couldn't breathe. His COPD was getting the best of him.

We spent the night there just to make sure and left the next morning. It was a beautiful, sunny, spring-like day. We drove back to my house, and out of nowhere he started laughing.

"Mr. Ron, that was a close call. You believe it's just another step in workin my way home?" He stopped laughing and gave me the kind of piercing stare that penetrates the soul. "One day you gonna know that feelin."

Once again I brought up the subject about his moving back in with us. It was the only way I could think of to protect him and his worldly goods, as he liked to call them.

"Your room is waiting for you to return," I said.

He answered that he'd think about it.

I offered to keep his car parked safely in my garage and suggested he take taxis or get a driver when he needed to go somewhere. That seemed to hit his hot spot. He refused both and held out his hand, wanting his keys back.

"Why don't you keep your money in a bank?" I asked.

"I's afraid some homeless fella will rob it!" He laughed and then started coughing and sputtering, "Lord, have mercy!" It clearly hurt him to waste valuable breath on laughter.

"And you're not afraid someone will steal your car in the parking lot of your motel? Why don't you take the money out right now and bless your children today?"

But against my pleading to stay or drive him back, he drove away.

I felt helpless dealing with his medicines, his dementia, his other health problems. All I could do was my best, but by the looks of things, I was failing. I feared that our lives, our story, could move from hope and redemption to tragedy any day or night. Some nights I couldn't sleep for worry that one of his dizzy midnight rides would end in tragedy.

I prayed that night for God to take him before he and his legacy burned up in a fiery one-car crash—or, God forbid, a multicar pileup. Visions of all the pages of his many accolades charred by the Devil's flames like those that had robbed him of Big Mama haunted me.

Beth thought I should get tougher—demand his keys and impound his car. She thought I was being foolishly optimistic and a little deluded, even going so far as calling me Ron Quixote. I listened, but she had not lived this fourteen-year friendship.

Was I guilty of seeing Denver in his glory and being blind to the real man he was today?

"No," I insisted. "I see the real Denver, the way millions of readers saw him before his amerism, heart attack, dementia, and countless meds. And I want to help usher him safely home."

99

DENVER

Now that I's outta the hospital, Mr. Ron asked me if I felt up to goin to the Cowboy Spring Gatherin out at Mr. Rob Farrell's ranch. I been goin there 'bout twelve years now, and I really enjoyed them cowboys. The first time when I seen all them white boys on horses carryin ropes, it made me a little nervous. But the worstest time was when that cowboy brought his black helper I knowed back in Angola. I figured for sure he was gonna blow my cover, but he didn't. Like Mr. Ron told me, God made stutterers for that job.

A couple of times over the years I done slept in a Indian tepee. I'd be willin to bet I is the onliest black that's done that. Think about it. Did you ever see a black cowboy and Indian picture show?

Now that me and Mr. Ron gots a little age on us, we just stays at Rocky Top instead of the tepees. It's real peaceful there, and I always visits Miss Debbie's grave and stone. Mr. Ron and I picked it up right off the ranch and placed it at her head. It's kinda shaped like a church. I can read it now, and I know she'd be proud. Some of it say she was a best friend to a multitude. I ain't sure what that means, but I bet it's got something to do with me. On the bottom of her stone it say she fought the fight, finished the race, and kept the faith. Hope somebody can say something nice like that 'bout me. When the wildflowers is bloomin, I picks a few and puts 'em in a jar by her stone. I remember when she offered to teach me to read, but I told her I didn't want to rely on the words of man; I just wanted to listen to the Lord. But I'm glad I can read now so I know what her stone say.

I told Mr. Ron I'd go out there to the Gatherin with 'im, but when he come by this mornin for me to follow him out there, I wasn't feelin too well. "I'll drive out later," I told him, "when I gets to feelin better." He say he'd get somebody to drive me.

I knowed he was worried that it was gettin a lot harder for me to take good care of myself. I prob'ly needed to have a talk with Mr. Ron. Maybe I should quit smokin . . . Naw, I'm just messin with you. Even Ray Charles could see that!

I talked about all that with the man at the front desk. He say he don't mind helpin me, but he thought it might a good idea to move back home.

I fell back asleep, and when I woke up I looked at my phone. Mr. Ron done called me fourteen times, so I called him back.

"You worry me when you don't answer your phone," he said.

"I was sleepin," I told him, "and all this medicine don't let me wake up easy."

He say all the cowboys be askin 'bout me and wonderin when I'm gonna show up. Say he could send somebody to bring me if I was feelin up to it. They was holdin up supper till I got there and wanted me to sing at cowboy church on Sunday mornin.

100

RON

By early afternoon there was no sign of Denver. I called repeatedly, hanging up and pushing Send as I had on so many days over the last ten years. No answer. Frustration morphing into concern, I called the front-desk manager. He had not seen Denver all day, though Denver's car was still parked by the front door. But he also said that Denver had started feeling bad that he was disappointing me and my friends. So he'd gotten in his car, started the motor, then said, "I gots the whirlies."

Denver used that word to describe how he felt when he was dizzy—like when you're spinning one of those tops you start with a string. He'd told the manager, "The whirlies ain't good for no drivin, so tell Mr. Ron to go on ahead and send somebody to get me in the mornin." Then he'd turned and crawled back into bed.

Before our chuck-wagon supper, I called and left another message, this time asking the front-desk manager to check Denver's room. His meds were a problem, and I knew it wasn't unusual for him to sleep all day, but I still wanted to hear his voice and know whether he was coming or not.

Around ten at night with still no word, I left another message for the night manager to please check on Denver and tell him to call me regardless of whether he felt like coming. If he was feeling okay, I had a friend who'd said he would drive him out.

At 2:23 the next morning, the phone woke me from a deep sleep. Vida was in hysterics. "He's dead!" she said.

The police had called her to say they found Denver unresponsive in his bed around midnight. No evidence of foul play.

I was speechless. A profound sadness engulfed me, like being in the eye of a hurricane at peace while the world around spun out of control. My prayer had been answered and it didn't feel good; it was more like guilt. I could have done more. I should have prayed differently.

Vida told me he was being held at the city morgue until funeral plans could be made and we could move him elsewhere. That was not how I'd planned on picking him up. God's plans had trumped mine. And the Cowboy Spring Gathering, the few days in spring I looked forward to most, would now serve as the marker for another irreplaceable loss.

I slipped into my jeans and pulled on my boots for the drive back to Dallas, stopping by the barn to unload my saddles and tack. Climbing the stairs to Denver's apartment in what used to be the hayloft, I thought of making it a small museum to honor him. For a moment I was lost gazing out his window onto the moonlit canyon we had often hiked down to the river. I closed my eyes and I saw us—two friends, best friends, walking down the river trail together. Downstairs I sat and prayed on the long red bench by the barn door, Denver's favorite spot on the ranch. We had spent hours there, sometimes talking, sometime whittling, sometimes saying nothing.

As I drove the two-mile winding rock road to the front gate, I stopped first at Debbie's grave to deliver the sad news. Beth must have turned off her ringer, because it rang and rang with no answer. I prayed one of the cowboys would be up early feeding horses. I needed to tell someone—someone who knew him, loved him, and could feel my pain and offer a hug. But this was not a night for luck.

All the way home from Rocky Top, with hardly a car on the road, I drifted in and out of my imaginary movie of our lives together. Reel after reel played in my head—the day I first laid eyes on him, when he threatened to kill everyone in the room, the life-changing catch-and-release meeting at Starbucks, the hours spent painting together or sharing a platform to speak about Debbie's dream. For ten years we had sat at the breakfast table nearly every single morning sharing our life stories and me absorbing his profound wisdom—Denverisms. Tears poured as I remembered the standing ovation he received at Debbie's service when he first spoke the profound words I would hear again and again: "Whether we is rich or whether we is poor or something in between, this earth ain't no final restin place. So in a way we is all homeless, ever last one of us, just workin our way home."

I purposely drove the hundred miles slower than the limit, my wet eyes unable to focus, the movie still playing in my mind. I didn't want it to end—not this way. But I also thought it could have been worse, and then I praised God for that as the credits rolled. Before the screen went dark, I heard him say he loved me. He was a strong man who used that word sparingly because it took all his strength to say it. For most of his life, his strength had been his weakness, causing him to miss out on important things like true friends. It's a little ironic he was such a true friend to me. I'm glad I told him.

Now the screen was dark, and the house lights were slowly rising. I heard the distant music from his piano as I sang out loud one of the spirituals he used to sing:

> I am trav'ling tow'rd life's sunset gate,
> I'm a pilgrim going home;
> For the glow of eventide I wait,
> I'm a pilgrim going home.

Evening bells I seem to hear
As the sunset gate draws near!
Evening bells I seem to hear
As the sunset gate draws near.

I shall rise again at morning dawn,
I shall put on glory then;
With the shadowy veil of death undrawn,
I shall put on glory then.

I guess if I'd been black and driving a white Escalade, I'd have been pulled over during that drive. As Denver often said, I had no place to go and plenty of time to get there. *Lord, help me keep it between the lines.*

It was breaking dawn as I drove across the Interstate 30 bridge into Dallas. The spiritual beauty of a morning sunrise—the dawning of a new day—quickened my spirits. How had I not thought of nor seen the beauty and joy of the moment the gates swung open and Denver went walking in. A sad smile broke free as I thought of me stopping to tell Debbie on my way out. She already knew. Finally, my spirits soared as I pictured Debbie wrapping the man of her dream in a big hug before raising a hand-scribbled cardboard sign:

Welcome Home Denver.

Afterword

Denver joined Miss Debbie in heaven on March 31, 2012. The *Dallas Morning News* page two headline read, "LA Skid Row Hits Skids Again." I don't know why that hit me the way it did. There are so many like him to save and so many like him who can actually save a selfish, arrogant nation from ourselves. In our case, I believe Denver and I were thrown together by Debbie's dream to save each other.

It's funny that I dreamed about Debbie every night from the day she entered heaven until the day Denver moved in with me. Though I tried and tried, sadly, mysteriously, I never dreamed of her again. There must be something to that. I assume one day she will have an answer for me.

It had been exactly 5,169 days since I first laid eyes on Denver in the dining hall of the Union Gospel Mission. I remember nearly every one of those days—some of the best of my life.

Tracy, Denver's daughter, wanted me to handle the details and preach at his funeral. It pleased me that she understood the depth of our friendship. We talked and planned as she made her way to Texas on a three-day train ride.

His body was prepared by the mortuary he'd slept behind for months in the bushes until meeting Pastor Stafford. We dressed him in the suit he'd worn to the White House. I made sure his hat was on to keep his amerism warm. His hands clutched our first-edition hardback, the one I'd signed for him.

Pastor Stafford and I conducted the service. TV crews and newspaper reporters stood outside the church filming and interviewing.

Nearly five hundred attended, including the Academy Award–winning producer of *The Blind Side*, Gil Netter. Thousands more watched a live stream on the Internet. Many had never met Denver but felt they knew him through reading our book. Some flew from other states; others drove hundreds of miles to honor the wise man of Debbie's dream.

I listened for hours to stories from those whose lives had been impacted by his story of hope and redemption. I vowed to them all to keep his and Miss Debbie's memory alive.

Denver and I had talked often about him being buried beside Debbie in our little Brazos de Dios cemetery at Rocky Top. Tracy rejected that idea—afraid wolves might gnaw his bones. Strangely, Denver once told me the same thing. Honoring her and the pastor's wishes, we buried him in a cemetery just south of Fort Worth, surrounded by African American brothers and sisters whose ancestors, like his, had been slaves.

With his motor safely in heaven, his body was carried to his final resting place in a black, lacquered, horse-drawn hearse worthy of a king. A parade of mourners celebrating his life walked in procession behind a New Orleans jazz band with gospel singers belting out "When the Saints Go Marching In."

———

On October 20, 2017, five years after Denver joined Miss Debbie in heaven, the film we had worked on and dreamed about opened in theaters nationwide. It carries the name of our first book, *Same Kind of Different as Me*. It is a beautiful story of hope, redemption, and friendship. Most of all, I believe it illustrates beautifully that it's not the color of our skin that divides us, but the condition of our hearts. I pray that everyone who sees it will walk away with new eyes to see the homeless through the lenses of God—and may they be inspired to leave their comfort zones and look for their own Denver and make a difference.

Beth and I have started a charitable foundation to meet emergency needs of the homeless and to keep Debbie's and Denver's torches burning brightly. Visit us at SKODAM.org.

Acknowledgments

Thanks to my publisher who has blessed me with multiple opportunities to share my stories. And to Debbie Wickwire who saw the value in telling this story and helped me see I did not have to tell it all. And last, to my wife, Beth, who encouraged and pushed me to sit still long enough to write down all the great Denver stories I've been telling her since we met seven years ago.

MORE DENVER!

If you've enjoyed Denver's story in *Same Kind of Different as Me* and *Workin' Our Way Home*, turn the page to read a sample chapter from *The Hundred Story Home*, by Kathy Izard. You'll learn how Denver helped Kathy solidify her calling to serve the homeless and sparked her efforts to build Moore Place, a "housing first" living space for homeless individuals and families in Charlotte, North Carolina.

CHAPTER 9

Going for a Ride

*"The only important thing in a book is
the meaning that it has for you."*
—W. SOMERSET MAUGHAM

I picked up Ron and Denver on Wednesday, November 13, 2007, at the Charlotte airport, trying to appear confident. Our little group of moms had been overly successful, and the planned small event for one hundred guests at church had mushroomed into over one thousand people who wanted to come support the homeless. We had moved the event twice to accommodate the expanding crowd and finally booked Charlotte's largest ballroom. The past few months I had lost a lot of sleep wondering why I had ever listened to that whisper to invite Ron and Denver to Charlotte.

When the dynamic duo got into my car, however, they were not exactly living up to their press. The pair billed as having an amazing and "unlikely friendship" arrived for our event in a silent feud. In the car on the way to lunch, Ron explained the rift.

A couple of nights before, they were honored guests at a fundraising dinner in Texas. Former first lady Barbara Bush had read their book and invited them to "A Celebration of Reading" promoting literacy.

News of this high-profile engagement shocked me. I had no idea they were in such demand when I sent my email six months before. Ron laughed, telling me Denver's famous quote about the Texas event: "I done gone from livin' in the bushes to eatin' with the Bushes. God bless America, this is a great country!"

Although Denver had now been off the streets for years, he still had a habit of wandering off when it suited him. The night of the big event for the first lady, Denver had been seated at the head table with former president George Bush. During dinner, Denver had gotten up from the table and simply walked home. As Ron related all this on the drive from the airport, he was obviously still fuming that he and the Secret Service had spent hours searching for the missing honored guest.

Denver, listening in the back seat, shot back: "Mr. Ron! I lived on those streets for years! You think I can't find my way home?"

I delivered Ron and Denver to their hotel, making plans to see them later at Kim's house for the reception with sponsors. I was panicked by the thought only one of the authors would show up, but I trusted Ron to deliver Denver.

Two hours later I was unloading boxes of programs for the luncheon to the hotel ballroom where True Blessings was going to be held. I noticed Denver out in front of the hotel, with Ron nowhere in sight. My palms started to sweat.

How could Ron have left Denver alone to wander off again?

I hurried over to make sure he didn't escape. Denver was leaning against the hotel's stone facade, and he did not appear to immediately recognize me as the same woman who had picked him up hours earlier at the airport.

"White folk look alike," he would say.

Cloaked in a black shirt, black sport coat, black slacks, and signature black hat, he looked ominous. I took it as a warning sign he was preparing to slip into Charlotte's downtown and avoid the tedious meet-and-greet schedule ahead of him. I needed to think quickly to keep Denver from disappearing.

"Denver, you need a ride somewhere?" I asked.

He studied me before answering. "You got homeless people here?"

"Sure, do you want me to take you to the Urban Ministry Center?"

Why hadn't I thought of that before?

Of course I should show Denver the Urban Ministry Center; it was the perfect plan. Inspiring scenes from his book *Same Kind of Different as Me* ran through my head. I imagined taking him to the soup kitchen where Denver would surely motivate some grateful Charlotte homeless person. Denver would be motivational. Transformational. And I would get to witness it.

Denver stepped toward my minivan. As he opened the door, I reached in to move the thick folder of notes and lists filling the passenger seat. With this herculean task of lunch for one thousand, I had put my organizational skills into overdrive, filling two pages of a yellow legal pad with to-do items to check off by category and day.

As I got behind the wheel with my lists in my hands, I felt Denver examining me. I looked from his stare to my overly exact schedule and back. My anxiety clearly outlined in those lists looked a little ridiculous to me now.

"Denver, I have every minute of today scheduled, but this ride is not on the schedule," I confessed.

Denver nodded as if he already knew that, and then he flashed a grin I had not seen since he arrived.

"We are going for a ride!" he exclaimed, emphasizing *ride* in a long, southern drawl.

We arrived a few minutes later at the Urban Ministry Center in the middle of the afternoon. As we walked toward the buildings, I explained all we were doing for Charlotte's homeless. I was sure Denver would be impressed.

He wasn't.

Leading Denver on a tour of the center, I proudly gave a monologue about all of the UMC's innovative programming. In the art room dozens of paintings by homeless artists were on display. The works were vibrant in color, rich in texture, and layered with meaning.

Denver passed them without comment.

The Neighbors weren't flocking to Denver either. I had been certain Neighbors would somehow recognize this formerly homeless man, now a celebrity author, and swarm us when we arrived. But everyone ignored us, intent on their own mission—surviving the day. In his dapper sport coat and hat, no one seemed to consider Denver had anything in common with them, least of all a shared history of homelessness. For his part, Denver wasn't even trying to connect his story with the homeless waiting in line.

Where was the wise man from the bestselling book?

The visit became increasingly uncomfortable. As my tour dragged on, we passed photos of our soccer team hanging on the walls. All our players competed locally and internationally while still enduring homelessness. Visitors always would remark about the players' commitment to the team in the face of this obstacle. Again, Denver had no visible display of emotion as he studied the players' proud smiles in those photos.

Moving outside the building, we came to our vegetable garden. It was at the end of the season, but Neighbors were tending collards and kale alongside volunteers. Witnessing this side-by-side interaction usually sparked conversation, but Denver peered only briefly over the fence before walking back into our main building.

Trailing behind him, I couldn't understand why Denver didn't think what we were doing was as extraordinary as most visitors did. It was maddening to think I had imagined a much different scene, sure that Denver would change someone's life at the UMC. My fantasy had been to see him wrap his arm around one of our Neighbors and whisper something utterly profound. In all honesty, I was also hoping to receive some message as well. Some praise for my ten years of dedicated volunteer service here.

One of Ron's most remembered Denverisms, however, said it all: "If you really serious 'bout helpin somebody, crawl down in the ditch with 'em, bandage up their wounds, and stick with 'em until they is strong enough to crawl up on your back and get out."

Denver's silence during that tour was disturbing. Was there a message in that? Was he communicating by not speaking? Weren't we helping? All of our art, soccer, and gardening programs as well as services were designed to build relationships with Neighbors and restore their dignity. Most cities had just soup kitchens and limited services, but in our thirteen years the UMC had developed extensive programming far beyond this basic first-aid response.

Yet Denver had not asked a single question, made one comment, or expressed a word of admiration about our innovations.

Frustrated, I turned to leave.

Denver finally spoke.

Motioning to the stairway in front of us, he asked, "Can we go upstairs now?"

I was beyond frustrated. Angry even. I couldn't believe Denver was finally showing interest when there was nothing to see. "There's nothing up there. Just offices."

Denver looked from the stairs to me and then back again. All these years later, I still hear his question, and the ones that followed it, as clearly as I did that day: "Where are the beds?"

"The beds?" I asked, utterly confused.

As I started the long, complicated explanation of how Charlotte has several shelters, Denver's dark face silenced me.

Clearly, I wasn't getting his point.

"You mean to tell me you do all this good in the day and then lock them out to the bad at night?"

His accusation left me gutted.

Denver patiently allowed me my discomfort. He watched me silently wrestle with my new awareness before quietly asking, "Does that make any sense to you?"

Of course it made no sense. I was flooded with shame.

Denver's next question would change the trajectory of my path forever. It was the question I had been waiting for and looking to answer ever since my dad died nine years before.

"Are you going to do something about it?"

I wanted to look behind me to see exactly who he was talking to, but there was little doubt. Denver was staring at me and only me. I had come here for Denver to talk to someone else. To be prophetic to someone else. To transform someone else. I was going to witness that miracle.

Now, Denver was talking to me—just me.

"Do I need to say anything else?" Denver whispered.

My no was barely audible, but we both heard it loud and clear.

Steering the car back to the hotel, I tried not to look at Denver, but his words were still ringing in my ears. I had totally forgotten why we went to the UMC—to keep Denver from wandering off before the cocktail party.

Instead, he had wandered into my life and hijacked my conscience.

From the passenger seat Denver was studying me. "You know, you don't have to be scared."

He kept talking, adding cryptically, "They already know they are coming."

"Who?" I asked, still reeling from the magnitude of his assignment.

At that moment we arrived at the hotel's circular drive. Denver stared at me with utter certainty as he said, "The people who are going to help you—they already know they are coming."

And with that, Denver opened my car door and walked away.

———

Denver showed up for the reception that night and acted as though nothing had happened. I did too. Maybe we could just forget the whole thing.

The next morning I arrived in the hotel ballroom early with all of my lists to set up for True Blessings. My daughters were out of school for the day so they could help, and my sister Louise had flown in that morning from Washington, DC. There were dozens of volunteers assembling centerpieces and putting out programs when Dale entered the vast ballroom. Full of excitement for the day, he headed straight for me.

"Dale, I took Denver on a tour of the UMC yesterday. . . ." I began.

"What did he think?" Dale looked eager to receive the same affirmation I had wanted.

"Well, that's the thing. He really wasn't impressed. He thought we should be doing more." I hesitated as Dale's face fell. "He told me we should have beds and talked about locking them out to the bad at night."

As I floundered to find the right words, Dale tried to track my point, "Beds?" He was trying to connect the dots. "Do you mean housing? That's not what we do, Kathy."

"But maybe we should? If you had heard him yesterday, Denver was so. . . ."

We were interrupted by a volunteer, and I didn't try to circle back. Dale and I would need to talk later because hundreds of guests were beginning to fill the room. My biggest concern now was whether Denver, who was supposed to inspire the crowd to give to the UMC, would tell a thousand people we actually were not doing a very good job.

Ron Hall spoke first and entertained the crowd with stories of his unlikely friendship with Denver. He was a masterful storyteller who spoke as if the thousand guests were simply friends on his living-room couch.

As Ron finished, Denver mounted the stage with all the fervor of a Southern Baptist preacher. Once more he was dressed in his signature black outfit, including his hat. Denver began softly and built to a crescendo that was part prayer and part song. The crowd had gone reverently silent as we all were now in Denver's church and he was delivering a sermon.

Denver was his best self, stepping off the pages and bringing to life quotes from their book and gospel songs. His preaching peaked when he bellowed: "Charlotte, y'all need to do more! Y'all need to build some beds!"

I'm glad I couldn't see Dale's face in that moment. Some in the crowd seemed a little confused. Beds? Had Denver just said we should build beds? The many UMC volunteers in the room knew we didn't have a single bed. Those who were hearing about the UMC for the first time, however, seemed to take it in stride, not understanding this would be an incredible mission shift.

A longtime donor, Dave Campbell, seated next to Dale, leaned over and asked, perplexed, "Are you launching a capital campaign?"

Dale whispered back truthfully, "I have no idea what he is talking about."

Denver continued preaching, even though our event timekeeper was frantically signaling that his time was up. Denver dismissed her, saying, "I see you, but I's got more to say!"

It didn't seem to matter that Denver ran on a little long, because as the one thousand guests exited, they were buzzing about what felt more like a tent revival than a fund-raising lunch. It didn't take long to realize everyone gave with such generosity that the Spirit must have moved the audience as well.

A small group of us led by Angela gathered in the room we had set up as "the bank" to open piles of pledge envelopes. We gasped as we pulled out checks for $500, $1000, and even one pledge card promising $50,000.

Angela showed me a check she was holding, and we both teared up. It was one of the largest we received, and it was signed by Charlie.

I was stunned. In all the planning I'd forgotten to discuss with him what our personal pledge would be. Charlie and I had never given a gift like that to any charity. It was beyond generous. Considering our four girls and mounting tuitions, it was a little crazy.

After I picked up the phone to call him, I could hear him smiling on the other end. Although he hated receiving surprises, Charlie excelled at giving them. "I was proud of you," he said simply.

Everyone involved with planning True Blessings was realizing our gamble had paid off. Our free lunch raised over $350,000 in one hour.

It was astounding. In the thirteen-year history of the organization, the UMC had never held a fund-raising event and never received pledges of that magnitude. Nonprofits all over Charlotte held fundraisers regularly for the arts or children's causes, but not to help homeless people. What exactly had Ron or Denver said to inspire so many? In all my nervousness I couldn't remember a word that had been said.

But like everyone there, I felt the effects.

I had expected to feel a sense of relief and enormous accomplishment at the end of True Blessings. But exactly the opposite was true. At 9:00 p.m. that night, I was restless.

More restless than I had ever been in my entire life.

I had not mentioned my conversation with Denver to anyone except Dale, mostly because it felt crazy. Why was I continuing to hear the words of a formerly homeless man from Texas tell me that I should become personally responsible for housing the homeless in Charlotte?

It sounded as unlikely as building an ark, and I definitely wasn't Noah.

It was time to confess. Charlie, Louise, and I were in our den recounting True Blessing's highlights. If one of them could understand the prophetic conversation with Denver, I thought it would be Louise—the family minister. At age thirty-two, Louise had shocked us all with the revelation that she was going into the ministry and was accepted to Harvard Divinity School.

I imagined Charlie's reaction would be one of rational cynicism. What would Charlie say if he knew I thought the entire purpose of this True Blessings event was for me to meet Denver? Because of my family history of mental illness, it felt mildly dangerous to believe I should listen to Denver's voice, which I was still hearing.

I felt the conversation would go better if Louise was in the room to back me up. She had felt a calling once, so she might be able to verify this call from Denver—or dispel it.

Hesitantly I began telling them the story of how I had taken Denver on a tour that didn't go as planned. I finished with Denver's insistence that I build beds.

They both were silent.

Louise spoke first. "So you feel Denver had a message for you?"

To hear her say it sounded crazy. I decided it was time to turn in.

Charlie and I were brushing our teeth, standing side by side at the double sinks, looking at each other's reflection. Silently we finished and held each other's gaze in the mirror until he spoke first.

"You know the funny thing? I'm not sure Louise got it." He paused. "But I did."

I wanted to cry with relief.

If Charlie had called me foolish or made one of his excellent rational arguments, I am sure I would have dropped the whole idea that night. At that moment the dream of doing something was too fragile. I honestly wanted someone I trusted to talk me out of it.

All it would have taken was a little loud logic to silence that brief whisper of purpose.

Instead, Charlie remembered our evening at the Outward Bound fundraiser and asked the perfect question: "So is this going to be your forty-year thing?"

I couldn't sleep that night. Denver's words more than made sense. They began to map a journey for a forty-four-year-old life that had lost direction.

The next morning I picked up Ron and Denver to take them to the airport. I was distracted during the drive, trying to figure out a way to talk to Denver one more time before he left. I wasn't sure Denver even realized how he had disrupted my life with his charge to build beds. As they got out of my minivan with their suitcases at the airport, I pulled Denver aside before he walked into the terminal.

"Denver, can I ask you something?"

He stopped and gave me another one of his intense, unnerving stares. I had no idea if Denver even recognized me as the woman he had taken "for a ride."

"If I do this," I asked, searching for the right words, "if I build the beds, can I name it after you?"

Denver looked back at me with clear understanding and an obvious memory of our conversation. "I would like that," he said.

He then paused to consider before adding, "But you better hurry because I'm old."

About the Author

Ron Hall has dedicated much of the last ten years of his life to speaking on behalf of, and raising money for, the homeless. Formerly an international art dealer, Ron is a *New York Times* bestselling author and writer/producer of the Paramount/ Pure Flix film *Same Kind of Different as Me*. A Texas Christian University graduate, Ron was honored in 2017 with the Distinguished Alumni Award. In addition to traveling and speaking, Ron and his wife, Beth, run the Same Kind of Different as Me foundation (SKODAM.org), which meets emergency needs for those who are less fortunate.

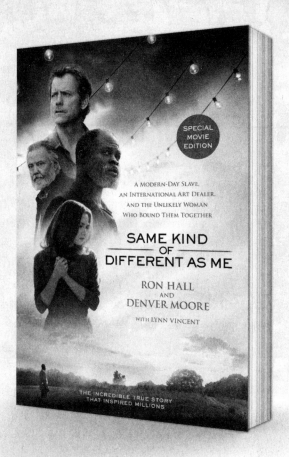

ALSO AVAILABLE FROM
Ron Hall and
Denver Moore

ISBN: 978-0-7180-9179-8

Take the next step.
Help somebody today.

DONATE, DISCOVER, AND MAKE A DIFFERENCE AT

samekindfoundation.org

"The Same Kind of Different As Me Foundation is the '911' for those experiencing homelessness and the agencies that serve them."

- RON HALL, AUTHOR, SCREENWRITER, AND MAN WHO LIVED THE STORY

We are fully committed to restoring the lives of the homeless, hungry, abused, and hurting. Our foundation work was birthed from the thousands of responses we received from readers whose lives were impacted by reading our #1 *New York Times* bestselling book, *Same Kind of Different As Me*, published in 2006, or watching the major motion picture.

INTERESTED IN SCHEDULING RON AS A GUEST SPEAKER OR PRESENTER?

Contact Mark P. Fisher • 443-907-2828 / Mark@InspiringGrowth.biz